Knowledge Driven Development

The majority of IT projects necessitate the incorporation of domain knowledge into working software. This knowledge needs to be consistently managed across the project's activities and outputs. This book assesses how two well-known software development methodologies – Waterfall and Agile – attempt to meet this challenge. Both approaches exhibit a number of strengths, but also some weaknesses.

An alternative model, the Project Knowledge Model (PKM), is put forward. The model scopes the knowledge relevant to the project into a specified number of data points assisting in its digitisation. It establishes a connection between enterprise knowledge and project knowledge for continuous improvement and accelerated project delivery. It can assist existing methodologies in managing knowledge better and has been further developed into a new methodology: Knowledge Driven Development (KDD). Case studies and examples are interspersed throughout the text for better understanding.

Taking these concepts further, a Generic Knowledge Management Frameworks (GKMF) is also described which has the potential to manage generic knowledge and assist in skill development.

Manoj Kumar Lal works as a Consultant at Tata Consultancy Services, India. He has spent two decades working extensively in the field of IT project delivery, with specialisation in business analysis and quality assurance working primarily in insurance domain. He is accredited in various activities of software development. His area of interest is quality assurance and digitisation of knowledge.

CAMBRIDGE–IISc SERIES

Cambridge–IISc Series aims to publish the best research and scholarly work on different areas of science and technology with emphasis on cutting-edge research.

The books will be aimed at a wide audience including students, researchers, academicians and professionals and will be published under three categories: research monographs, centenary lectures and lecture notes.

The editorial board has been constituted with experts from a range of disciplines in diverse fields of engineering, science and technology from the Indian Institute of Science, Bangalore.

IISc Press Editorial Board:

Amaresh Chakrabarti, *Professor and Chair, Centre for Product Design and Manufacturing*

Diptiman Sen, *Professor, Centre for High Energy Physics*

Prabal Kumar Maiti, *Professor, Department of Physics*

S. P. Arun, *Associate Professor, Centre for Neuroscience*

Titles printed in this series:
- *Continuum Mechanics: Foundations and Applications of Mechanics* by C. S. Jog
- *Fluid Mechanics: Foundations and Applications of Mechanics* by C. S. Jog
- *Noncommutative Mathematics for Quantum Systems* by Uwe Franz and Adam Skalski
- *Mechanics, Waves and Thermodynamics* by Sudhir Ranjan Jain
- *Finite Elements: Theory and Algorithms* by Sashikumaar Ganesan and Lutz Tobiska
- *Ordinary Differential Equations: Principles and Applications* by A. K. Nandakumaran, P. S. Datti and Raju K. George
- *Biomaterials Science and Tissue Engineering* by Bikramjit Basu

Cambridge–IISc Series

Knowledge Driven Development
Bridging Waterfall and Agile Methodologies

Manoj Kumar Lal

CAMBRIDGE
UNIVERSITY PRESS

University Printing House, Cambridge CB2 8BS, United Kingdom

One Liberty Plaza, 20th Floor, New York, NY 10006, USA

477 Williamstown Road, Port Melbourne, vic 3207, Australia

314 to 321, 3rd Floor, Plot No.3, Splendor Forum, Jasola District Centre, New Delhi 110025, India

79 Anson Road, #06–04/06, Singapore 079906

Cambridge University Press is part of the University of Cambridge.

It furthers the University's mission by disseminating knowledge in the pursuit of education, learning and research at the highest international levels of excellence.

www.cambridge.org
Information on this title: www.cambridge.org/9781108475211

© Manoj Kumar Lal 2018

This publication is in copyright. Subject to statutory exception and to the provisions of relevant collective licensing agreements, no reproduction of any part may take place without the written permission of Cambridge University Press.

First published 2018

Printed in India

A catalogue record for this publication is available from the British Library

ISBN 978-1-108-47521-1 Hardback

Cambridge University Press has no responsibility for the persistence or accuracy of URLs for external or third-party internet websites referred to in this publication, and does not guarantee that any content on such websites is, or will remain, accurate or appropriate.

I dedicate this book to our Guru Maharaj Param Sant Shri Chaturbhuj Sahay, founder of Ramashram Satsang (ramashram.com), Mathura, India, who gave me spiritual strength to persevere, complete this piece of work and take it to a logical stage to be able to publish it. I pray to him to give enough strength to fellow innovators to carry on with increased enthusiasm until they fulfil their dream of displaying their innovations to the world.

Contents

Figures	*xi*
Tables	*xiii*
Foreword	*xv*
Preface	*xix*
Acknowledgements	*xxiii*
Overview of the Book	*xxv*

1. Knowledge Driven Development: What is the Proposition?   1
    1.1 Knowledge Driven Development (KDD): A Background   1
    1.2 Waterfall, Agile and KDD Methodologies: A High Level Overview   4
       1.2.1 Waterfall Methodology   4
       1.2.2 Agile Methodology   5
       1.2.3 KDD Methodology   5
    1.3 Case Study: Customer Self-Service   9
       1.3.1 Implementation using Waterfall methodology   10
       1.3.2 Implementation using Agile Methodology   14
       1.3.3 Implementation using KDD Methodology   18
    1.4 Difference in Approach among Waterfall, Agile and KDD   26

2. Project Delivery and Supporting Methodologies   30
    2.1 IT Industry from Technology and Domain Perspective   30
    2.2 Information Technology: A Knowledge-Based Industry   32
    2.3 IT Project Delivery: An Introduction   34
    2.4 IT Project Delivery Methodology Landscape   38

3. Project Delivery Pain Areas and the Way Forward   46
    3.1 Context   46
    3.2 IT Project Failures   48
    3.3 Project Delivery Pain Areas   50
    3.4 Project Knowledge   52

4. Project Knowledge Model: Context and Definition — 59
4.1 Traditional Project Knowledge Management — 59
    4.1.1 Project Knowledge Management in Waterfall Methodologies: Document Driven — 60
    4.1.2 Project Knowledge Management in Agile Methodology: Collaboration Driven — 61
4.2 Project Delivery Activities and Project Knowledge — 62
    4.2.1 Project Delivery Activities — 62
    4.2.2 Activities Mapped to End-to-End Project Delivery — 63
    4.2.3 Project Delivery Activities: Inherent Interactions — 66
4.3 Project Knowledge Model: Definition — 68
    4.3.1 Knowledge Evolution and Project Knowledge — 68
    4.3.2 Software Project Knowledge Building Blocks — 71
    4.3.3 Project Knowledge Building Blocks Mapped to Knowledge-Intensive Phases — 76
    4.3.4 Project Knowledge: Away from Documents and towards a Model — 76
    4.3.5 Project Knowledge Model Defined — 85
4.4 Project Knowledge Model: An Example — 93

5. Project Knowledge Model: A Differentiator — 97
5.1 Project Knowledge Model Characteristics: Traceability and Flexibility — 97
5.2 Advantages of the Project Knowledge Model — 98
5.3 Reason for Delay in Discovering Project Knowledge Model — 118
5.4 What Does it Really Mean for Project Delivery? — 119

6. Project Knowledge Model *vs* Project Documents — 121
6.1 Project Knowledge Model and Project Documents — 121
6.2 Comparison of Project Knowledge Model and Project Documents — 125
6.3 Document Excerpt and Equivalent Project Knowledge as per the Project Knowledge Model — 132
6.4 Output of Project Knowledge Model — 136

7. Extending Project Knowledge Model to Cover End-to-End Project Delivery – KDD — 140
7.1 Introduction — 140
7.2 KDD Focus Area — 141
7.3 KDD Core Values — 142

	7.4 End-to-End Project Delivery Using Quality Gate	153
	7.5 Tracking Project Delivery Quality via Key Performance Indicators (KPI)	164
	7.6 Fitment for Different Types of Domains and Projects	167
	7.6.1 Domain Relevance	167
	7.6.2 Project Type Relevance	167
	7.7 KDD differentiators	167
8.	**Extended KDD: Pre-Requirement and Post Delivery**	**169**
	8.1 Business Case (Pre-Requirement)	169
	8.2 Service Management (Post Delivery)	170
9.	**KDD Compliance with Standards of Project Delivery**	**172**
	9.1 Quality Assurance Framework	172
	9.1.1 Six Sigma	173
	9.1.2 CMMI	175
	9.2 Project Management Framework	180
	9.2.1 PMP	180
	9.2.2 PRINCE2	184
	9.3 Service Management Framework	187
	9.4 Enterprise Architecture Framework	187
	9.4.1 TOGAF	188
	9.4.2 Zachman Framework	189
	9.5 Business Analysis Framework	193
	9.6 Test Management Framework	194
10.	**Enabling DevOps**	**198**
	10.1 What Is DevOps	198
	10.2 DevOps Focus Area and Assistance by KDD	199
11.	**Addressing Contemporary Concerns of Project Delivery**	**203**
	11.1 Shift Left	203
	11.2 Knowledge Management	205
	11.3 Digitisation	209
	11.4 Collaboration	209
	11.5 Agile Way of Working	209
	11.6 Systems Thinking	210
	11.7 Lean Way of Working	211
	11.8 Software Engineering Modelling	211
	11.9 Machine Learning and Artificial Intelligence	211
	11.10 Internet of Things (IOT)	212

12.	**Helping Existing Methodologies**	**214**
13.	**Technology Enablers: Tools and Automation**	**220**
	13.1 Automation Potential in Project Delivery	220
	13.2 Tools Landscape in Project Delivery Environment and PKM	223
	13.3 PKM: Conceived as ALM Plus Enterprise Knowledge Management	226
	13.4 Benefits of Automation	228
14.	**Suits Factory Model: Needs Cultural Change**	**233**
	14.1 Bringing IT Project Delivery Closer to Process-Based Industry	233
	14.2 Implementing the Factory Model	235
	14.3 The Need for Cultural Change	238
15.	**Global Relevance of KDD: GKMF Assisting Skill Development**	**241**
	15.1 KDD and Generic Knowledge Management Framework	241
	15.2 Examples of Generic Knowledge Management Framework	245
	15.2.1 Password Management in IT Industry	245
	15.2.2 Plantation: Agriculture	247
	15.3 Generic Knowledge Management Framework: Used in Skill Development	248
	15.3.1 Portal Development	249
	15.3.2 Insurance Industry	252
	15.3.3 Agriculture Industry	254
	15.4 Towards Another Ontology Framework	256
16.	**Lean KDD: Elimination of Requirement and Test Design?**	**257**
	16.1 Revisiting KDD: Elimination of Test Design Phase	257
	16.2 Influence of Business Rule and Scenario on Project Delivery	258
	16.3 Lean KDD: without Requirement and Test Design	259
17.	**Conclusion**	**261**
Appendix A:	Illustrative Non-Functional Attributes	265
Appendix B:	Compliance of PKM with GKMF	267
Appendix C:	Project Estimate and Business Rule/Scenario Framework	272
Appendix D:	Inventory Relationship for Setting up of Security Questions – as per Example in Chapter 6	274
Appendix E:	KDD: Response to Criticism	281
Glossary		286
References		290
Index		293

Figures

1.1	Evolution of knowledge	1
1.2	Levels of knowledge	2
1.3	Levels of knowledge covering its evolution	3
1.4	Waterfall project delivery phases	4
1.5	Agile project delivery phases	5
1.6	KDD project delivery phases	6
1.7	Scoping of project knowledge in KDD	7
1.8	Project knowledge management activities	8
1.9	Project requirements	10
1.10	Project Knowledge Model of case study	23
1.11	Comparing project delivery attributes of Waterfall, Agile and KDD	27
4.1	Project delivery activities	63
4.2	Project activities mapped to end-to-end project delivery	64
4.3	Project delivery activities: inherent interactions	66
4.4	Levels of knowledge	69
4.5	Evolving 8 generic building blocks into 18 for software project delivery	72
4.6	Building blocks mapped to knowledge-intensive software development phases	76
4.7	Relationship between four forms of project knowledge	77
4.8	Project knowledge tree	81
4.9	Reusable enterprise knowledge	85
4.10	Digitised project knowledge data points	87
4.11	Project Knowledge Model	88
4.12	Activities to manage project knowledge	89
4.13	Project Knowledge Model quantified	90
4.14	Enterprise knowledge reuse: an example	93
5.1	Traditional review and review in PKM	100
5.2	Knowledge maturity in Waterfall, Agile and KDD	108
6.1	Project knowledge management in project delivery	122
6.2	Project Knowledge Model	124

6.3	Output of the Project Knowledge Model	137
7.1	Inventory and relationship driven project knowledge	142
7.2	End-to-end project delivery activities	144
7.3	Execution and management related activities	149
7.4	Relationship between project delivery phases in KDD	150
7.5	Fault tolerant evolution of knowledge	153
7.6	KDD project delivery governance: quality gate approach	154
9.1	Standards of project delivery	172
9.2	Requirement viewpoint of project delivery	192
10.1	Collaboration between Dev and Ops in KDD	200
13.1	Digitised project knowledge for creating the software	222
13.2	Benefit from KDD automation	229
13.3	Visualisation of the Project Knowledge Model	230
14.1	Typical steel manufacturing process	235
14.2	Project delivery factory model	237
15.1	Generic Knowledge Management Framework	242
15.2	Knowledge maturity: domain agnostic	242
15.3	Knowledge maturity in IT industry	243
16.1	KDD and redundancy of test design	258
16.2	Relevance of business rule and scenario in IT project delivery	259
16.3	Lean KDD	260
17.1	Knowledge gap in Waterfall, Agile and KDD	262
17.2	Knowledge life cycle	263
17.3	From Project Knowledge Model to Generic Knowledge Management Framework	264

Tables

1.1	Comparison of Waterfall, Agile and KDD	23
1.2	Comparison of project delivery attributes with Waterfall, Agile and KDD	28
2.1	Existing project delivery methodologies	39
2.2	Frameworks and standards enabling project delivery	44
3.1	Pain areas in project delivery	50
4.1	Project knowledge building blocks	70
4.2	Rationale for evolution of software project knowledge into 18 building blocks	73
4.3	Building block definitions	74
4.4	Requirement inventory	80
4.5	Relationship between requirement and communication	80
5.1	Advantages of the Project Knowledge Model	98
5.2	Enterprise knowledge building blocks and relationships	110
5.3	Maker-and-checker mechanism across the four portions of project knowledge	117
6.1	Comparison of Project Knowledge Model and project document	125
6.2	Output of the Project Knowledge Model	138
7.1	Understanding project knowledge via inventory and relationship	143
7.2	End-to-end project delivery activities	144
7.3	Relationship between different phases of project delivery	150
7.4	KPIs to monitor project delivery quality	164
9.1	KDD compliance with Six Sigma	173
9.2	KDD compliance with CMMI	176
9.3	KDD compliance with PMP	180
9.4	KDD compliance with PRINCE2	184
9.5	KDD compliance with TOGAF	188
9.6	KDD compliance with BABOK	193
9.7	KDD compliance with seven principles of testing	195
12.1	Existing project delivery methodologies and how PKM assists	214

13.1	Features of project delivery and the Extended Project Knowledge Model	226
15.1	Building blocks of GKMF and PKM	243
15.2	Password management via eight building blocks	245
15.3	Rice seedbed preparation via eight building blocks	247
15.4	Business scenario for 'customer alteration' process	249
15.5	Business rule for 'customer alteration' process	251
15.6	Business scenario for 'retirement due to incapacity' process	252
15.7	Business rule for 'retirement due to incapacity' process	254
15.8	Business scenario for 'preparation of seedbed' for rice	255
15.9	Business rule for 'preparation of seedbed' for rice	255
16.1	Project Knowledge compartments	257
A.1	List of non-functional attributes	265
B.1	Project Knowledge analysis for finding knowledge at the highest level of abstraction	267
D.1	Intra-relationship of process step	274
D.2	Inter-relationship of process step	274
D.3	Intra-relationship of business data	276
D.4	Inter-relationship of business data	276
D.5	Inter-relationship of business rule	278
D.6	Intra-relationship of scenario	279
D.7	Inter-relationship of scenario	279
D.8	Inter-relationship of message	280

Foreword

When we think of the challenges in software engineering, we focus on the various technical activities: requirements, architecture, design, implementation, verification etc. Various management dimensions also receive attention: processes, planning, change management, quality, teamwork, competency, domain understanding, customer interaction, value focus and so on. Clearly, each one of these is very important, even critical, to successful software engineering.

However, there is another dimension that is central to software engineering: contextual knowledge and how it flows through the engineering process, into the final product. It is easy to see why this dimension is central if we examine the nature and role of software. Software is the agent of operations for systems. It implements/enables the concept of functioning of its target system, which could be a business function, embedded system and/or user task. The technical activity stream in software engineering as a whole is aimed at developing this contextual knowledge about the target system, and then ensuring that it is addressed accurately and consistently by the resulting software solution.

This book introduces Knowledge Driven Development (KDD), a path-breaking software engineering technology (best practice) that manages and ensures the systematic flow of contextual knowledge into software solution. As the author Manoj Kumar Lal illustrates beautifully through the case studies in Chapter 1, even software projects that diligently follow modern best practices are extremely likely to face challenges associated with managing this flow. The problem is that contextual knowledge evolves continuously as the project progresses (In Agile, this means that knowledge relating to software generated by a particular Sprint continues to evolve even after the Sprint completes), and that consistent shared understanding of relevant contextual knowledge needs to be maintained across all team members (even in large distributed teams) to avoid quality problems. Readers will find that the typical problems described by him are familiar to them as commonplace in the projects that they execute, and that these problems lead to significant productivity losses and quality problems. Every project, large or small, will benefit substantially from a structured approach to managing the consistent flow of contextual knowledge into software solutions.

The book goes on to introduce precisely such a structured approach. Contextual knowledge about the target system is captured through a Project Knowledge Model (PKM) classified into 18 'building block' types, and a further n^2 matrix of 171 possible relationships among them. This leads to a highly granular view of the contextual knowledge about the target system, with the advantage that different parts of the software solution and associated enabling systems use different identifiable subsets. This granular view of contextual knowledge creates a logical and consistent PKM structure that makes it easier for subject matter experts providing the contextual knowledge to review and check its completeness and correctness. As the contextual knowledge evolves, this granular model facilitates change tracking and application to relevant software solution and enabling artefacts. For larger and more complex target systems, this building block PKM approach may be applied again at the subsystem and even component level.

The major and path-breaking value of KDD is that it generates a contextual knowledge inventory, the PKM, that is delivered along with the software solution. Today, given a software artefact, there is no way to easily determine the target system knowledge embodied in it, other than to reverse engineer it – which is often extremely difficult to do. This is a major contributor to software obsolescence. By making that target system understanding an explicit companion artefact to software, the Project Knowledge Model revolutionises the software life cycle and increases the utility of the software. PKM is the knowledge equivalent of structured programming: once we get into the practice of creating and managing the PKM as a primary project artefact, we would be surprised that people would ever carry out engineering activities without explicitly capturing the associated Project Knowledge Model.

The term Knowledge Driven Development might conceivably be misinterpreted as referring to 'yet another SE methodology'. The book goes into painstaking detail to counter that, by indicating how this best practice is compatible with different software life cycle models, development methodologies and software engineering standards. This eliminates potential barriers to adoption in the minds of readers, and provides guidance on how KDD can be integrated into existing practice.

Foreword xvii

While this book is likely to be of special interest to practitioners, project managers and those engaged in process definition, the careful conceptual breakdown and detailed presentation style make it highly suitable for academic use as well. Software engineering students and even faculty will also benefit substantially from the specific insights it gives them into the ground realities and challenges of practical software engineering. There is often a tendency in academia to assume that the primary challenges in engineering software are technical. This book introduces them to the reality that basic communication and consistency management are often far greater threats to software quality than gaps in engineering competence! The author's grounding in the trenches of real-world software development shines through from every page, and serves as an excellent orientation for them, not only in the challenges but also on the possibility of deep, well thought-out innovative solutions to those challenges.

In short, Knowledge Driven Development is a substantial contribution both to software engineering practice and to the literature on the topic. It is a rare gem that not only introduces a new best practice, the maintenance of a Project Knowledge Model, but backs it up with a powerful elaborate conceptual structure and detailed practice guidance. It is reasonable to expect that this will become a widespread and indeed indispensable software engineering best practice over the next decade.

Swaminathan Natarajan
Chief Scientist
Tata Consultancy Services Research

March 2018

Preface

Let's visualise IT project delivery as consisting of two segments. The first, dealing with requirement gathering and analysis, and detailing the solution from the business and technical perspective. The second, dealing with coding, testing and implementing the software. The first represents project knowledge and the second relates to its technical implementation. Software engineering focuses on both. While there has been a significant advancement in technical implementation, project knowledge has not matured at the same rate. Project knowledge is still plagued with gaps in effective representation, communication, competency and quality assurance, and there is significant opportunity to improve this area.

We try to manage project knowledge largely through experienced associates, strong adherence to processes and documentation, and robust communication with stakeholders. In this book, I have gone deeper into this by decomposing knowledge and representing it via data points. I have conceptualised the Project Knowledge Model (PKM) to manage the project knowledge in a structured manner. PKM catalogues the entire project knowledge and integrates it together with an exhaustive traceability mechanism. PKM has the potential to assist all the existing project delivery methodologies. It digitises project knowledge which, in turn, assists in the technical implementation of the software as well.

I have expanded PKM to cover end-to-end project delivery and evolved a new methodology of project delivery, named Knowledge Driven Development (KDD). KDD is driven by PKM and blends the Waterfall and Agile project delivery concepts. The bridging of the gap between Waterfall and Agile project delivery is an underlying theme that runs throughout this book and is a positive spin-off from the digitisation of project knowledge.

Taking the knowledge decomposition concept beyond IT, I have also evolved a Generic Knowledge Management Framework (GKMF) which has the potential to manage generic knowledge and assist in skill development.

This book introduces PKM, KDD and GKMF with a case study and examples. It elaborates PKM and explains how the model may help the project delivery, regardless of the project delivery methodology followed. The idea is still conceptual and untested but matured enough to be presentable. Objective of this book is to present the idea in a meaningful manner to enable further work on it.

What inspired me the most to work towards this methodology were the numerous instances of lost time, misdirected effort and the ensuing delays in project delivery. This provided great opportunity to improve and I started thinking how project knowledge management can assist in this regard.

As an experienced project delivery practitioner, being inclined towards spirituality, I had a firm belief that knowledge in its original form is the same, however, it may be manifested differently in different domains or companies within the same domain. It has been an enlightening journey trying to simplify the knowledge required to deliver an IT project. My experience of working in almost all the roles of IT project delivery over the last twenty years gave me an insight into core purpose of this book: simplification of project knowledge.

I have evolved KDD based on my experience, research and interacting with experts in project delivery. I have compared KDD with other project delivery methodologies and have provided information on its compliance with different standards and frameworks which are widely accepted in the project delivery environment. It seems to me that the individual ideas mentioned in the book may not be all new, but when looked at from an end-to-end IT project delivery perspective, the concept certainly creates an offering that is currently not available in the industry or in academia to the best of my understanding. I consider KDD as an innovation that attempts at a new way of delivering IT projects.

The target audience of this book are:

- Students of computer science
- Students of information technology
- Students of information science
- Students of software engineering
- Students of quality assurance
- Students of knowledge management
- Students of project management
- Students of business analysis
- Academicians of software engineering
- Project delivery practitioners of IT companies

- Change management teams of organisations
- Standards bodies related to IT industry

The academic courses where this book can be used are:
- Software engineering
- Knowledge management
- Project management
- Requirement management
- Software quality assurance

After reading this book, the reader may be able to appreciate how project knowledge can be simplified using PKM. They may realise that PKM is the main offering that can assist evolving KDD as well as assist existing methodologies. They may also be able to use one or more features of PKM to help in project delivery. Additionally, it may help them coming up with topics for their research and training projects.

The book is better read sequentially. However, it is useful to revisit chapter 1 (case study) after reading the entire book. A basic knowledge of software engineering is needed for the reader to appreciate the contents of this book. The book may require close attention from the reader as the book details a new concept.

I am taking KDD, which is driven by PKM, to the IT industry and academia through this book and hope it will prove to be a step enabling the IT industry to mature, from being knowledge-based to process-based.

For those starting their IT careers, it is natural to think of IT projects as purely intellectual activities. For the those of us that have spent many years working on projects we will have experienced many other dimensions such as personal experience, culture, ego, taste and politics. All these need to be focussed towards meeting project delivery objective. The book provides a technique (in the form of PKM) that may be used either independently (via KDD) or following traditional delivery methodologies (PKM assisting Waterfall and Agile). Whereas no technique alone can ensure project delivery success, PKM may be a refreshingly simple technique assisting the team in their endeavour towards a successful project delivery.

Acknowledgements

I am greatly indebted to my wife, Sujata; children, Sumi and Shreya; and parents, Tripti Narain Lal and Prabha Devi, as I have stolen from them years of quality time to work on this book. They have been fully behind me in this journey, with their constant encouragement.

I acknowledge Phil Knaggs, who took pains to review every single sentence of the book so that it is readable and understandable to an interested reader. The quality of the contents of book has been greatly enhanced by the valuable feedback from Simon Richards. I am also grateful for the feedback received from Chris Reeve, Steve Rice and Phil Sisson.

I acknowledge Professor R Srinivasan, Professor Sujit Chakravarty, Dr Krishna Chandra Jha, Professor Claudio B. Cunha, Professor R Zhang and Professor Sandra D. Eksioglu for their kind reviews of the sample chapters of the book.

I acknowledge support of my colleagues at Tata Consultancy Services who kept my motivation high and provided useful inputs from time to time. It is difficult to name all of them, but there are some names I must mention: Dr. Swaminathan Natarajan, Dr Balamuralidhar P., Sushant Kumar Pati, Chandraasekhar Mallari, Ravi Babu, P. M. Dhanesh, Anupam Karar, Anupam Upadhyay, Ashok Bohra, Tara Prasad, Shrikrishna Kulkarni and Anil Narayanan.

From among friends and family, mostly software professionals, I am grateful for the assistance provided by Ajay Rajhans, Dheeraj Kumar, Anupam A.K., Kumar Ambuj, Manish Kumar, Purnendu Kumar, Prabhakar Lal and Rajiv Jha.

I acknowledge the support of Vikram Verma, Dashrath Chaudhary, Ashok Kumar Labh, Rameshwar sharan, Dr R. S. Prasad, Professor D. K. Singh, Professor J. Nagabhushanam, Kailash Bihari and Dr Parasnath Chaudhary, who have been a guiding force for this book to see the light of the day.

I am grateful to Professor Kesava Rao and Kavitha Harish for their guidance to get the sample chapters reviewed and accepted by IISc Press. Manish Chaudhary, Gauravjeet Reen and Hardip Grewal from Cambridge University Press have been kind enough to guide me through the different stages of publishing.

Overview of the Book

Generally, there are two types of people in the world: one who follow processes and methodologies as written in books, and the other who enjoy breaking rules and doing things differently. The latter can also be split into two categories: those with good intentions and those with bad intentions. The first category produces innovation and the second category produces criminal behaviour. Society has all these kinds of people. In a healthy society, a majority of people follow processes, some have honourable intentions in breaking rules and only a very few have criminal intentions.

This is evident in software project delivery as well. Let's see how it happens there. Almost all projects select a project delivery methodology (there are many to choose from). There will be a set of people in the project who will understand the intent of the methodology and try to follow it while performing their assigned tasks. There will be another set of people who will have the maturity to understand that certain portions of the project delivery can be better accomplished by slightly tweaking the methodology steps and they will propose this to their colleagues. There will also be a few people who, for less honest reasons, will argue against the methodology steps or suggestions for change. They might propose something that will make their task easier, even if it becomes difficult for the majority of the team to accommodate their proposal. They will take excuses of someone's failure and justify delays from their side. They will create an opaque boundary around their work so that the transparency in the project progress is hindered.

While there may be a majority of people falling under type one (process followers), there are significant number of people falling under the second type, category one (rule breakers with good intentions) and category two (rule breakers with bad or selfish intentions). A fine balance between all these types of people needs to be maintained by the project management. That is why success and failure of a project today is largely in the hands of the project manager, even if the team is highly skilled and experienced.

Depending only on the project management to drive a project is not the best solution. The industry is keen to solve this issue at a strategic level. A major roadblock is that the IT industry is still knowledge-intensive. The existing project delivery methodologies leave a significant portion of project delivery to interpretation, giving an opportunity to type two, category one and two people (rule breakers with good and bad intentions) to influence the project delivery adversely.

In contrast, for process-based industries (e.g., manufacturing), end–to-end processes are clear and unambiguous, leaving almost nothing to interpretation. Industries mature from being knowledge-based to process-based gradually.

For a successful project delivery, it is essential that the entire team is fully aligned to the chosen delivery methodology. The methodology should be prescriptive enough so that the project team is always clear about how exactly to perform the current and future steps. The methodology should also recognise the fact that project delivery deals with human beings and not machines (like the manufacturing industry) and be flexible enough to accommodate their preference, where relevant, without bringing any ambiguity to the overall framework of the methodology.

The existing project delivery methodologies struggle to be prescriptive. IT delivers projects for all the other industries and primarily covers two types of activities other than the management activities. One activity is knowledge related, such as requirement gathering, and business and technical solutioning. The other activity is execution related, such as build and test, which makes sure the software being developed meets the requirements. Methodologies cover both types of activities and ways to manage them. Execution related activities are enabled by the latest technological advancements in the programming languages, database and supporting tools. In the knowledge related activities, the methodologies restrict themselves to generic guidelines (such as requirements must be atomic and unambiguous), as knowledge seems to differ not only across domains but also within companies in the same domain. Therefore, it is difficult to be prescriptive about capturing and maintaining project knowledge. Managing these activities becomes a challenge as the knowledge related activities are difficult to quantify and, thus, measure. For example, it is difficult to say that 80% of the solution design is complete as the solution evolves.

I have developed a new methodology that is focused on bringing prescriptiveness to a significant extent to the knowledge-based activities.

Overview of the Book

Be it any domain, the entire knowledge, needed for a successful project delivery is scoped into a specified number of data points (detailed later in the book). The data points digitise the project knowledge. The project knowledge activities are now better managed as they are easily measurable via the data points. This has made it possible to develop a prescriptive methodology, comparable to methodologies of process-based industries. Knowledge Driven Development (KDD), as I have named it, is, as far as I am aware, the first prescriptive methodology for the IT industry.

The book has four logical units as follows:
1. Unit 1, chapter 1 to chapter 3: This unit starts with a case study executed by following Waterfall, Agile and KDD after a brief explanation about the methodologies. It carries on introducing the reader with the general aspects of software engineering, pain areas of project delivery and importance of knowledge in project delivery.
2. Unit 2, chapter 4 to chapter 8: This unit defines the Project Knowledge Model (PKM), the main proposition of the book. It extends PKM to cover end-to-end project delivery and explains KDD in detail. It also tries to bring out the differentiating factors of PKM and KDD.
3. Unit 3, chapter 9 to chapter 14: This section of the book analyses the various standards, frameworks and methodologies of project delivery and tries to bring out two important take-aways. One, KDD is compliant with the existing standards and frameworks. Two, concepts of PKM can assist existing project delivery methodologies since PKM digitises project knowledge.
4. Unit 4, chapter 15 to chapter 17: The concept of KDD is extended beyond IT via a new Generic Knowledge Management Framework (GKMF). GKMF, although introduced earlier in the book, is explained via examples in this unit. This section explains how GKMF can assist in skill development initiatives. GKMF also helps conceptualising Lean KDD which is introduced at a high level and has a good potential to simplify project delivery further.

Introduction of PKM, KDD and GKMF and its various aspects are explained through the chapters in the following manner:

Chapter 1: 'Knowledge Driven Development: What Is the Proposition?' introduces KDD via a case study, bringing out the salient features of the typical Waterfall and Agile project delivery methodologies and contrasting them alongside KDD methodology.

Chapter 2: 'Project Delivery and Supporting Methodologies' discusses the history of project delivery through knowledge-based and process-based industries. The chapter explains how an IT project is delivered and lists the delivery methodologies and their advantages and limitations.

Chapter 3: 'Project Delivery Pain Areas and the Way Forward' examines the pain areas in IT project delivery, along with the role of project knowledge for smoother project delivery.

Chapter 4: 'Project Knowledge Model: context and definition' details PKM, which is the key to KDD.

Chapter 5: 'Project Knowledge Model: A Differentiator' explains how PKM uniquely assists and accelerates the project delivery.

Chapter 6: 'Project Knowledge Model *vs* Project Documents' illustrates how PKM can replace the current documentation regime.

Chapter 7: 'Extending Project Knowledge Model to Cover End-to-End Project Delivery: KDD' explains end-to-end project delivery driven by ten quality gates for eight phases. Four phases are entirely driven by PKM and the remaining phases are highly influenced by the model.

Chapter 8: 'Extended KDD: Pre-Requirement and Post Delivery' discusses how PKM can be expanded to cover activities that occur before the requirements are detailed and after a project is delivered and the software is in the support, maintenance and enhancement phase.

Chapter 9: 'KDD Compliance with Standards of Project Delivery' looks into various standards of project delivery and analyses how KDD complies with it. The standards are taken from different areas such as quality, project management, business analysis, test design, architecture and service management.

Chapter 10: 'Enabling DevOps' explains how KDD establishes an interactive and fruitful relation between development and service management.

Chapter 11: 'Addressing Contemporary Concerns of Project Delivery' looks at the recent popular techniques in the industry in project delivery and analyses how PKM addresses the issues they are trying to solve. The topics dealt with in this chapter include Shift Left, Knowledge Management, Digitisation, Collaboration, Agile and Lean.

Chapter 12: 'Helping Existing Methodologies' revisits the project delivery methodologies explained in chapter 2 with the focus on understanding how PKM can help these methodologies.

Overview of the Book xxix

Chapter 13: 'Technology Enablers: Tools and Automation' explains how to automate project delivery using PKM at a conceptual level.

Chapter 14: 'Suits Factory Model: Needs Cultural Change' describes how KDD helps bringing the IT industry closer to a process-based industry by enabling a factory model. This chapter also identifies major areas in the change of mindset that is needed to make the factory model work.

Chapter 15: 'Global Relevance of KDD: Assisting Skill Development' elaborates on the Generic Knowledge Management Framework (GKMF) that has evolved from the KDD thinking process. GKMF has the capability to manage knowledge of any domain or organisation. It will assist skill development significantly if it is used to capture domain knowledge.

Chapter 16: 'Lean KDD: Elimination of Requirement and Test Design?' analyses KDD to suggest that test design may be redundant and the GKMF to suggest that business rules and scenario can be used to specify requirements. This gives rise to Lean KDD as explained in this chapter.

Chapter 17: 'Conclusion' summarises PKM, KDD and GKMF proposition.

PKM, the core of KDD, that also helps bridging the gap between Waterfall and Agile methodologies from knowledge perspective, is a new concept. I have explained this model through different chapters of the book as follows:
- Chapter 1 explains how PKM works via a case study.
- Chapter 4 defines PKM and provides an example.
- Chapter 5 lists advantages of PKM.
- Chapter 6 demonstrates how a document excerpt can be converted into PKM.
- Chapter 7 explains how PKM can be expanded to cover end-to-end project delivery, resulting in evolution of KDD.
- Chapter 12 explains how PKM can help the existing methodologies.

A glossary of terms is provided. The words 'software' and 'product' are used interchangeably in the book. The words 'information' and 'knowledge' have also been used interchangeably. Project delivery and software development are used interchangeably. Methodology, method, model, life cycle and framework are popular terms used to specify Waterfall and Agile in related literature, this book uses methodology to specify them.

Examples throughout the book is illustrative and I do not claim them as factually correct. Their main purpose is to help reader understand the related concept. The way banking industry digitised its work from paper general ledgers to software, I visualise IT industry to digitise the project knowledge from project documents to the PKM. 'Digitisation of project knowledge' is used in this context throughout the book.

The following copyrights and trademarks have been used in this book:

BABOK
CMMI
DSDM
IIBA
ISTQB
ITIL
JAD
JIRA
Microsoft Project Plan
Microsoft SharePoint
PMBOK
PMP
PRINCE2
RUP
SAFe
SAP
Shift Left
Six Sigma
TOGAF
Zachman Framework

Each copyright and trademark belongs to its respective owner.

CHAPTER 1

Knowledge Driven Development: What is the Proposition?

This chapter contextualises Knowledge Driven Development (KDD), a new software development methodology, in the broader scheme of knowledge management and software development. Through a case study, KDD is contrasted against the traditional Waterfall and Agile methodologies at high level. The idea is to introduce the reader to the overall KDD way of delivering a project so that they are mindful of it while going through subsequent chapters of the book.

1.1 | Knowledge Driven Development (KDD): A Background

Knowledge remains relevant to us in various forms right from childhood until the end of active life. In the early stages we gain knowledge via primary and secondary *education*. When we reach adulthood, we learn necessary *skills* to prepare ourselves for the profession of our choice. When we join an organisation, we accomplish tasks and start gaining *experience* in the skill acquired. There are primarily two types of tasks – repeatable or specialised tasks and tasks to optimise repeatable or specialised tasks. Figure 1.1 illustrates this.

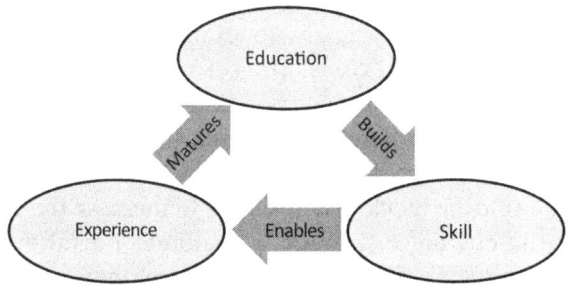

Figure 1.1 | Evolution of knowledge

From a structural perspective, knowledge has four levels which can be captured by eight knowledge constituents named as building blocks, two at each level. Figure 1.2 identifies levels of knowledge and the related building blocks.

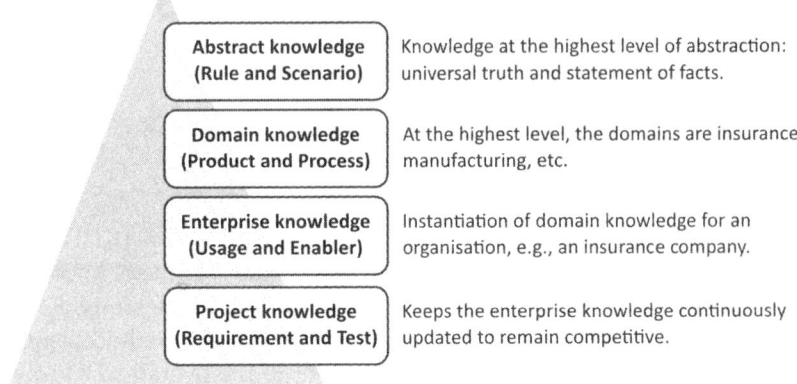

Figure 1.2 | Levels of knowledge

Rules and scenarios are sufficient to capture knowledge at the highest level, i.e., abstract knowledge. They are mostly universal truths and statements of fact. The addition of products and processes contextualises the rules and scenarios which capture knowledge at a lower level, i.e., domain knowledge. Knowledge about insurance, banking and manufacturing are examples of domain knowledge. Enterprise knowledge is instantiation of domain knowledge for an organisation. The 'usage' building block provides a mechanism to customise domain knowledge for the organisation via user interface, reports and communications and 'enabler' building block automates 'usage' primarily via IT applications. Knowledge about a banking company, for example, represents its enterprise knowledge. At the last level comes project knowledge. The objective of project knowledge is to keep the enterprise knowledge updated to maintain the competitive advantage of the organisation. Project knowledge is driven by specific requirements and a way to prove that the requirements are met is via the 'test' building block. An initiative to increase the self-servicing capability of the customer through a customer portal is an example of project knowledge as the portal will help maintain the competitive advantage of the organisation.

Knowledge levels are contextual. Project knowledge in one situation can be viewed as abstract knowledge in another. Forcing users to change the password at regular intervals may be project knowledge in the context of an enterprise initiative. The same requirement may represent abstract knowledge for a specific project to force password change for the users of a specific IT application. For the same project, an example of project knowledge can be that the users must change password every six months and a warning message for the same must start appearing in the last 15 days of the six month period.

The number of building blocks required to capture a particular knowledge level will be the cumulative blocks of that level and the preceding levels. For example, to capture project knowledge completely, it requires a total of eight building blocks, two from the project knowledge building blocks and the remaining six from the previous knowledge levels. As we go down in the level, the granularity of information in the building blocks increases. For example, business rules and scenarios in project knowledge will be more detailed than that of an abstract knowledge.

For a particular situation, these four levels of knowledge provide a framework to capture fit-for-purpose knowledge. These four levels of knowledge are ingrained in the three forms of knowledge (education, skill and experience) as illustrated in Figure 1.3.

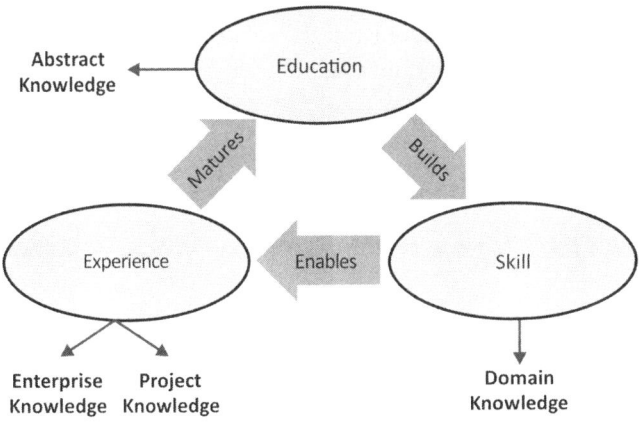

Figure 1.3 | Levels of knowledge covering its evolution

This understanding of knowledge is set to bring about the next level of maturity in knowledge management. I have named this framework as

'Generic Knowledge Management Framework' (GKMF). It paves the way for knowledge digitisation in the form of inventory and relationships of knowledge captured in building blocks. Using this framework, a wide range of knowledge, from school textbooks to process manuals used in an organisation, can be digitised. This can replace the traditional storage of knowledge in the form of documents. Chapter 15 deals with GKMF in detail.

This book aims to implement GKMF to software development in the form of a new project delivery methodology called Knowledge Driven Development (KDD). KDD falls under the purview of 'experience' and deals with the lowest level of knowledge abstraction which is 'project knowledge'. KDD is a new methodology on its own and at the same time its concepts can assist both Waterfall and Agile methodologies. KDD is introduced at a high level in the next section.

1.2 | Waterfall, Agile and KDD Methodologies: A High Level Overview

1.2.1 | Waterfall Methodology

The Waterfall methodology is the oldest project delivery methodology. It follows a structured approach and is typically split into five phases as illustrated in Figure 1.4. In this methodology, a phase can only start when the previous phase is completed and the related documents are signed-off. There is an elaborate change management mechanism to handle changes to the signed-off documents.

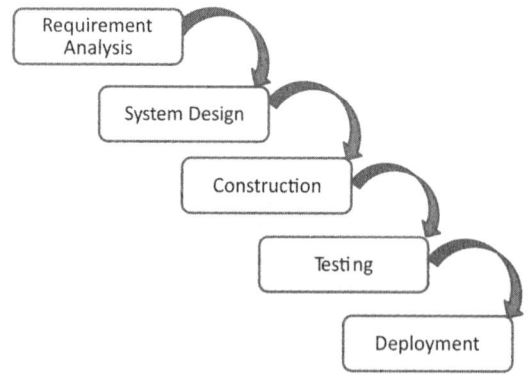

Figure 1.4 | Waterfall project delivery phases

1.2.2 | Agile Methodology

An Agile project does not place emphasis on exhaustive documentation as a reliable source of communication and, instead, relies on face-to-face collaboration for effective and faster project delivery. It also delivers work in iterations so that the customer has early visibility and any deviation can be corrected in time. Figure 1.5 represents the concept of Agile project delivery.

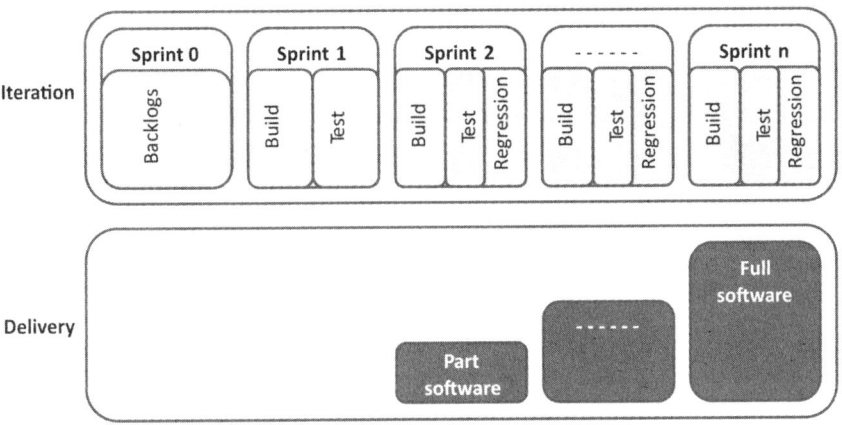

Figure 1.5 | Agile project delivery phases

1.2.3 | KDD Methodology

KDD is a project delivery methodology based on digitisation of the project knowledge and blends the structure of Waterfall and the dynamism of Agile. Figure 1.6 represents different phases of project delivery in KDD.

As indicated in Figure 1.6, KDD has the base structure of Waterfall, blended with Agile in the form of bidirectional interaction between phases and parallel execution of application design and test design. This is made possible as KDD provides an alternate mechanism for managing the project knowledge which is currently contained in documents such as Business Requirement Specification (BRS), Functional Specification Document (FSD), High Level Design (HLD) and Test Cases of the project. These documents are the output of the four knowledge-intensive phases: requirement analysis, solution design, application design and test design. The alternate mechanism, known as Project Knowledge Model (PKM), scopes the project knowledge into a set number of knowledge data points. KDD drives the end-to-end project delivery via the knowledge data points, digitising the project knowledge. Bidirectional traceability across the KDD phases ensures the requirements are always kept updated with the progress in design phases and any modification of requirement is propagated to the design phases in a scientific manner.

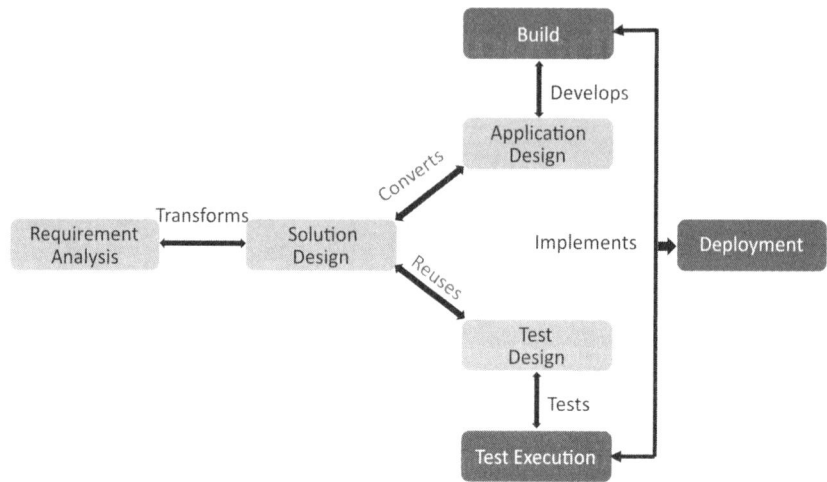

Figure 1.6 | KDD project delivery phases

Project knowledge, as per GKMF, can be captured in eight building blocks. When customised to software development, a typical implementation of PKM has 18 building blocks as listed in the Figure 1.7. Inventories of each of the 18 building blocks (individual requirements are the requirement inventories) are linked together to create 171 relationship types (such as requirement to test case, screen to communication, business rule to product, etc., listed in Figure 4.10 of chapter 4). The 18 building blocks and the 171 relationship types add to form 189 data points of project knowledge. As the project knowledge is made more transparent via catalogued information when compared to documents, its quality assurance is also simplified. As explained in chapter 5, the quality assurance is digitised into 327 data points. With a provision to capture effort in the draft, review and rework mode across different phases of software development, KDD provides for extreme quantification in project delivery.

Requirements are transformed into solution design that contains sufficient information to build the software. Post solution design, application design and test design start in parallel. However, application design is completed last as it traces the test cases produced during test design phase so that test cases are statically tested before a single test case is executed. Solution design is converted from business to technical language in application design. Solution design is reused for test design. These are the four knowledge-intensive phases of project delivery, creating the catalogued knowledge repository.

The remaining two phases of project delivery, i.e., build and test execution, are driven by the catalogued project knowledge repository. Figure 1.7 provides a list of building blocks across the project delivery phases and relationships between different phases from knowledge perspective.

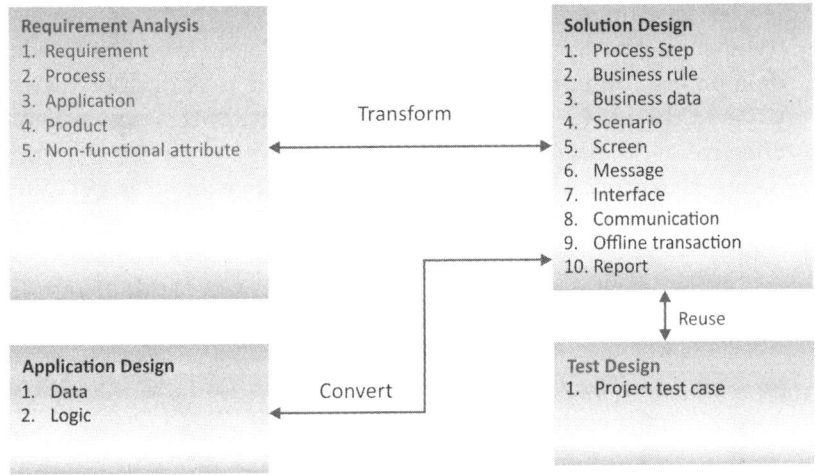

Figure 1.7 | Scoping of project knowledge in KDD

Let's now try to understand how KDD manages end-to-end project delivery. At the start of the project, the subject matter experts (SME) select the relevant building blocks out of a total of 18. Before using PKM in an organisation, its list of applications, processes, products and non-functional attributes is added to the model.

Figure 1.8 provides a common-sense approach to complete each of the four knowledge-intensive phases. The following steps drive phase completion:

1. Select the project knowledge and quality assurance data points relevant for the phase. Selection is done by project SMEs and is based on considerations such as the nature of the project and its budget. Many times, it is done for all the phases together in a single step at the start of the project.

2. Complete relevant information about the selected data points. Mandatory attributes of the data points ensure that the information is fit-for-purpose and is not incomplete (a generic issue with the document production regime where the author is not forced to write a specific piece of information as the document is in free-form text). Enterprise knowledge, which is also in the format of inventories and relationships, can be directly reused for adding project knowledge, if available and relevant.
3. Analyse the negative relationships extracted from the model and update the data points, if relevant. An example of negative relationship is a test case not linked to any requirement.
4. SMEs should perform a manual review of the latest project knowledge data points and update it if relevant. Negative relationships review, prior to the SMEs' review, helps making the SMEs' review more effective, as otherwise a significant effort of SMEs is spent in detecting defects that are clerical in nature (e.g., a requirement not being tested by any test case) in PKM.

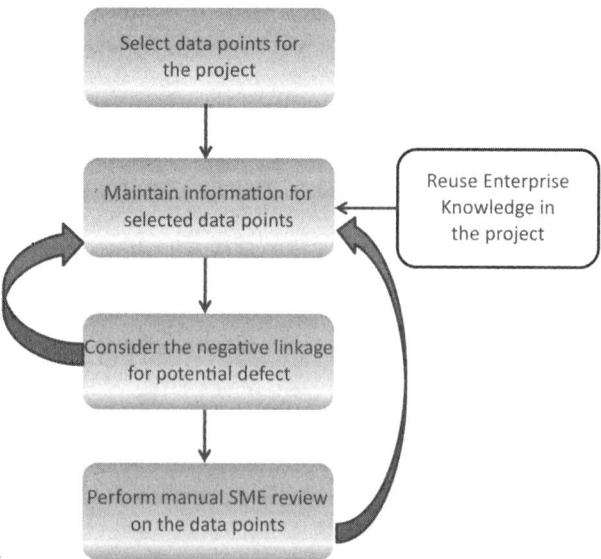

Figure 1.8 | Project knowledge management activities

Having understood how project knowledge is managed, it is easy to appreciate how build and test execution is managed. The entire project, if necessary, is split into manageable chunks primarily based on business processes. For each chunk, build is completed by coding the application design inventories having a provision for review and rework. Similarly, for each chunk, related test cases are executed, with a provision for raising defects and taking the defects to closure that might involve updating the build. PKM comes to assistance in ensuring almost a real-time update of the related data points across the four knowledge intensive phases as the project knowledge is now digitised.

1.3 | Case Study: Customer Self-Service

There are many IT project delivery methodologies in use today. They fall under two broad categories: Waterfall and Agile. KDD methodology attempts to use the best of both and primarily focuses on digitisation of the project knowledge.

Let us try to understand how a project is typically delivered using Waterfall, Agile and KDD through a case study based on an imaginary project.

Project Overview: An insurance company is undertaking a strategic programme to introduce self-servicing capability to its customers via an online portal. The first phase of the programme is complete. It has introduced a skeletal portal with generic features such as online registration, user login and a landing page. The company is now embarking on the second phase of the programme where customers will be provided with a facility to view and update their details. It is assumed that the feasibility and business case for the programme are already complete and the work for this case study begins with requirement detailing.

The project is aimed at implementing customer self-service via a web portal to allow changes consisting of:

1. Change of personal details (e.g., surname, date of birth) which need documentary evidence before the details are updated.
2. Change of contact details (e.g., address, mobile number).
3. Change of bank details (from where the premium for the policy is paid).
4. Change of beneficiary details (i.e., changing recipient of policy amount in case of death of the policy holder).
5. Monthly report showing the percentage of changes originating from the portal against the total number of changes which include other channels namely, phone, email and mail.

The changes mentioned can be performed either by the customer or an authorised representative of the customer using the portal. Post completion of the change, an email notification must be sent to the customer with a copy to the authorised representative, where relevant.

The alteration functions are currently performed via a call centre as well as via back office using phone, email and mail (post) as channels.

Figure 1.9 provides a pictorial view of the requirements.

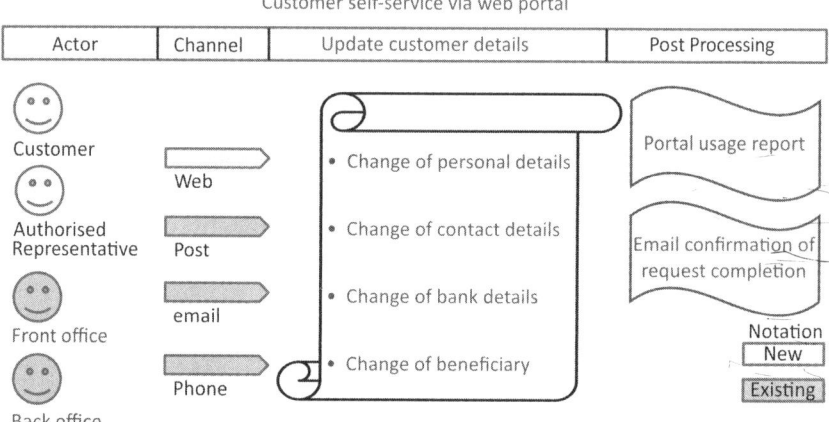

Figure 1.9 | Project requirements

We will now see how the project was delivered using Waterfall, Agile and KDD delivery methodologies, contrasting them with one another. The description below is illustrative and should help visualise how a project is delivered under these methodologies.

1.3.1 | Implementation using Waterfall Methodology

For this case study, the project team consisted of a project manager, a business analyst, a business system analyst, a system analyst and a test analyst. The project was executed in the following different phases to deliver the customer alteration functionality as detailed earlier.

Requirement Analysis: The business analyst interacted with the Operations team to detail the requirements. It soon became obvious that the requirement for processing documentary evidence needed more clarity. It was decided that for the updates requiring documentary evidence, an automatic task in the CRM application would be created, putting the request in a pending status. Once the document was received, the pending task would be closed and the related transaction would be marked as complete with an email sent to the customer, copying the authorised representative where the request for the update was raised by the authorised representative. A Business Requirement Specification (BRS) document was prepared and issued to Operations team to agree and sign-off. After several interactions, the Operations team signed-off the BRS document. This marked completion of the requirement analysis phase.

System Design: The business analyst walked through the signed-off BRS with the business system analyst. The business system analyst prepared the Functional Specification Document (FSD) and had it reviewed internally by his peers. Post incorporation of review comments, he sent it back to the business analyst and the test team for their review and sign-off. The document was signed-off post their review and this marked end of the system design phase.

While writing the FSD, it was found that evidence processing (for the updates that require documentary evidence) still lacked complete specifications. It did not cater to the situation when the evidence was not received for the update request and it also did not specify how long should the system wait for the receipt of evidence. After discussing with Business, the FSD was elaborated as follows:

If evidence was not received within three weeks, a reminder email would go to the customer (and authorised representative, if relevant). If after a further three weeks the evidence did not come, the update request would be rejected and an email would be sent, informing the customer (and the authorised representative if relevant). The email would mention that a new request needed to be raised for the required update if the customer wished to pursue it.

This led to revising the BRS and having to go through the sign-off process again. The project was now slightly delayed, but the project manager thought the delay was within the tolerance and could be compensated for later.

Construction: The business system analyst walked through the signed-off FSD document with the system analyst. Post walk through, the system analyst raised many points as follows:

1. The system analyst suggested that email communication may not be required additionally if the update is processed online, confirming the update in the user screen itself. It was discussed with the business analyst and the suggestion was accepted.

2. The system analyst suggested that facility to add or delete the authorised representative of the customer should be available to the customer. This was accepted by the business analyst and it was agreed to add it as a new requirement.
3. The system analyst suggested the use of Sort Code and Post Code search and check utilities so that the chances of capturing bad data were reduced. The project manager accepted it.

The project manager had not anticipated so many changes in the project and had not made any allowance for them in the project plan. To try to deliver the project as estimated earlier, he decided not to update the BRS and FSD documents and not to produce the HLD document. An email update detailing the new changes was sent to the project team and the system analyst was advised to carry on with the build immediately.

The system analyst completed the build and unit test and this phase was treated as complete.

Testing: While the system analyst was busy in build, the test analyst was designing functional and non-functional test cases which finally got a sign-off from the business analyst. The test team flagged that there were no requirements on response times. As the portal needed to interact with the Contract Engine (i.e., the policy administration system used to administer customers' policy since inception to claim), CRM application, post code and bank sort code utility, specific requirements on response times were detailed.

Operations elaborated that the report should also be generated online for a given date range in the reporting application. This resulted in additional work to be done in the reporting application.

As the project was running behind schedule, the project manager decided to implement these changes without updating the BRS and the FSD. An email update detailing the new changes was sent to the project team and the system analyst agreed to a timeline by which the changes would be delivered.

The testing team, in the meantime, created test cases for these new requirements.

The system analyst confirmed build and unit test of the additional work and the test analyst commenced the functional and non-functional tests. The following defects were detected:
1. When any of the interfacing application was down, the portal was not displaying an error message consistently. It was agreed to display the message in the same font and size.

Knowledge Driven Development: What is the Proposition?

2. The customer could add an authorised representative even when there was an existing one with an active status. The development team fixed this.
3. A copy of the email went to the active authorised representative even if the customer raised the update request. The development team fixed this.

After functional and non-functional testing was done, user acceptance test (UAT) started. UAT raised the following points:

1. It was found out during a meeting with the development team that the customer details were being retrieved from the Contract Engine whereas the Operations team had clearly mentioned them to be retrieved from the CRM applications as that was where the latest details would reside at any point in time. The business analyst had not added this in the BRS, assuming it to be an implementation detail that the project team would know anyway.
2. The UAT team insisted that when doing online reporting, there should also be a provision to produce a pdf copy, with a facility to print the report.
3. The UAT team stated that the customer's unique id must be visible in all the screens of the portal.
4. The UAT team raised a defect that the email confirmation was not sent when the change was about the office phone number only.

The project manager agreed to fix the first three defects. The fourth one was rejected as it had been decided earlier in the system design phase that for updates not requiring documentary evidence, the email will not be sent. BRS was not updated as the project was lagging in schedule and the UAT team was informed about it via email. They had forgotten about the previous decision while creating test cases.

The system analyst fixed all these defects and suggestions and the UAT team re-tested them. This marked closure of the testing phase.

Deployment: With the UAT being complete, the solution was deployed and the project documents BRS and FSD were archived. During the closure of the project, it was realised that the test case to requirements traceability was not available (it could not be done due to lack of time). It was decided to prepare one for project closure compliance.

Project Output: The following were the outputs of the project:
1. Working software (delivered late with respect to actual plan).

2. Project documents (BRS and FSD not up-to-date, and HLD not produced).

Observations: The following key observations can be made:
   1. The project execution through phases clearly demonstrated that knowledge in the project matures over time and it is not possible to freeze the requirements in the requirement analysis phase. One reason for so many changes in the later phases of the project was lack of involvement of all project stakeholders from the beginning.
   2. The project execution also demonstrated heavy reliance on the experience and skill-set of the individuals in the project. The experienced system analyst, who had managed the application for a long time, discovered many amendments in the requirements as the business analyst was less experienced and had not been able to consider the relevant points at the beginning of the project.
   3. Project documentation that was being done rigorously at the start of the project could not continue as updating and subsequent re-approval was a time-consuming process. We saw the team's reliance on old, out-of-date documentation led to raising a wrong defect (in UAT), resulting in wastage of project effort.
   4. Testing team's effectiveness was limited as almost equal number of defects were raised during UAT. One of the reasons for limited effectiveness may be – testing team could not validate test cases against the HLD document as it was not produced in the project due to lack of time.
   5. At the end of the project, the BRS and FSD documents did not represent the actual knowledge that was implemented in the software as they were not updated. For that reason, the IT maintenance team would not rely on the project documentation and must crawl through the code for any debugging, maintenance and future requirement needs.

1.3.2 | Implementation using Agile Methodology

For this case study, an Agile team was formed, which followed Scrum with Extreme Programming. The project team consisted of a scrum master, a product owner, a test analyst and a system analyst to deliver the project. In the project kick off workshop, it was decided to deliver the project in two Sprints. The first Sprint would deliver the contact details, bank details and beneficiary details update and the second Sprint would deliver personal details update that included document evidence processing. Reporting was also planned to be covered in the second Sprint.

Sprint1: The product owner started writing user stories based on the understanding in the project kick off workshop. It became obvious very soon that an authorised representative of the customer would not be available in the system for many customers and, therefore, there was a need to provide a facility to add or delete the authorised representative. The system analyst, while going through user stories on change in address and change in bank details, observed that sort code and post code utilities should be used to reduce the probability of capturing bad data. The system analyst also indicated that to retrieve customer details, CRM application was needed to be used, based on his knowledge of the applications. The test analyst stressed the need to capture response times as there were interfacing applications and to ensure it was not far from the industry standard. While reviewing the prototype, the product owner suggested showing customer id on all the screens. Build and test case creation continued concurrently.

As the team was co-located, defects were conveyed to the system analyst and corrective action was taken immediately. Formal logging and tracking of defects was not done, which saved a lot of effort.

During test execution, the test analyst raised a point that sending email for changes that did not require documentary evidence was not required as the confirmation message was already displayed while processing the change in the portal. The project team accepted it. The test analyst also observed the inconsistency in the error messages when the interfacing applications were down. The system analyst fixed it. As the teams were co-located, to save time, the defects were not raised in sheets or tool and were managed informally.

In the second half of the second week, the test analyst fell ill and was absent for the remainder of the week. Being the only person for testing, the team decided to deliver only contact details update (that had been tested prior to the illness) in this Sprint and move the bank details and beneficiary details update to the product backlog.

The fully functional contact details update (along-with add or delete authorised representative) was delivered as Sprint1, reducing the initial scope.

Sprint2: User stories for processing evidence for personal detail update were collaboratively created in the project as it was treated as one of the most complex functionality in the project and needed inputs from the system analyst. They visualised the happy path scenario when the document came in and the alternate scenario when the document did not come. If after three weeks the document did not come, an email would be sent to the customer and authorised representative (where relevant), informing that the request would be cancelled if the documents did not reach in the next three weeks. Post that, if the document was not received, the request was to be cancelled, informing the customer to raise a fresh request, if the customer wished to pursue it.

While finalising the user stories on the report, there was a need felt by the product owner to produce the report online in the reporting application. Also, a need to produce a pdf and a print facility was added in the user story.

Build was complete in time. Test execution revealed that:
a. No email was being sent post personal detail update.
b. The task was automatically created in CRM application for updates requiring documentary evidence but with status as blank. It should have been 'pending'.
c. The reminder email was sent not exactly after three weeks in all the cases. Public holidays incorrectly increased the elapsed time. The requirement was to send it in three (calendar) weeks' time post request creation.
d. Date of receipt was not in the DD/MM/YYYY format.

The project team agreed to fix these bugs. However, the system analyst expressed inability to fix it in the timelines of this Sprint. The project team decided to deliver only reporting as a part of this Sprint and move the evidence processing to the product backlog.

Sprint3: Bank details change (build done, to be tested), beneficiary details change (build done, to be tested), evidence processing (bugs to be fixed and re-tested) formed the part of Sprint3. The test analyst detected a defect that an email was sent to the authorised representative if there was an active one linked to the customer, even if the customer raised the update request. The system analyst fixed this.

Sprint3 was handed over for regression testing. It was realised that the email was being sent post update of contact detail where documentary evidence was not needed (delivered in Sprint1). The system analyst fixed this.

The project was completed and user stories and high-level test cases were archived.

Project Output: The following were the outputs of the project:
1. Working software (delivered in three Sprints rather than two Sprints as planned initially).
2. Project documents (only two documents, i.e., user stories and high-level test cases, that too, at high level).

Comparison between Waterfall and Agile

1. Significant advantage of co-location and involving stakeholders early was demonstrated in the Agile methodology when compared to Waterfall. The effort on exhaustive documentation and defect management formalities were reduced to a minimum, which allowed for more time for software development.
2. In Agile, the effort taken to deliver the project was significantly reduced, with the only compromise being on exhaustive documentation of the Waterfall methodology. The exhaustive documentation is, anyway, incomplete for most of the projects following Waterfall methodology.
3. However, structured analysis of Waterfall has some advantages over the relatively informal approach of Agile. The effort spent on documenting requirements and solutions helps the project team to gain a common minimum understanding of the project before a single line is coded for the project. This understanding helps in reducing rework and oversight during the build and test phases of the projects following the Waterfall methodology.
4. Effectiveness of regression testing is demonstrated better in the Agile methodology when compared to the Waterfall methodology. In Agile, the regression test may start evolving from second Sprint itself, whereas in Waterfall, the regression test can only be performed when build and system testing is complete for the current project. Some Waterfall projects are delivered in chunks and regression test can therefore be performed from the second chunk of the project. However, the second Sprint in the Agile projects may be a couple of weeks after the first Sprint, in the case of Waterfall projects, the second chunk may be much longer than a couple of weeks after the first chunk limiting the effectiveness of regression for Waterfall projects.
5. In Agile, the quality and completeness of user stories and test cases is not adequate enough for them to be reused by the service management team with any confidence. In comparison, the document set in the

Waterfall project is quite comprehensive and detailed, with a good potential for reuse (although the documents are generally out-of-date).
6. Agile has a heavy reliance on the team members and any absence results in costly delays. This is relatively less visible in Waterfall projects where the team size is comparatively larger and milestones are not on a daily or weekly basis, so unplanned absences can be accommodated to some extent. The shorter Sprint duration and smaller team size in Agile affects the project immediately in case of any unplanned absence.
7. Nature of defects, particularly in Sprint2, indicated that the system analyst was not skilled and experienced enough, resulting in delays. As the team size in Agile is smaller when compared to Waterfall, there is almost no opportunity for a system analyst in Agile to learn and do any research to see what can be the best solution. Experienced team members are needed to execute a project in Agile.

1.3.3 | Implementation using KDD Methodology

For this case study the project team consisted of a business analyst, a system analyst, a test analyst and a project manager. For a project of this nature and complexity, inclusion of business system analyst was not felt necessary. Solution design is driven by business analyst with input from system analyst. There was a single point of contact from the customer, who was available to the project on a need basis.

Project Initiation: Project SMEs sat together in the project kick off workshop and decided how many project knowledge data points were fit-for-purpose for the project delivery. It was agreed that 80 out of 189 knowledge data points were required for the project of this nature and budget. A sample of selected data points were: requirement and relationship between requirement and test case. A sample of data points not selected for the project were: product (customer alteration does not depend on the product selected) and relationship between communication and message (not necessary for a project of this nature).

This exercise had given the project team an opportunity to consider all types of information (data points) that the project would need for the software development. Selecting from a complete project knowledge base reduces the chances of oversight during project scoping and hence saves potential rework.

Requirement Analysis: For this project, the building blocks selected for the requirement analysis phase were: requirement, application, process and non-functional attributes. The list of applications, processes and non-functional attributes for the organisation were already available in PKM in its enterprise knowledge base area. Based on the understanding gained in the project initiation workshop, the following activities were accomplished in this phase:

1. Select in-scope applications: In the project kick off workshop, only the Contract Engine and the Member Portal were selected as applications required to deliver this project. Additional applications identified as impacted during the requirement analysis phase were as listed below:
   a. Sort code utility: to validate sort code of the bank reducing the potential to capture bad data.
   b. Post code utility: to validate post code of the address reducing the potential to capture bad data.
   c. Reporting application: to provide online reporting.
   d. CRM application: to manage evidence processing via automated task creation.

   Applications related to analytics, for example, were not selected as it was out of the scope for the project.

2. Select non-functional attributes: While browsing through the list of non-functional attributes in PKM, 'response time' was added in the project scope due to multiple interfacing applications.

3. Select processes: From the available list of enterprise processes, the obvious ones such as Personal, Contact, Bank, Beneficiary details update, were selected. While browsing through the list of processes, the process 'Add authorised representative' invoked some discussion. It was finally selected to accomplish the requirement related to authorised representative being able to perform customer alteration. As few customers had an existing authorised representative, it was agreed to allow the customer to add authorised representative through the portal.

4. Revamp requirements to accommodate revised list of applications, non-functional attributes and processes as agreed in the previous steps. For example, a new requirement was added to validate post code.

5. For requirement review, KDD prescribes the first cut of transformation of requirements into solution design. During this, the requirements are split into inventories of building blocks (data points) of solution design such as business rule, interface and so on.

The evolution and transformation of 'evidence processing' requirement is interesting to consider. This resulted in creating the following inventories in the solution design area:
a. A business rule was created stating that if the document did not come in three weeks, an email must be sent to customer and authorised representative (if relevant) to give another three weeks, after which the request would be cancelled.
b. Three communications were created: reminder email for sending the evidence, the confirmation email when the evidence was received and the cancellation email when the evidence was not received even in the six weeks period from creating the request.
c. A process step was created to add a task in the CRM application for evidence processing with a status of 'pending subject to receipt of the documentary evidence'.
d. An interface between the portal and CRM application was created so that a task was created in the CRM application when a request was created in the portal for change in personal details requiring documentary evidence.

This exercise also helped to update the requirements so that no important aspect of the evidence processing requirement was missed.

Another example of transforming requirements was the requirement around 'Add authorised representative' where a business rule was added that the authorised representative can be added for a customer only when there was no existing active authorised representative related to that customer.

6. All the inventories thus identified of requirements, non-functional attributes, applications and processes, were interlinked and negative relationship mechanism of PKM was used to ensure the knowledge catalogue was consistent and integrated. Negative relationships indicated that the non-functional attribute 'response time' was not linked to any requirement. A requirement was created, as a result, and then linked to the non-functional attribute. Additionally, the inventories of building blocks and their relationships were manually reviewed to ensure that no gaps existed.

In KDD, requirements are handled in this phase scientifically considering scoping parameters such as applications, non-function attributes, and processes.

Solution Design: The existing inventories for the solution design building blocks (data points such as business rule, interface, process step, business data) that were created during requirement analysis phase are evolved and completely specified in the solution design phase.

During solution design, it was realised that the online report should be produced in pdf format which allows for printing. This required a change in requirements and report building block which was achieved effectively through the positive relationship (traceability) mechanism of PKM.

The non-functional attribute 'response time' was expanded to the next level. For example, 'response time' of a maximum of 5 seconds was agreed to action personal details update. This was a complex transaction as it needed creating a task in CRM with pending status before the action was completed. A response time of a maximum of 2 seconds for transactions not requiring documentary evidence was thought to be reasonable.

The solution design building block inventories were also linked to each other. For example, the response time inventory was linked to the process step that created an automated task in the CRM application.

The negative relationship mechanism of PKM revealed that customer id was not linked to any of the screens. It was decided that the customer id should be displayed on all the screens and therefore the necessary linkages were established.

Another example of the negative relationship mechanism was that the email (inventory of communication building block) confirming successful update was not linked to any business rule highlighting a potential gap in project knowledge. This was linked to a business rule that stated an email after successful update would go to the authorised representative only when they initiate the request.

The manual review process highlighted that the same message was displayed on the screen as well as in a subsequent email when updates were executed online by the customer. In this case, the email was not deemed necessary and the requirement and linkage were amended accordingly.

The manual review also highlighted that inconsistent error messages existed when the interfacing application was not working. These error messages were rationalised so that they had the same font and size that was linked to all these three interface failure scenarios (CRM, post code utility and sort code utility).

The project knowledge is kept up-to-date with exhaustive traceability mechanism. KDD caters for this gradual evolution of requirements into solution design scientifically.

Application Design: Post solution design, application design and test design run concurrently.

As a part of application design, all the inventories of solution design are mapped to the physical data and logic (data points) of the related application (identified during requirement analysis phase). The mapping process ensured that CRM and not the Contract Engine is used to retrieve customer details. Also the test cases were mapped to application design data points once the test design was complete.

The negative relationship review identified that the business rule that prevented more than one active authorised representative was not linked to any data point of the application design. The system analyst added the validation (an inventory of the 'logic' building block) and linked it to that business rule, fixing the issue. Additionally, a test case to check the format of the email was not linked to any application design inventory. The system analyst added the validation and linked it to the test case.

There was no obvious issue detected in the manual review of application design data inventories and their linkages.

Application design ensured that all the inventories of solution design were linked to the application design inventories. It also ensured that all the test cases are statically tested by the system analyst before even a single test case is executed.

Test Design: All the information required to create the complete list of test cases (from unit test to UAT) was available from solution design inventory and relationships. With the help of the PKM, the solution design information was reused to create test cases. The list of scenarios available as output from solution design became the basis for creating test cases using the Orthogonal Array Test Strategy (OATS) technique.

Negative relationship mechanism was used to ensure exhaustive coverage of test cases with requirement and solution design. Manual reviews indicated some oversights that were immediately corrected by the test analyst.

Build: Application design helped in build. As and when portions of build were complete, the test team supplied the unit test cases to be executed. Any defect was resolved in the build phase itself. Once the build was completed, it was handed over to the test team.

Test Execution and Defect Management: In this phase, system test, system integration test, non-functional test and UAT were executed. All the test cases along with the necessary test data were already available in the test case repository prepared during the test design phase. There was only one defect raised in this phase. The remaining test cases were passed in the first attempt. The defect was that the email was sent to the active authorised representative even if the customer raised the update request. This was due to oversight by the system analyst as even though he linked the related business rule to logic, there was a coding error.

Knowledge Driven Development: What is the Proposition? 23

Deployment: As a part of project deployment, the software was deployed and handed over to the service management team. The relevant portion of the project knowledge was moved to the enterprise knowledge.

Project Output: The following were the outputs of the project:
1. Working software (delivered in time as planned).
2. PKM consisting of digitised project knowledge as represented in Figure 1.10.

Digital project knowledge consists of:
- **80** data points
- **11** inventories of enterprise knowledge reused
- **155** inventories
- **2343** relationship
- **398** negative relationship defects
- **16** manual reviews
- **22** activities to manage all

Figure 1.10 | Project Knowledge Model of case study

Comparison of Waterfall, Agile and KDD

Table 1.1 compares the three methodologies based on the case study.

Table 1.1 | Comparison of Waterfall, Agile and KDD

Parameters	*Waterfall*	*Agile*	*KDD*
Project knowledge scoping	No such consideration: at the discretion of SME.	No such consideration: at the discretion of SME.	Provides a scientific basis for project scoping, which enables the SME. KDD has a concept of scoping the project knowledge via 189 data points (assuming 18 building blocks). It gives a sense of completeness while capturing the project knowledge. For the case study, 80 of them were considered fit-for-purpose by the project SME.

Contd.

Parameters	Waterfall	Agile	KDD
Project knowledge digitisation	Primitive: via documents.	Primitive: via high level documents, wiki and face-to-face interactions.	Scientific, via PKM as represented in Figure 1.10.
Easy maintenance of project knowledge	Need multiple documents to be updated for a small change, the main reason BRS could not be kept updated until the end of the project.	Mostly undocumented and managed by updating backlogs where relevant.	Catalogued inventories and exhaustive traceability assist in easier maintenance of the project knowledge in PKM.
Effective review	Traditional document review by the SMEs. A lot of their effort goes towards removing clerical (e.g., consistency related) mistakes for which SME skills may not be required.	Reviews are managed informally most of the time, lacking in rigour and exhaustiveness.	Significant portion of clerical errors are detected by negative relationship review. The review is more effective as the knowledge is digitised. Test execution went almost defect free (with only one defect detected) as the development team statically tested it before the start of test execution.
Effective requirement management	Lots of requirement related changes were identified in later phases but BRS could not be updated due to lack of time.	Backlogs were used to manage requirements better than that of in the Waterfall methodology.	Requirements are sense checked in the requirement analysis phase with other high-level building blocks – non-functional attributes, processes, applications. It is transformed into solution design and through traceability are linked to application design and test design. Every requirement is traced until test cases via exhaustive traceability making requirement management easier when compared to Waterfall and Agile.

Contd.

Parameters	Waterfall	Agile	KDD
Consolidated project knowledge	It is split into various documents with different versions.	No consolidated detailed project knowledge is stored.	Consolidated project knowledge is available in the PKM. Exhaustive traceability integrates the project knowledge. It assists in quality assurance and collaboration as the project knowledge is consolidated and digitised. In the case study, whereas the inconsistency of the error messages was detected in Waterfall and Agile during testing, in KDD it was detected during the manual review in the solution design phase itself.
Enterprise knowledge reuse	Not in a structured way.	Not in a structured way.	The enterprise knowledge is digitised and has the same format as project knowledge making it easy to be reused. In this case study, the list of applications, non-functional attributes and processes was reused from the enterprise knowledge.
Test case consolidation	Test cases are spread across development team, test team and user acceptance team.	There is a lot of informal testing so that time is saved in creating test cases, raising defects and taking them to closure. However, it is difficult to prove traceability with requirement and solution knowledge.	Using the solution design knowledge, end-to-end (unit test to user acceptance test case) test cases are created at one go in the same format. This helps optimising duplication, better prioritisation and traceability to requirement and solution design knowledge.
Reuse across project knowledge	Direct reuse is difficult from the document set.	Lack of exhaustive documents would mean almost no reuse across project knowledge other than relevant experience of the team.	As the project knowledge is digital, reuse is easy. As demonstrated in this case study, solution design inventories are reused for creating test cases.

Contd.

Parameters	Waterfall	Agile	KDD
Easy prioritisation based on project budget	It is difficult to customise a document based on budget.	Backlogs help in prioritisation.	Selection of the most relevant data points addresses the issue of budget directly. This case study had 80 data points of the project knowledge in-scope. If there was less budget, the less important data points could be removed.
Parallel execution of application design and test design	Test design completion is dependent on the output of application design, hence both cannot be done in parallel.	Once the user stories are known, solution design, application design and test design as well as build and test execution run in parallel but not in a structured way.	Solution design contains the project knowledge in business language at the lowest level. This allows parallel execution of application design and test design.

1.4 | Difference in Approach among Waterfall, Agile and KDD

Having understood the essence of KDD via the case study, let us understand the difference in approach between these three methodologies by an analogy of constructing a building.

Waterfall would manually create a blueprint of the building before construction, using pen and paper with instruments like scales and T-squares. Any amendments in the blueprint are an effort-intensive activity.

Agile would start constructing the building without a detailed blueprint. It requires a rough blueprint, created at the time of starting the construction.

KDD would create the blueprint first using state-of-the-art software, where creating and editing the blueprint is much simpler. Post production of the detailed blueprint, doing the construction as per the blueprint is visualised in KDD, but during the construction if there is a need to update the blueprint, it is updated in real-time.

Agile and KDD both deliver the project in less effort than the Waterfall methodology. But the difference is that whereas Agile ignores the project knowledge management of Waterfall methodology via documents, KDD provides a viable alternate and manages project knowledge by cataloguing it.

KDD brings agility in project delivery in an interesting way. Splitting of the work via PKM into data points instead of producing monolithic documents is a feature of KDD. Requirement analysis is one of the four compartments completely specifying the project knowledge and it is executed in a scientific manner as explained earlier. This helps in giving an early view of the project complexity and helps in agility from that perspective. Having a single repository of the project knowledge addresses the issue of communication gap.

This approach of KDD reduces the need to deliver a piece of working product every two or three weeks as is done typically in Agile. KDD encourages chunk-wise project delivery if the project is complex, but the duration of a chunk in the case of KDD resembles Waterfall more, that is, the duration may be months rather than weeks. KDD manages these project deliveries much easier, due to transparency in project knowledge. The Agile approach of delivering a working product in couple of weeks does not allow the team enough time to think about the architectural stability of the code and other finer aspects that are required for stable and maintainable code.

KDD supports splitting a big project in chunks in its unique way. The project knowledge is managed by the data points as explained earlier. Its build and execution are driven by splitting the project in multiple chunks primarily driven by business processes. Due to the exhaustive traceability mechanism of KDD, the complete project knowledge about the chunks and inter-chunks dependency is more transparent than in any other methodology. This helps driving complex projects via KDD.

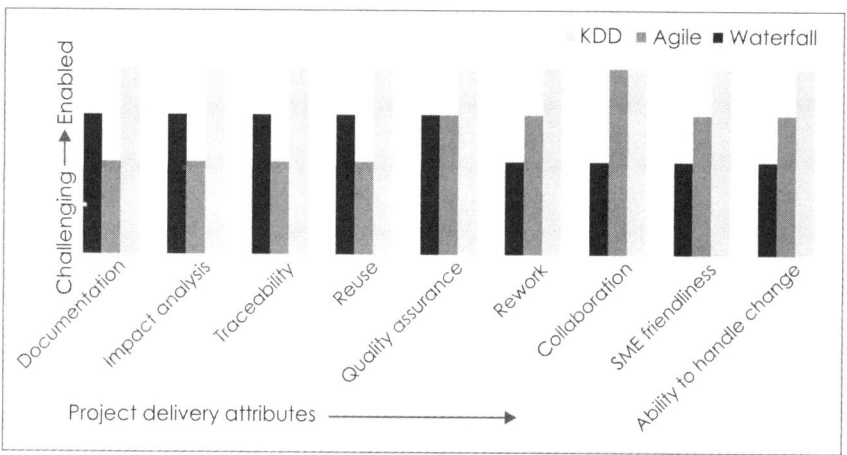

Figure 1.11 | Comparing project delivery attributes of Waterfall, Agile and KDD

Figure 1.11 compares important project delivery attributes with the three project delivery methodologies detailed above.

Table 1.2 provides the rationale behind the comparison of the project delivery attributes identified in Figure 1.11.

Table 1.2 | Comparison of project delivery attributes with Waterfall, Agile and KDD

Project delivery attributes	Rationale of comparison
Documentation	Waterfall prescribes exhaustive documentation, Agile has high level documentation. KDD relies on PKM from which the documents can be extracted. As the document-set from KDD can be extracted from the same source (PKM), it will be consistent.
Impact analysis	Documents, that are difficult to be kept updated, are used for impact analysis in Waterfall. In Agile, impact analysis is mostly informal and sometimes may be challenging due to the absence of exhaustive documentation. In KDD, digitisation of project knowledge makes impact analysis easier.
Traceability	Normally, 5 to 10 relationships are traced in the Waterfall methodology. Traceability is difficult to maintain in Agile as the project knowledge is not captured in detail. In KDD, up to 171 relationships of traceability can be maintained.
Reuse	There is limited reuse in Waterfall as the project knowledge is in the form of documents that is difficult to be kept updated. In Agile, reuse is lesser than Waterfall as it may not have exhaustive documentation. In KDD, as the project knowledge is digitised, reuse is easy. Enterprise knowledge can be reused in KDD as it is in the same format as the project knowledge.
Quality assurance	Quality assurance in Waterfall methodology is via manual review. In Agile we expect associates to be experts in their area and quality assurance is mostly via peer review and informal interactions, as and when required. Co-location of the project team assists in this regard. In KDD quality assurance of the project knowledge is also digitised. Potential defects due to negative relationship are extracted from PKM. This assists in quality assurance, significantly making the subsequent manual review more effective.
Rework	Rework through documents is time consuming in Waterfall. Rework in Agile is easier as it does not have too much of documentation overhead. In KDD, due to structured project knowledge, rework is more effectively managed.
Collaboration	Collaboration is via documents and its formal review, and the handover takeover mechanism in Waterfall. In Agile, the team is co-located and collaborates when needed without much formality. In KDD, PKM becomes the single source of project knowledge, promoting collaboration amongst various project teams.

Contd.

Project delivery attributes	Rationale of comparison
SME friendliness	SME would struggle to help keeping updated the project knowledge that is present in the document form in Waterfall. A good amount of their effort may be wasted correcting clerical defects in the documents. In Agile, the team is supposed to be sufficiently skilled for the job and the ability of SME to assist the project quality increases. Also, it provides an informal environment where progress may be more, given same effort. In KDD, SME is enabled by the digital project knowledge provided by PKM. Any defect will be quickly identified by the SME. Negative relationship review output, extracted by PKM also assists SME as they may not have to look for clerical defects.
Ability to handle change	There is an elaborate change management process in Waterfall to handle change. However, it may be challenging to update the documents and keep them consistent. It is better to handle change in informal Agile environment where the team is co-located and there is not much overhead of document changes. KDD is even better at handling changes as the project knowledge is digitised via PKM. Here the change might only mean a couple of new or updated inventories and relationships.

CHAPTER 2

Project Delivery and Supporting Methodologies

This chapter introduces the reader to the technology and domain aspects of an industry and then details it for IT industry. It elaborates the knowledge-based nature of the IT industry and the factors limiting its natural movement to a process-based industry. It then provides a general overview of the IT project delivery. It also lists project delivery methodologies, standards, guidelines and frameworks used in various scenarios to manage the IT projects.

2.1 | IT Industry from Technology and Domain Perspective

Information Technology (IT) is nascent industry. Let us look at various industries and their ages:

1. Agriculture (12,000 years old)
2. Modern Banking Industry (700 years old)
3. Modern Insurance Industry (350 years old)
4. Modern Pharmaceutical Industry (200 years old)
5. Modern Steel Industry (150 years old)
6. Information Technology (60 years old)

Industries have matured with research and experience contributing to enrichment of knowledge in the industry. Old industries have matured enough to have standard and well-defined processes for delivery of various projects. Also, their processes are not generic but detailed and prescriptive. For example, in an agricultural plantation, separation between two plants is well-defined and prescriptive. It primarily depends on plant types. But this would not have been the case a few thousand years ago. At that time the practice must have gone through several phases of research and experience to come to the optimal separation between two plants. Agriculture, then, could be termed as a knowledge-based industry but now it is a process-based industry.

One of the greatest revolutions in the maturity of industries has been the Industrial Revolution where mechanisation proved immensely beneficial for mass production. Another revolution of a similar or even greater scale is being brought about by the introduction of computers (including smartphones and apps), which has started impacting every aspect of our lives. Computers have brought in the IT industry to the fore.

The IT industry itself is a new industry and is barely 60 years old. IT is a support industry which assists other industries. Predominantly, IT automates manual, repeatable processes via software.

An industry has two components at the highest level. These are the implements and the way of using the implements effectively. The implement in IT is 'technology' and the knowledge about how to effectively use an implement is 'domain'. In agriculture, the tractor is an example of implement and the knowledge about the process of tilling effectively using a tractor is an example of domain. In manufacturing industry, machines are implement and the knowledge of using these machines to produce outputs is domain.

In IT industry, computers, printers and programming languages are technology and the knowledge of using them to produce outputs is domain. Over the last 60 years, the processing power of computers has been increasing at an exponential rate. Storage power has increased tremendously. Programming languages have matured from assembly language to object oriented languages.

Let us now look at the domain side of the IT Industry. Building incredible things by passion and investment is one thing, but standardising it by defining matured processes for continued and repeatable delivery is another. IT domain is primarily about standardisation of processes for building commercial software. There are numerous standards, guidelines, methodologies and frameworks being developed from the last 40 years and some have matured over this time. Any good book on software engineering will explain this in detail. Methodologies are touched upon in this chapter and standards of project delivery are dealt with in chapter 9.

One of the important measures of effectiveness of the processes of an industry is how well it can store the information and be used for a specific output. Taking an example from the insurance industry, for issuing a life insurance policy, information provided in the proposal form is used to issue the policy without any manual intervention (most of the time). A similar level of maturity in IT processes can be: when requirements are known in sufficient detail, it should be easy to make a software product out of them. Currently, it takes multiple times the effort of requirement gathering to deliver the software, which is not so in the insurance industry. This clearly demonstrates the difference in maturity in insurance industry (process-based industry) and IT industry (knowledge-based industry). The constraining factors in IT industry preventing it to become closer to process-based industry are:

1. The IT industry spans across numerous domains, making it difficult to create effective and domain-agnostic processes to assist project delivery. Due to this fact, current methodologies remain shallow and indicative when it comes to detailing *how* to do things.
2. Project knowledge is core to the maturity of IT industry as it drives project delivery. Currently, the lowest logical unit of project knowledge is a document or sections of a document. Documents are not the best way to create and maintain project knowledge since they are costly to produce and update in terms of time and resources. This has become evident by the reducing usage of the Waterfall methodology.
3. 'The knowledge required for IT project delivery remains a prerogative of subject matter experts.' This is a wrong notion and it contributes to slowing down the maturity of IT processes. Software is driven by algorithms which are explicit knowledge. It should be possible to store the knowledge in a way that can directly assist in software development.
4. There is a vast array of technology on which software is built. Although technology only covers the implementation aspects of the software, it plays a part in limiting the industry to come up with a set of common standards and guidelines.

Having discussed the domain of IT industry, let us understand its knowledge-based nature in detail in the next section.

2.2 | Information Technology: A Knowledge-Based Industry

From time immemorial it has been a quest for human kind to discover higher levels of knowledge. Knowledge is relevant in every aspect of human life. Knowledge maturity takes a similar path in any industry. It takes early shape via inventors and innovators. Post that, practitioners give standardisation of the concept and implementation. After some time, it stabilises via standard processes. Inventors and innovators start thinking about the next levels and the cycle goes on. Industries mature via knowledge maturity cycles and after the maturity of multiple cycles, it moves from knowledge based industry to process based industry. This movement reduces the need 'to do things differently' in the process based industry as the processes are standardised. Introduction and standardisation of telephone, mobile and smartphone are the examples of maturing knowledge and thereby maturity of the telecommunication Industry.

In knowledge-based industries, there is a wide variation between what is written in the text and what happens in reality. This may be because the industry has not matured enough to have stable and standard processes and there is too much left to the discretion of the person executing the work. Delivery of work, both in terms of effort and quality, therefore depends on the skill and experience of the team involved. In contrast, for a process-based industry, there is less variation between what is written in texts and what happens in reality. This is because the processes have matured over time and are standard and detailed, reducing the need for differences in interpretations. Machines drive the delivery with the support from the person in process-based industry, whereas in the knowledge-based industry the person drives the delivery with the support from machines. The percentage of effort on research and development is greater in the knowledge-based industry.

Let us consider steel industry that is matured enough to be termed as a process-based industry. During the period 1860 to 1980, it matured through many innovations like Bessemer process, Open Hearth Furnace and Electric Arc Furnace. Now there are standard and efficient ways to produce steel, although there will always be scope for improvement.

Now let us consider Information Technology (IT) industry, which is still evolving and can be termed as a knowledge-based industry. IT started its journey around 60 years ago at commercial levels. It delivers software products to different industries to automate their business processes. The IT industry is maturing at a very fast rate and has multiple standards and guidelines covering various areas of the industry. However, the following indicators suggest that it is still maturing and has not yet become a process-based industry:
1. Variation of effort and quality to deliver similar projects is significant.
2. People still drive a project. Machines (i.e. tools) play a secondary and not a primary role.

3. The effort on research and innovations is significantly greater when compared to the process-based industries like electric bulb manufacturing industry.
4. There are too many methodologies of project delivery indicating the need for consolidation and rationalisation.
5. In-spite of all the standards and guidelines, software project delivery is largely dependent on the experience and temperament of the project team. The project leader primarily drives the working style of the team.

To understand these indicators better, let us discuss how projects are delivered in IT industry in subsequent sections.

2.3 | IT Project Delivery: An Introduction

Almost all industries deliver projects. Some of the examples of project delivery are:
1. Building a residential house (Civil domain)
2. Setting up a gift shop (Retail domain)
3. Launching a satellite (Space Science domain)
4. Launching a new life insurance product (Insurance domain)
5. Commissioning of a factory (Manufacturing domain)

Like all industries, the IT industry also delivers outputs, generally via projects. Almost all the companies across domains (such as retail or manufacturing) use IT to automate their business processes, subject to cost-benefit analysis, which in most of the cases is in favour of automation. Typical examples of an IT project are:
1. To replace manual ledger entry with software (Banking domain)
2. To enable customers of an insurance policy to do self-service (e.g., change in address) via a portal (Insurance domain)
3. To order books online from a publisher (Print Media domain)
4. To order food online from a restaurant (Catering domain)
5. To automate inventory management for a food superstore (Retail domain)

For the purposes of this book, let us restrict ourselves to the IT project delivery that deals with automation of business processes. IT projects in embedded domain such as industrial automation is not dealt with here, primarily due to my lack of experience in that area.

Companies usually have their own IT department to deliver the IT projects. An IT department can either deliver the projects on its own or get them delivered by IT service providers. It either buys the software (off-the-shelf) from IT vendors or builds it in-house or it can have an external supplier develop a bespoke implementation. The change management department closely works with the IT department to deliver the IT project. Change management functions are: business project management, business analysis and user acceptance. The IT department functions are: IT project management, system analysis and build, quality assurance and service management. These functions are detailed below:

1. **Business Project Management:** This is mainly involved during the initial stage of the project where the idea is expanded from Business perspective and with inputs from IT, a cost-benefit analysis is done. Cost-benefit analysis helps determine if it is viable to become an IT project.
2. **Business Analysis:** This function is responsible for gathering requirements from relevant user departments and presenting them in a structured manner by producing relevant documents. This is supported by business analysts under the guidance of business architects.
3. **User Acceptance:** This function ensures that the product meets the requirements specified by business analysts. It is planned and executed by a dedicated team, usually consisting of users from the related departments. It is popularly known as UAT (User Acceptance Test) team.
4. **IT Project Management:** A business project usually has IT as a significant component in the project. There will be a few aspects of the business project where IT will have little to do, for example, user training for a particular skill to be able to use the IT applications being developed. The IT project is managed by this function and it usually reports to the business project management.
5. **System Analysis and Build:** Business system analysts interpret requirements and help produce the solution design with the assistance of the business analyst. The design is then developed into working software using various IT technologies by system analysts. System analysts work under the guidance of technical architects.
6. **Quality Assurance:** This function ensures that the software is built as per the requirements and solution design. It tests both the functional and non-functional aspects of the product managed by test analysts. This function of IT department is similar to user acceptance function in the Business and is usually more detailed than user acceptance.

7. **Service management:** They own the maintenance and enhancement of the product once it is in production.

The main stakeholders the IT and change management departments need to deal with are:

1. **Business:** They are primarily the front office and/or back office teams who stand to gain from usage of the IT product being built or enhanced. IT products aim to automate the business processes of the business teams. Business teams help business analysts in finalising the requirements of the project.
2. **IT Vendors:** There are established software products from IT vendors in almost all the domains that are sold 'off-the-shelf'. Policy administration system from different IT vendors is an example in the insurance domain. The product may also be domain agnostic. An example may be Customer Relationship Management (CRM) product that can be used in any domain for managing customers. Some of the products such as Application Lifecycle Management (ALM) tools assist in automating the IT project delivery itself. The IT vendor may also sell hardware (e.g. servers). The products may need customisation to suit the requirement of the company although the assumption is that it will be minimal.
3. **IT Service Providers:** Some of the IT functions may be costly to implement in-house and the IT department may find it more cost-effective to procure them from IT service providers. An example of this would be outsourcing of testing services.
4. **Third Parties:** As a part of project delivery, the IT department may need to get the facilities of third parties, for example usages of post code search functionality from the Post Office, credit check functionality from Experian.

Having understood project delivery functions and their main stakeholders, it becomes easier to understand how an IT project is delivered. The IT project delivery has following activities:

1. **Initiation:** When an idea is generated either by the Business or the IT team, usually all the aspects of it are appropriately captured in a pre-defined format. The idea is analysed and a high-level cost-benefit analysis is done leading to a business case. If the idea is complicated, it is broken into multiple ideas or a feasibility study is done before doing the cost-benefit analysis. If the cost-benefit justifies, the next set of activities are initiated. Business architect, technical architect, business project manager and senior management of the company drive this activity.

Project Delivery and Supporting Methodologies

2. **Requirement Analysis:** Business analysts produce business requirements with inputs from Business. This allows for the detailed understanding of the idea. The business case is revalidated with inputs from business and technology experts.
3. **Solution Design:** Business system analysts, with the help of system analysts, expand on the requirements and undertake detailed design in the form of processes, screen prototypes, logical data model, letter or report templates, etc. Solution design provides detailed information on the product to be manufactured in business language.
4. **Application Design:** System analysts convert the solution design which is in business language to technical language via algorithms, system use cases, physical data models, state transition diagrams, class diagrams, sequence diagrams, etc.
5. **Test Design:** Test analysts read requirements and solution design and create test cases to prove that the software developed complies with the requirements set out. This includes functional and non-functional tests. Non-functional tests cover the overall behaviour of the software from different perspectives such as usability, security, maintainability, portability and performance.
6. **Build:** System analysts, after the completion of application design, write the code using appropriate programming environment and create the software. They also perform unit and integration tests to demonstrate that the software is working.
7. **Test Execution:** Test analysts run the test cases and ensure that the software meets the requirements and solution design. This includes user acceptance test (UAT).
8. **Implementation:** Once the software is tested, it is implemented in production. After a pre-defined period of warranty support, it moves to service management, who own the maintenance until the application is decommissioned.

Let us now list down the roles of project delivery. There are two types of roles – worker and specialist roles.

Worker roles are:
1. Business analyst: Responsible for detailing requirements.
2. Business system analyst: Responsible for solution design.
3. System analyst: Responsible for application design and build.
4. Test analyst: Responsible for test design and test execution.

Specialist roles are:
1. Project manager: Ensuring the project is delivered mainly with the help of worker roles and specialist roles.

2. Database administrator: Responsible for administering database on which the software is based upon.
3. Release manager: Responsible for maintaining version of code base and documents and also moving the code to production.
4. Architect: Business, technology and data architects are experts in their areas.
5. Non-functional test experts such as performance test expert.

The core software development consists of two areas. One relates to specifying details of the product to be delivered through requirement, design and test specifications. This is known as project knowledge (which is the subject of this book) and is different for different domains. The other is about actually delivering the product using relevant technology that may or may not be same in different domains.

With a fair understanding about the IT project delivery, its knowledge-based orientation and stakeholders, let us now consider the current landscape of IT project delivery methodologies.

2.4 | IT Project Delivery Methodology Landscape

There are three layers of evolving processes to execute a software delivery project. They are:
1. Set of methodologies coming from either Waterfall (structured and sequential) or Agile (empirical and iterative) family, covering software project delivery.
2. Industry standard frameworks and standards (e.g. CMMI) to assist project delivery.
3. Company-specific methodologies that are customised to suit their needs.

These currently drive project delivery.

First Layer: Generic Project Delivery Methodologies

Project delivery methodologies started with the Waterfall methodology. This methodology is structured and sequential, where the next phase starts once the previous phase is agreed to be complete. Requirements can rarely be correctly written at the first attempt and, on most occasions, the requirements continuously evolve, making the use of Waterfall methodology challenging. This started giving rise to the next generation of methodologies that accommodate changes, shed elaborate documentation, split the work into smaller chunks so that early results can be shown faster and increase the collaboration with customers. These are the set of Agile methodologies and are more experience-based (empirical) than structured.

Every single methodology is a result of its inventor's attempt to solve a real problem on ground. As the problems are always contextual, the methodology works best in that context but not so well in other contexts.

At the highest level, any methodology must either be sequential or iterative. Waterfall represents sequential and Agile represents iterative methodology. Also, any methodology must either be empirical or structured. As mentioned earlier, Waterfall represents structural and Agile represents empirical methods. From output perspective, methodologies suggest either delivering the entire software in one go or deliver it in increments. Waterfall typically delivers in one go and Agile delivers in increments. We have used Waterfall and Agile in the book which covers all the six characteristics of project delivery. We have now learnt enough on the methodologies to predict them. Three factors below primarily influence them:

1. Eight generic activities of project delivery mentioned above.
2. Six characteristics of project delivery mentioned above.
3. Importance attached to these activities and characteristics. For example:
   (a) Focus on test activities resulted in V-model, Test Driven Development (TDD) and Behaviour Driven Development (BDD)
   (b) Focus on iteration results into Prototyping and Spiral models.
   (c) Focus on increments are demonstrated in Scrum and Extreme programming.

The list [1] in Table 2.1 covers a wide range of methodologies.

Table 2.1 | Existing project delivery methodologies

Methodology	Characteristics	Strength	Weakness
Waterfall	• detailed planning • exhaustive documentation • each phase has its own deliverables • next phase starts when the previous phase documents are signed-off	• structured approach • customer knows what to expect at the end of the project • easy to understand for the project team	• does not support natural evolution of requirements • a lot of effort spent in re-factoring planning and core project documents • customer does not get an early view of the software • low tolerance for design and planning errors

Contd.

Methodology	Characteristics	Strength	Weakness
Agile	• time-boxed iterative delivery • face-to-face communication • constant feedback loop	• faster response to changing requirements. • faster turnaround as time saved on exhaustive documentation • communication gap reduced due to face-to-face communication • greater customer satisfaction due to direct and frequent engagement	• lack of exhaustive documentation results in more effort in the maintenance phase • not suitable for bigger and complex projects • if the entire team is not sufficiently skilled and experienced, project might not deliver as expected
Prototyping	• build one or more demo versions of the software product • project owner is actively involved • requirement understood primarily via prototype before design starts • prototype matures till it is agreed to be stable.	• accurate identification of application requirements • early feedback from the project owner • improved user experience • early identification of missing or redundant functionality	• leads to unnecessary increase of the application's complexity as the scope may increase • increased programming effort as the prototype may be discarded • Lack of documentation makes it harder to regression test
Spiral	• focuses on objectives, alternatives and constrains • has 4 major phases: planning, risk analysis, development and evaluation • emphasises risk analysis • evaluates multiple alternatives before proceeding to the planning stage	• early identification and reduction of project risk • suitable for complex projects • strong documentation	• costs generated by risk handling • dependent on accurate risk analysis • spiral may go on indefinitely.
Rapid Application Development	• less emphasis on planning tasks and more focus on development • time-box approach	• applications are developed fast • code can be easily reused	• poor documentation • high development costs • code integration issues

Contd.

Project Delivery and Supporting Methodologies

Methodology	Characteristics	Strength	Weakness
Extreme Programming (XP)	• pair programming • unit testing • fast consecutive releases • collective ownership • open workspace • project owner decides the priority of tasks	• application gets very fast in the production environment • frequent releases of working code • reduced number of bugs • smooth code integration • continuous feedback from the project owner	• lack of documentation • developer's reluctance to pair programming • developer's reluctance to write tests first and code later • requires frequent meetings • lack of commitment to a well-defined product leads to project owner's reluctance
V-Model	• introduces testing at every development stage • highlights the importance of maintenance	• low bug rate • easy to understand and use	• vulnerable to scope creep • relies heavily on the initial set of specifications
Scrum	• iterative development • time-box approach known as 'Sprints' • daily meetings to assess progress known as 'daily scrum' • self organising development team • tasks are managed using Backlogs: product backlog and Sprint backlog	• delivers products in short cycles • enables fast feedback • self organising development team	• lack of documentation resulting in issues with regression testing • requires experienced developers • hard to estimate at the beginning the overall effort required to implement large projects; thus cost estimates are not very precise
Dynamic Systems Development method	• iterative development • MoSCoW prioritisation of tasks • time-box approach • non-negotiable deadlines • strict quality standards set at the beginning of the project • project team and project owner share the workplace (physical or virtual) • test early and continually	• focuses on addressing effectively the business needs • post project implementation performance assessment • complete documentation • active user involvement	• requires large project teams as it has multiple roles to cover • requires very skilled developers • relatively new methodology, not many experts available • may require very large number of iterations particularly if the existing application is being replaced

Contd.

Methodology	Characteristics	Strength	Weakness
Rational Unified Process	• iterative and incremental development • prioritise risk handling • adequate business modelling • change management • performance testing	• accurate and comprehensive documentation • efficient change request management • efficient integration of new code • enables reuse of code and software components	• requires highly qualified professionals • development process is complex and poorly organised
Lean Software Development	• iterative development • discards all components that do not add value to the product • amplify learning • customer focus • team empowerment • continuous improvement	• reduced project time and cost by eliminating waste • early delivery of working code • motivated project team	• project is highly dependent on individual team members • a team member with strong business analysis skills required
Test-Driven Development (TDD)	• unit testing driven • testing scenarios are developed before actual coding • repeated short development cycles • suitable for debugging legacy code developed with other techniques	• less time spent on debugging • higher quality code • by designing tests, the developer empathises with the user • less defects get to the end user	• tests are focused on syntax and overlook actual functionality • requires more code than most methodologies • writing unit tests increases costs
Behaviour-Driven Development (BDD)	• driven by behavioural aspects and not by implementation details • unit testing • focuses on business value • genuine collaboration between business and development	• easy to maintain • usability issues are discovered early • reduced defect rate • easy to integrate new code	• Team should have scripting skill • project owners are reluctant to write behaviour scenarios

Contd.

Methodology	Characteristics	Strength	Weakness
Feature-Driven Development (FDD)	• iterative development • application is broken down into features • no feature should take longer than two weeks to implement • uses milestones to evaluate progress	• multiple teams can work simultaneously on the project • scales well to large teams • good progress tracking and reporting capabilities • easy to understand and adopt	• individual code ownership • iterations are not well defined • may not lead to well-designed systems
Model-Driven Engineering (MDE)	• uses domain model • models are automatically transformed into working code • knowledge is encapsulated in high level models • emphasises reuse of standardised models	• high degree of abstraction • increased productivity • delivers products with a high degree of compatibility and portability • shorter time-to-market, lowers maintenance costs	• requires considerable technical expertise • documentation is readable only by domain experts • difficult to implement version control on modelling environment
Kanban	• make work visible • limit work in progress • manage the flow of work	• flexible planning • reduced cycle time • visual metrics • continuous delivery	• not fit for projects requiring some level of planning • outdated boards can lead to issues • no idea when the work will complete, it only shows the current status
Joint Application Development	• emphasises determination of system requirement • involves the project owner and end user in the design and development • JAD meetings • prototyping	• accelerates design • enhances quality • promotes teamwork with the customer • creates a design from the customer's perspective • lowers maintenance costs	• relies heavily on the success of the group meetings • does not have a documented approach for stages that follow system requirements determination and design
Scaled Agile Framework (SAFe)	• scaled agile practices • three levels – team, program and portfolio • influenced by agile, lean and system thinking	• handles large projects • builds incrementally with fast learning cycles • decentralise decision making	• highly prescriptive • manager oriented agile

Second Layer: Generic Frameworks and Standards

Based on experience and research, various frameworks and standards have evolved to aid project delivery methodology from different perspectives. Build phase of Software Development Life Cycle (SDLC) is not considered here as this is varied and dependent on the technology (e.g. programming language).

Some of the known frameworks and standards are listed in Table 2.2.

Table 2.2 | Frameworks and standards enabling project delivery

Framework / Standard	Description
PRINCE2	PRINCE2 (an acronym for **PR**ojects **IN** **C**ontrolled **E**nvironments) is a structured project management method. It emphasises dividing projects into manageable and controllable stages. It is used extensively by the UK Government. It is also used in the private sector.
PMP	Project Management Professional (PMP) is an internationally recognised project management methodology offered by the Project Management Institute (PMI). The certification examination is based on the PMI Project Management Body of Knowledge (PMBOK) describing the methodology.
ITIL	ITIL is a widely accepted approach to IT Service Management (ITSM) This framework has worldwide use. ITIL gives a series of best practices based on experience from both the public and private sectors, locally and worldwide. ITSM is constantly evolving. The evolution is driven by technology and the vast range of organisational environments in which it operates.
TOGAF	TOGAF® is the de facto global standard for enterprise architecture. The Open Group Architecture Framework, or TOGAF, is intended to provide a structured approach for organisations seeking to organise and govern their implementation of technology. The objective of TOGAF is to employ a conceptual framework to ensure that software development projects meet business objectives, they are systematic and their results are repeatable.
CMMI	Capability Maturity Model Integration (CMMI) is a process improvement training and appraisal programme.
BABOK (IIBA)	Business Analysis Body of Knowledge (BABOK) represents the collective knowledge of the business analysis community and is a written guide reflecting current best practices and techniques. It is owned and maintained by International Institute of Business Analysts (IIBA).
TBOK (ISTQB)	ISTQB® is International Software Testing Qualifications Board and has started activities for the creation of a comprehensive and consistent TBOK (Testing Body of Knowledge). It is working on TBOK and will be publicly available shortly.

Third Layer: Customised Methodology for an Organisation

At the last layer, organisations having the budget devise their own delivery methodologies. This results in a customised methodology and is often a hybrid of two or more of the methodologies we have discussed. These are usually owned by the change delivery function of the organisation that is responsible to deliver changes to Business.

CHAPTER 3

Project Delivery Pain Areas and the Way Forward

This chapter provides the context of the book and summarises how a new methodology of IT project delivery has evolved. It lists out some major failures of IT projects in the past, mentions the challenges in project delivery and identifies the root causes. It explains the reduced usage of the Waterfall project delivery methodology, having failed to keep project documents updated in real-time. It also explains the downgrading of the importance of project documentation in the Agile methodology. It introduces an alternate way of creating and maintaining project knowledge which is currently present in documents.

3.1 | Context

Maturity in software project delivery is still low despite having numerous methodologies available to drive it. Methodologies generally fall under two families: Waterfall and Agile. The latest global data from the Standish Group [2], tracking over 50,000 projects during 2011–2015, shows that the success rate of Waterfall is 11% and Agile is 39%.

The book has taken the scientific structure of Waterfall and the dynamic approach of Agile, combined it with PKM and evolved a new IT project delivery methodology, which I refer to as Knowledge Driven Development (KDD).

An important reason for project failure is lack of availability of 'fit-for-purpose' information and timely communication across project stakeholders. In Waterfall methodology, the information and its communication are accomplished by project documents stored in a commonly accessible location. Documents change under version control with a sign-off mechanism, making it difficult to keep the document up-to-date in a continuously evolving project delivery environment. If a defect in the document is detected, say, today. It might take a month before the new version of the document is released addressing the defect (due to the sign-off mechanism). The other limiting factor is the document itself as it is written in free-form text and keeping it consistently updated involves significant effort. In Agile methodology, the situation is not better as the documents are not meant to be exhaustive enough to be considered as containing 'fit-for-purpose' information. The information is primarily communicated through face-to-face discussions, making it person dependent. Agile assumes fully skilled team members, and any attrition or absence might be a challenge. The only reliable source of information is code, which is written in technical language that only the technologists in the project can understand.

KDD resolves the issue of the lack of availability of 'fit-for-purpose' information and its timely communication in project delivery through its newly developed PKM.

KDD visualises the end-to-end project delivery consisting of knowledge related and execution related activities across different phases as follows:
1. Requirement analysis: Knowledge related
2. Solution design: Knowledge related
3. Application design: Knowledge related
4. Test design: Knowledge related
5. Build: Execution related
6. Test case execution and defect management: Execution related

These six phases are managed by four activities of project management:
1. Task management
2. Quality management
3. Risk management
4. Configuration management

PKM covers the knowledge related phases, which then drives the entire project delivery. This model has the following constituents:
1. Data points of project knowledge with the flexibility to be customised to suit any project. A subset of project knowledge data points is identified as enterprise knowledge data points to be reused in the project delivery environment.
2. These data points completely specify the software from business, technology and test perspective, and are quality assured by negative relationship (extracted from PKM) review and manual review.
3. The project knowledge data points and their quality assurance are managed by three types of activities of project delivery: draft, review and rework.

The model creates a single source of project knowledge which replaces the documents effectively. It ensures that enterprise knowledge and project knowledge collaborate with each other and create an environment of continuous improvement in project delivery.

Once the project knowledge is detailed and quantified, it can drive build and test phases. It can also assist performing project management activities better. PKM can easily expand to cover end to end project delivery and evolve into a new methodology – KDD. KDD has the potential of:
1. Bringing the much desired quantification in the project delivery environment due to cataloguing project knowledge and its quality assurance.
2. Ensuring exhaustive traceability that integrates the entire project knowledge together. It ensures easier impact analysis and information update.
3. Taking the IT industry from knowledge-based to process-based where the project delivery is standardised like that of manufacturing industry, for instance.
4. Ensuring seamless transfer of the software from the development to the service management team as the project knowledge is digitised via the data points of PKM.

The book introduces this new methodology (KDD) based on PKM. The book also explains how PKM having digitised project knowledge, can assist existing methodologies. The PKM and KDD can be used to improve the capability of delivering future projects.

3.2 | IT Project Failures

Even though there are so many project delivery methodologies, the IT industry is full of examples of inefficiencies and ineffectiveness in the end-to-end project delivery. Some examples of the known failures worth noting are:
1. [3] The National Health Service (NHS) is the public health service of UK. The National Programme for IT (NPfIT) in the NHS was launched in 2002 to bring the use of information technology in NHS into the twenty-first century through the introduction of integrated electronic patient records systems, online 'choose and book' services, computerised referral and prescription systems and the underlying network infrastructure. It was the largest public sector IT programme ever attempted in the UK, originally budgeted to cost approximately

£6 billion over the lifetime of the major contracts. After a history marked by delays, stakeholder opposition and implementation issues, the programme was dismantled by the Government in 2011, almost ten years after it was launched.
2. [4] In 2004, a UK food retailing giant reported its first ever half-year loss of £39 million, when it wrote-off £260 million of IT expenditure. The new system was implemented into production but proved to be unworkable.
3. [5] In 2004, a new government welfare management system in Canada, costing $200m was unable to handle a simple benefits rate increase. The contract allowed for six weeks of acceptance testing and never tested the ability to handle a rate increase.
4. [5] In September 2004, flights across the UK were grounded after an air traffic control computer failure at West Drayton control centre. The National Air Traffic Services' Flight Data Processing System failed at around 0600 BST for an hour, after overnight testing of an upgrade. Thousands of passengers experienced delays as airlines worked to clear the backlog of flights. Planes had to be grounded at airports including Gatwick, Heathrow, Manchester and Inverness.
5. [6] The Akash, a low-cost tablet was officially launched in India on 5 October 2011 as a part of the initiative to link 25,000 colleges and 400 universities in an e-learning programme. It aimed at providing a US$35 tablet suitable for poor students. This project did not meet the expectation.
6. [7] The massive 'Universal Credit' project in UK was intended to replace a hotchpotch of existing benefits and tax credit top-ups with a simple, single monthly payment to the claimants. The Department of Work and Pensions (DWP), UK ceased all Agile software development on Universal Credit. One of the reasons of failure may be that the project did not fully adapt to the Agile methodology.

It has become clear that IT industry is still maturing in the area of project delivery (whether it is Waterfall or Agile) and in the phase where it is learning fast from its mistakes. Most of the time, the issues are not technical but with humans. Although there are great technology enablers and multitude of delivery methodologies, humans are still in the driving seat and directly influence the success or failure of a project. This is a typical trait of knowledge-based industry.

Let us now understand the typical problem areas that contribute to IT project failures.

3.3 | Project Delivery Pain Areas

Despite availability of various methodologies, standards and frameworks, a significant number of software project deliveries still fail to achieve their stated objectives. One of the reason is lack of effective project knowledge management. Pain areas in software project delivery primarily related to project knowledge are detailed in Table 3.1.

Table 3.1 | Pain areas in project delivery

Pain	Description of the pain
Lack of effective communication among all the project stakeholders.	For an effective project delivery, timely communication is imperative. Documents, being the source of project knowledge is communicated via various mechanism such as email, configuration management tool. The issue is that documents can't be kept updated in real-time that also limits the effectiveness of the means of communication. Agile projects, where communication is based on face-to-face interactions instead of documents, are effective only in a small team and it is difficult to scale up in size effectively.
Lack of reliable, single version of truth with respect to the project.	The project documents in the Waterfall methodology try to bring out the single version of the truth in a project. The sign-off mechanism, needed to keep the documents orderly and under version control, also makes it difficult to keep the documents updated in real-time. The information may get out of date in matter of days. This compromises heavily on the ability to make the project documents as the single version of truth. In Agile, the project truths remain in the minds of the people and it does not even have a framework that we have in Waterfall. Lack of a single version of truth results in significant effort being wasted for review and rework.
Lack of an effective mechanism to track project progress to ensure it delivers to stated timelines.	Tracking usually depends on inputs from the project teams and there are reasons to believe that sometimes the team will not give a realistic status and also that sometimes the team does not know the real status: they just hazard a guess. The project manager does not have many options other than believing the team members, which may cause costly project delays.
Every year a new theme claims remedy for the pain areas, to be replaced with another one next year.	These are mainly exaggerated by the technology product vendors to enable them to sell their products and the customer may not gain proportionate benefits. It is difficult to distinguish the real innovation from the hyped and dummy ones. Initiatives such as IT application rationalisation, business process re-engineering and, service oriented architecture claimed to solve all the problems, but were not as successful as they initially intended to be. This resulted in a significant number of failed projects in these areas.

Contd.

Pain	Description of the pain
Ineffective traceability resulting in costly impact analysis.	Traceability is hard to be maintained between sections of documents and its complexity increases significantly when the number of entities (e.g. requirement, business rule, test cases) to be traced increases. It is generally seen as a liability, done ex post facto mainly for compliance reason and hence does not really help a project due to the way it is implemented in practice.
Limited reuse of information from the previous projects.	It is rare that all the documentation of the previous projects is kept updated. Even when we assume the documents are updated, retrieving information from these documents is a tedious task. The project team often feels that it is easier to create document from scratch rather than trying to look for previous project documentation for reuse. In the Agile world, similar experience helps to reuse information, but it is a huge challenge to recollect the detailed information of the previous project.
Limited reuse of information from previous phase to the next phase of the project.	Information about the software evolves during subsequent phases of project delivery. It should be intuitive to reuse information from the previous phase to the next phase. However, the reuse is impeded by the document regime in the Waterfall methodology and the dependence on memory of the project team in the Agile methodology. In the Agile methodology however, the impact is limited as there is not much demarcation between the phases. In Agile methodology, reuse for regression is crucial so that the incremental development does not impact existing functionality of the software.
Costly manual review to bring quality to the project delivery.	For code quality, there are numerous tools that help detecting errors to some extent. For document quality, there is no automated way of detecting an error. Error detection can come only through expensive manual review by the subject matter expert (SME). If enough attention is not given to extensive review, it may result in more number of defects in the later phases, increasing the cost of the project even further.
Project scope creep and lack of effective requirement management.	Requirements evolve and cannot be written correctly the first time itself. A majority of the requirements today are in a document format, which further impedes effective requirement management due to its inability to be kept updated in real-time. This also leads to scope creep and missing requirements.
Too many methodologies.	There are too many methodologies to choose from and sometimes the selection process becomes confusing. Also, different methodologies suit different types of projects. It is difficult and costly for a company to shift from one methodology to another.
Too many tools.	There are too many tools to choose from as for each methodology there are multiple tools that claim compliance with the methodology in their own way. Application lifecycle management (ALM) tools that cover end to end project delivery also suffer from certain limitations. They have evolved either starting as a requirement tool or as a testing tool. The result is they are more matured in one of these areas and their coverage is weak in solution design and application design.

Contd.

Pain	Description of the pain
Ineffective usage of tools.	There are two main issues with usage of tools. Different teams use different tools for the same purpose, creating confliction and, often, confusion. Many times, tools do not replace the manual work and outputs are further edited and copied in the project documents, leading to unnecessary rework.
Dependence on SME.	There is a large dependence on SMEs who are costly. There is no alternative, as the knowledge is not available in a readily usable form. Most of the time this gives SMEs the upper hand while negotiating for effort, sometimes giving rise to unethical practices.
Continuously changing requirements.	Requirements are the basis of all the subsequent activities in a project and when they change, it is like the base has changed. This results in changing all the subsequent artefacts and it becomes costlier to comply.
Varying team competency.	A project team will usually have team members with varying skills and experience. Sometimes it becomes an issue when the project is on the critical path and the best resources are oversubscribed.

The root causes for a majority of these pain areas are:
1. There is no matured and scientific knowledge management framework covering end to end project delivery.
2. Existing methodologies have not evolved further, beyond standards and guidelines. The project success is still very reliant on the experience of the project manager and the team.
3. Tools claiming end-to-end automation of project delivery lack sufficient maturity in linking the solution and application design information to requirements and test cases.

It is evident from these statements that maturity in the domain aspects of IT project delivery (also called 'project knowledge') is low and becomes the major cause of project delivery failure. Project knowledge covers four (requirement analysis, solution design, application design and test design) out of the six core project delivery phases as listed in section 3.1 of this chapter. The next section focuses on understanding project knowledge holistically.

3.4 | Project Knowledge

Project delivery almost always results in an intended output as well as the supporting by-products that are produced while creating the output. Let's understand this by examples.

1. Constructing a building is a project in the civil engineering industry. A constructed building is the output. There will be many by-products as a part of constructing the building such as detailed construction plan or blueprint.
2. Delivering software is a project in the IT industry. Working software is the output of the project and it will have many by-products such as requirement document, design document and test cases.

It is the by-products that drive the quality of the output and, if done properly, can help the output throughout its lifecycle (i.e., in delivery as well as in maintenance) and to execute other projects of a similar nature. If a detailed plan is maintained during the construction of a building, it will be of great help in later years for better maintenance of the building as it will tell the maintenance engineer where exactly the electric wires, drainage pipes and drinking water pipes are passing through inside the walls. A similar building to be built can customise this plan instead of creating a new one. Similarly, if there is a need to enhance the software and if the solution design document is up-to-date, the service management team can do the impact analysis for the enhancement without looking into the code.

The output produced is relatively more mature and stable as it is driven by ever maturing technology. It is the by-products that drive quality of the output and can be considered as the brain behind the output. Buildings are constructed by rods, cement, sand, bricks and water primarily, and software is constructed by programming languages and databases. These are the raw materials for the output, readily available and not so costly. It is the by-products that specify how to combine the raw materials in an optimal manner to create the desired outcome, increasing the value of the raw materials multi-fold. Knowledge and innovations play a greater role in producing the by-products. It is the maturity of by-products that drives the maturity of the industry and takes it from knowledge-based to process-based. For process-based industries, the by-products are standardised and repeatable in similar circumstances.

In IT industry, the by-products that are in the form of documents, are better understood via the Waterfall methodology as it is scientific and structured. The Agile methodology creates a void in this area as it does not have comprehensive documentation. As per the Agile Manifesto [8], output is preferred over documentation. Creating the by-products and keeping them updated during the lifecycle of the project delivery takes almost half of the total project effort (as implied in Figure 13.2 of chapter 13). All the by-products, when combined, represent the complete specifications of the software from business and technical perspective and can be called 'Project Knowledge'. If the project knowledge is kept updated, it makes the process of creating the software transparent. This has the additional benefit that it does not require a technology specialist to understand the details of how the software works. It becomes a reliable alternative to the code within the software.

Project knowledge is currently contained in the document sets that are created and maintained during different phases of software project delivery. Typical documents are:
1. Business Requirement Specification (BRS)
2. Functional Specification Document (FSD)
3. High Level Design Document (HLD)
4. Test Cases
5. Project Plan
6. Project progress report

It is worth noting that the first four documents represent the project knowledge whereas the last two documents detail the implementation aspects of the project knowledge.

As indicated earlier, creating the project documents and keeping them updated in real-time is a major pain area in project delivery and is mainly responsible for keeping the IT industry in the knowledge-based industry category. Some of the points worth mentioning in this regard are:
1. Over the decades, the industry has failed to maintain the project documents with quality, within the project budget. Documents do not therefore seem to be the best way to capture and maintain the project knowledge.
2. Projects try to keep the project knowledge updated and integrated by using the traceability matrix. The traceability matrix links together different pieces of information from different documents. For all practical purposes, its effectiveness is limited primarily due to two reasons. It is difficult to identify pieces of information suitable to be traced from the sections and paragraphs of a document in a majority of the cases. It is also difficult to ascertain the types of information (such as requirement, business rule) that needs to be traced. There needs to be a fine balance as when more types of information are traced, the transparency we have on project knowledge is better, but at the same time it makes the matrix difficult to be maintained (too many linkages to be maintained). Many projects produce the traceability matrix ex post facto (as it is an audit requirement), defeating the purpose of traceability.

3. It becomes difficult to create a framework to manage project knowledge as it is primarily dependent on the domain for which the software is being built.
4. In the initial stages of the project, there is a rigour in the documentation. In the later stages, coding and testing takes priority and the documentation becomes out-dated as it is not able to cope with changes. As a result, for coding and testing, the document fails to become a reliable source of project knowledge and to be of practical use. So the team stops using it. Instead, the team rather relies on individuals to understand the detailed requirements and solutioning. This increases the gap between what is written in the document and what is actually being built and the team gets the feeling that all the effort spent initially on the document has gone waste as it failed to deliver when it was needed most (i.e., in the coding and testing stages of the project delivery).
5. The absence of reliable project knowledge may cause experienced and skilled people in the project to start dictating terms in the project, often for their personal benefit, inflating or deflating the project effort. This brings about huge differences in effort and quality for similar work and is one of the reasons why the IT industry remains in the knowledge-based category.

An interesting phenomenon has occurred in the industry over the last decade. Citing the reasons of difficulty to maintain project documents, the proponents of Agile methodology have advocated keeping the documents only at high level.

A high-level document may be good for general understanding, but will be of less use to the workers in project delivery and service management. Unless the requirements for the software are specified completely, there is a fair chance that the software built will not perform what is required. It is often better to spend time to specify something with rigour before attempting to build it. This fits well with the evolving nature of knowledge that sees multiple iterations before it is built in a less costly manner. Let's take the example of building construction again. It is better to model a stable structure by multiple iterations rather than starting to create the building and demolish it multiple times if it does not meet expectation. It is worth believing 'if you cannot specify what you want, how can you build it?' in software development.

While project delivery based on Agile methodology has brought in much needed speed and better communication in project delivery, its insistence on keeping documentation at high level has resulted in creating a gap around project knowledge. With limited documentation, the only option for understanding the software is to consider the code, which can be interpreted by technology specialists who are relatively more expensive to hire. Agile has also reduced intellectual innovations around solutioning, design and testing, as focusing on software development is preferred over by-products (documents).

Agile is promoting the culture that 20-20 cricket matches have brought in. The 20-20 matches give results in a couple of hours instead of the traditional five days of a test match. However, this has inhibited the development of classic and sturdy batting and bowling styles, as every ball that does not result in either a run or a wicket is considered as a waste (which is not something that many would agree with). We are fast progressing to a culture where details are not always liked. Popularity of '100 latest news in 10 minutes' over a detailed discussion on a relevant topic, brief comments on Twitter and Facebook over detailed intellectual discussions are the indicators of this. In software delivery, it is important that someone somewhere has to think about the lowest level of details and it is better if that the thinking is done before the coding starts.

The biggest reason for keeping documentation at high level in Agile is the failure to keep it at low level as evident in Waterfall. The book details an alternate framework to capture and maintain the project knowledge at the lowest level, without the documentation regime.

I have extensively studied the entire project artefacts and conceptualised a model to digitise project knowledge. I have come up with the following hypotheses that forms the basis of digitisation of project knowledge:

- Building blocks or information types, such as requirement, test case and business rule can represent fit-for-purpose project knowledge currently contained in the documents.
- Fit for purpose project knowledge can be captured via a set of attributes for each building block. Requirement id, title, description, owner are examples of requirement building block attributes.
- Building blocks can be captured in the format of inventory (such as, 20 requirements for the requirement building block) and relationship (such as, Requirement_01 is related to Business_Rule_10).
- Knowledge contained in the building blocks can be quality assured by a mix of negative relationship and manual review process. Due to the inventory and relationship format of the project knowledge, it is easy to derive information such as 'a requirement is not linked to any test case'. This is an example of negative relationship. Defects can be

linked to inventory/relationship of the project knowledge digitising the quality assurance.
- With the project knowledge and its quality assurance digitised, it is easy to determine the number of activities (of the type draft, review and rework) covering it.
- Tracking these activities and taking corrective actions can digitise managing the project knowledge. This can easily be extended to cover the execution and testing activities as well.
- Building blocks and its specification via inventory and relationship mechanism can also be used to capture generic knowledge that can be used in skill development.

The model is named as Project Knowledge Model (PKM) and the project delivery methodology based on it is Knowledge Driven Development (KDD). The model can also assist the Waterfall and Agile methodologies in managing project knowledge better. The Generic Knowledge Management Framework (GKMF) describes how the same concept can be used to capture knowledge about anything and everything.

This book makes an attempt to prove these hypotheses.

The building blocks are domain agnostic. Hence they have universal applicability. They effectively replace documents as project knowledge. The project knowledge is now catalogued and not kept in free-form text in sections of documents, where any change needs to undergo the rigour of costly version control.

Complexity of design phase in project delivery is one of the main reasons why the IT industry is still seen as knowledge-based industry. Every project tries to solve a unique problem and it is the design phase where a unique solution is evolved making this phase challenging. Digitising the design phase through building blocks has brought in transparency, allowing management of this phase easily.

This way of creating and maintaining project knowledge promotes a cataloguing approach, where inventories of building blocks are linked together, forming a network of project knowledge. It can be kept updated more easily than a set of documents representing project knowledge. The impact for any change and its accommodation is easier as the entire project knowledge is well integrated. This brings order to the chaos caused by inconsistent and incomplete project documents representing partial project knowledge with limited reuse and impact analysis capabilities.

The model paves the way to bring digitisation in IT industry the way other industries such as banking have been digitised. The banking industry has moved from analogue manual ledger maintenance to doing it through software. In the same way, the IT industry can move from analogue project documents to the digital PKM.

IT Industry is moving fast and the documents are being replaced, at least partially, via model or sets of models such as BPM, Screen Prototype, Business Rule Engine and Use Case Model. From this perspective, PKM claims to be a model with the biggest scope – covering entire project knowledge.

This new methodology (KDD) has the potential to simplify project delivery to a great extent. As this is a new way of working for project delivery, people may be sceptical about its merits in the beginning. This book is an attempt to detail KDD at conceptual, academic and practical levels so that it is appreciated, discussed and adopted, to benefit project delivery. The remaining chapters of this book detail different aspects of PKM, KDD and GKMF.

CHAPTER 4

Project Knowledge Model: Context and Definition

Project knowledge, which was notionally introduced in the previous chapters, is fully contextualised and defined in this chapter. The chapter begins by explaining what currently happens in the traditional project delivery regarding project knowledge. The complete definition of PKM is provided. At the end, an example of PKM is given to explain how it might look.

4.1 | Traditional Project Knowledge Management

Knowledge, which is the combination of experience and research, is necessary to help IT industry, just as it is for all the other industries. IT industry will have two aspects: domain and technology. Domain is the collective knowledge, driven primarily by processes. Technology has implements such as programming languages that help putting that knowledge into useful outcome, most of the time it is software. Technology primarily helps in automating processes.

The automation that typically results in creation of software, is delivered via a project or programme. Knowledge plays a crucial role in software development and consists of business and technical knowledge. Typically, a software development project consists of four knowledge-intensive phases. The phases along with the document representing that phase is listed below:

1. Requirement analysis (business knowledge) – Business Requirement Specification Document
2. Solution design (business knowledge) – Functional Specification Document

3. Application design (technical knowledge) – High Level Design Document
4. Test design (business knowledge) – Test Case Document

This combination of knowledge is called 'Project Knowledge'. Let us now understand how the Waterfall and Agile methodologies manage this project knowledge.

4.1.1 | Project Knowledge Management in Waterfall Methodologies: Document Driven

Project knowledge is managed in the Waterfall methodology using documents. The main documents representing project knowledge are:
1. Business Requirement Specification (BRS) representing requirement analysis.
2. Functional Specification Document (FSD) representing solution design.
3. High Level Design (HLD) representing application design.
4. Test Cases representing test design.

Documents are authored by relevant stakeholders and are subject to review by the project team and SMEs, who may or may not be part of the project team. Post review, the documents are singed off and once a document is signed-off, changes to it are managed by version control. The next version of the document is also subject to the review cycle. Every time the next version of the document is signed-off, the information needs to be communicated to the entire project team. Recent technological advancements in document management have improved storage and retrieval capabilities as following:
1. Documents storage, version control and distribution are better managed by configuration management tools.
2. Usage of advanced search features and personalisation of search so that the contextual information can be easily extracted from the hundreds and thousands of documents stored in the folders.

Microsoft SharePoint is one of the technologies used for these capabilities.

The project delivery environment is dynamic, with new information emerging and the existing information is subject to change. Catering to these changes in the documents in a timely manner is challenging in the review, sign-off and version control regime. Obtaining the required level of quality in the documents and ensuring consistency across the project document set is not easy and is one of the biggest reasons for the reduced usage of the inherently sound and stable Waterfall methodology.

There is however, no alternative to documents as a mechanism to manage project knowledge in Waterfall methodology. In summary, depending on documents for project knowledge is today's necessary evil.

4.1.2 | Project Knowledge Management in Agile Methodology: Collaboration Driven

The rigour of exhaustive documentation is relieved in the Agile methodologies and the project documentation is kept at a high level. Agile projects often hold the project knowledge in the minds of the project team members making the project vulnerable to attrition. Agile projects also uses Wiki based knowledge capture mechanism. Its effectiveness is limited as it is unstructured in nature and the team can add/update any information they feel at any point in time. The project knowledge is also embedded in the software, but to decode and understand it requires technology experts who are expensive to hire. In summary, none of the four mechanisms (high level documents, knowledge in the minds of the project team, wiki based knowledge capture mechanism and software code) used to capture project knowledge in Agile methodology is cost-effective.

Knowledge sharing, however, is much better in Agile methodology since they insist on team collaboration using mechanisms such as:

1. Close collaboration with customer
2. Co-located team closely interacting with each other
3. Pair programming and daily Scrum meetings

As stated earlier, Agile gives less importance to complete and exhaustive documentation and relies more on direct (preferably face-to-face) interaction with the relevant stakeholders. This increases the reliance on the SME for the success of the Agile based projects. Also, without an appropriate platform (when compared to rigor of documentation in Waterfall), even an SME will not be able to extract 100% of the information, first-time-correct. Oversights in an Agile project often prove costly as they invariably lead to rework. Project knowledge sharing through unstructured collaboration may often be less effective than the counterparts in Waterfall methodology, where it is more structured and done via a walkthrough of the project documentation. This encourages personal heroism in Agile which the different quality models have tried to discourage through standardisation.

This puts the industry in an interesting situation. Project knowledge management through exhaustive documentation has limitations, causing reduced usage of Waterfall methodology. The alternate provided by the Agile methodology is not really an alternate. They focus on face-to-face interactions and getting the job done fast, leaving little for project knowledge, compared to their Waterfall counterpart. In effect, they increase the gap between the project development team and the service management team as there is no reliable documentation in the Agile methodology.

KDD provides a better alternative to project knowledge management which is currently achieved via project documents. We need a replacement for the documents and the recommendation from Agile to minimise it or almost get rid of it is often deemed unacceptable.

The subsequent sections elaborate on this alternative of the project knowledge management encapsulated in the Project Knowledge Model (PKM).

4.2 | Project Delivery Activities and Project Knowledge

Project delivery activities are investigated from knowledge perspective in this section. This has greatly simplified the understanding and relationship between different forms of project knowledge and how it can drive the project.

4.2.1 | Project Delivery Activities

Let us visualise the end-to end-project delivery from a knowledge perspective. The effort spent on project delivery goes in three types of activities related to:
1. Project knowledge (such as detailing the requirement)
2. Project execution (such as coding a specific module)
3. Project management (such as estimating for the project)

Knowledge is specified first in the project. Specifications are implemented and both the specifications and implementation need to be managed for effective project delivery.

Let us take the example of building construction. Here project knowledge relates to blueprints and drawings of the building. Project execution relates to constructing the building with the raw materials,

Project Knowledge Model: Context and Definition

guided by blueprints. Project management relates to monitoring the effort of the construction and blueprints so that the building is completed with quality and within budget.

Let us now understand the activities in the context of IT project delivery. Project knowledge is specified during requirement analysis, solution design, application design and test design phases. In the build and test execution phases, the knowledge is implemented as a working software. Knowledge and its execution are managed in an effective manner through project management.

Figure 4.1 illustrates this concept. It is interesting to note that project management effort does not actually fetch any output; it only supports the knowledge management (resulting in project knowledge) and execution (resulting in the working software) activities. The more enabled the teams are in these two activities, the less dependency will be on project management.

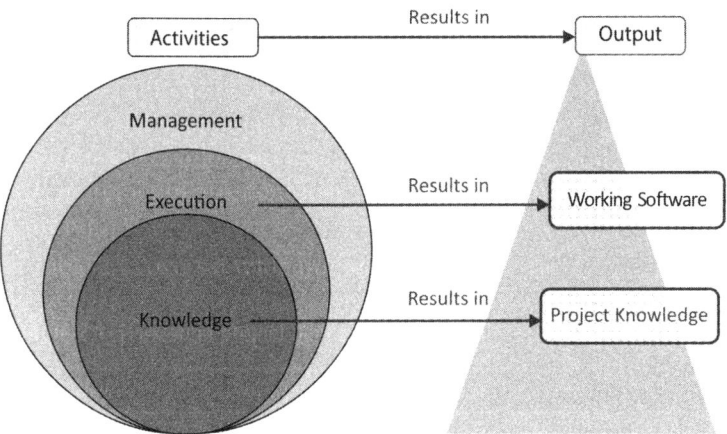

Figure 4.1 | Project delivery activities

4.2.2 | Activities Mapped to End-to-End Project Delivery

Let us continue to look at the project delivery from the knowledge perspective and revisit different phases of project delivery, including project management.

Figure 4.2 maps end-to-end project delivery with the three types of activities.

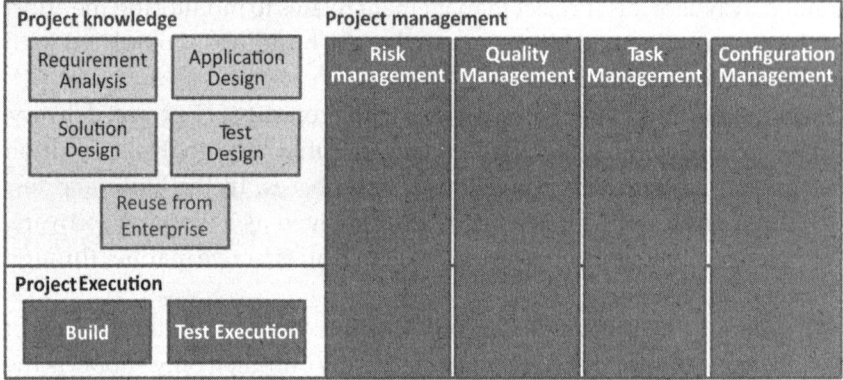

Figure 4.2 | Project activities mapped to end-to-end project delivery

Let's understand this in more detail.

Project Knowledge: Any information that is required while constructing the software is known as project knowledge. This is core to the project delivery, regardless of the delivery methodology. The project knowledge has four forms linked to the four knowledge-intensive phases of the project delivery. Reuse of enterprise knowledge is an important aspect of project knowledge.

a. *Requirement analysis*: In this activity, the customer specifies what is required out of the software and the service provider tries to understand the requirements by scoping the project and asking various questions and clarifications from the customer.

b. *Solution design*: Having understood the requirements, the service provider, with the help of the customer, undertakes solution design activities. The service provider expands on the requirement and details them in business language. This goes down to the lowest level of details, where customer inputs are required, such as screen prototype and error messages to be displayed. This activity uses methods such as use cases and process models to accomplish the tasks.

c. *Application design*: Once the solution is detailed, technology experts convert it from business language to technical language in the application design phase. This is assisted by models such as class diagram, interaction diagram and sequence diagram.

d. *Test design*: Solution details are reformatted into test cases and related artefacts such as test data in the test design phase.

e. *Reuse from enterprise*: Every organisation has a repository (of varying maturity and exhaustiveness) where the relevant information about various artefacts are kept, such as the list of IT applications, products and Security standards. Projects generally reuse this information, when available in the enterprise.

Project Execution: Activities in project execution result in creation of the working software. This is greatly influenced by the project knowledge activities as it executes the application design knowledge into working code that results in a working software. There are two main activities in project execution:
  a. *Build*: In build, the development team codes and conducts unit tests using the information from application design. In Waterfall methodology, application design and build phases are distinct and separate, whereas in Agile methodology these are done more or less simultaneously. However, these two are the generic activities in all the methodologies.
  b. *Test Execution*: In test execution, the test team executes the test cases designed in the test design phase. Again, in Waterfall methodology the distinction between the test design and test execution phase is more obvious than in Agile methodology but these two are the generic activities, irrespective of the methodology followed. Along with test execution also comes defect management.

Project Management: The project manager manages the time, cost, quality and scope of the project. Viewing from a knowledge perspective, let us redefine the role of the project manager. The project manager enables or facilitates the knowledge and execution related activities which, in turn, manages time, cost, quality and scope of the project directly. There are four main enablers for execution and knowledge related activities.
  a. *Risk Management*: Managing risk originating from either internal or external factors is an important part of project management. An example of internal risk is scope creep and an example of external risk is regulatory change. Risk needs to be managed to deliver the project on time, with quality and within budget. Risks mostly originate while executing activities of either project knowledge or project execution.
  b. *Quality Management*: Quality needs to be managed for each of the project knowledge and project execution activities. It is primarily achieved by internal and external review processes. Internal review

is performed by the project team members and external review is performed by an SME who may not be part of the project team. Detecting errors early is important as late detection might prove costly.

c. *Task Management*: Project knowledge and project execution activities need to be planned and managed through different sequential and parallel tasks. It needs to consider project estimate, task allocation and monitoring the progress.

d. *Configuration Management*: The artefacts created as a result of project knowledge and project execution activities need to be stored and maintained. The configuration management tools generally accomplish this. This includes documents and the source code which need to be configured appropriately for project delivery. Configuration management also includes release management and change management.

4.2.3 | Project Delivery Activities: Inherent Interactions

Having studied the main activities of project knowledge, execution and management, let us investigate how these activities interact with one another to deliver the project from the knowledge perspective. Figure 4.3 visualises all the activities and their interactions.

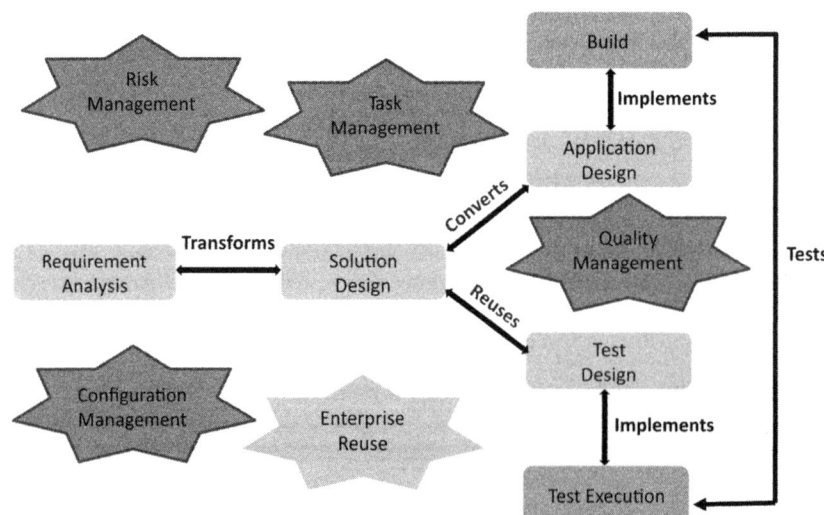

Figure 4.3 | Project delivery activities: inherent interactions

Interactions of Project Knowledge

Treating all the four phases (requirement analysis, solution design, application design and test design) related to project knowledge as a logical unit, we are now in a position to understand its interaction with the activities of project execution and project management.

Project knowledge plays an important role in identifying project risks. Any specific requirement, solutioning or technical aspects that pose a risk to the project are identified by project knowledge activities. All the project knowledge related artefacts are managed via a configuration management tool. Project knowledge activities are executed in different steps, managed by task management. An appropriate review mechanism is put in place to ensure that quality of the project knowledge artefacts is maintained.

Application design documents guide the developers to build the solution. Test cases prepared during test design are used in test execution. Any defect identified during test execution or build may result in updating project knowledge.

The interaction of project knowledge with project execution and project management ensures the software is delivered in accordance with the requirements.

Interactions within Project Knowledge

Requirements, solution design, application design and test design are different ways of looking at the same knowledge, that is, project knowledge. Together they form fit-for-purpose knowledge of the entire project from the business and technical perspective. All the four knowledge compartments are complete in themselves. As they represent the same knowledge from different perspectives, it is natural to have relationships between them.

Requirements are transformed or expanded into solution design using mechanisms like use cases, user stories and process models. Solution design is converted from business language to technical language in application design. Solution design details are reused in test design. Reuse from enterprise is relevant in all the four knowledge compartments, depending on how effectively an organisation manages its enterprise knowledge.

It is also interesting to look at the sequential and parallel relationships among these four knowledge compartments. The primary relationship between requirements knowledge and solution design knowledge is sequential. Unless the requirements are detailed to a sufficient level, there is no point in proceeding with solution design. However, once solution design is done, both application design and test design can start in parallel, the reason being that in solution design, all the inputs required from Business are specified completely.

It is not difficult to appreciate now that managing various activities and their interactions throughout the project delivery is not easy, particularly if documents manage the project knowledge. The project knowledge needs to be continuously updated in the dynamic project delivery environment and documents have limited effectiveness in this regard.

PKM digitises project knowledge and eliminates the need to create the project documents, making the execution of activities and their interactions seamless. The following section defines PKM.

4.3 | Project Knowledge Model: Definition

In this section, evolution of knowledge via 4 levels and 8 building blocks are discussed, which cover generic project knowledge: the most detailed level of knowledge sufficient for project delivery. When customised to the IT industry, 8 building blocks of project knowledge expand to 18 building blocks in a specific situation. These building blocks are mapped to the 4 knowledge-intensive phases of project delivery. This, then, gradually progresses towards a model to capture the project knowledge completely, replacing the traditional project documents.

4.3.1 | Knowledge Evolution and Project Knowledge

As touched upon briefly in chapter 1, knowledge evolves in four levels or layers. It is the last layer that can be used directly to accomplish a specific task and it is at operational level, named as the project knowledge. The four levels of knowledge are discussed below:

Abstract Knowledge: The abstract knowledge is knowledge at the highest level of abstraction, less in quantity but high on quality. It can be specified by two building blocks: Rules and Scenario. An example of rule may be: A product has three stages in its lifecycle, entry, servicing and exit. An example of scenario may be: There are three purposes for which human-made plantations can be used – commercial, gardening and agricultural purposes.

Domain Knowledge: The abstract knowledge may be domain agnostic or may belong to one or more domains, such as insurance, retail or agriculture. This

Project Knowledge Model: Context and Definition

knowledge can be further detailed for complete specification of the domain representing domain knowledge. Domain knowledge can be specified by two building blocks: Product and Process. Details of 'Claim' is an example of process in the insurance domain. Various tariff plans of mobile companies are an example of products in the telecom domain.

Enterprise Knowledge: Enterprise knowledge is instantiation of domain knowledge for a specific organisation or group, with more detailed information. Although it is instantiation of the domain knowledge, it is distinctly different so as to maintain its own brand in the industry. Enterprise knowledge can be specified by two building blocks: Usage and Enabler. Reporting specifications (usage) for senior management of an organisation represents enterprise knowledge. An example of enabler can be automation of these senior management reports via a reporting tool.

Project Knowledge: Project knowledge helps to keep the enterprise knowledge updated, creating and maintaining the competitive advantage of the organisation. It is the most detailed level of knowledge, sufficient to produce a desired outcome. Project knowledge can be specified by two building blocks: Requirement and Test. An example of project knowledge (requirement) is the detailed information to implement a regulatory change so that the enterprise knowledge remains compliant to that regulation. Detailed test cases to test these regulatory requirements are examples of test building block.

As indicated in chapter 1, this knowledge capture mechanism is named as 'Generic Knowledge Management Framework (GKMF)'. Figure 4.4 represents the four levels of knowledge and the associated building blocks.

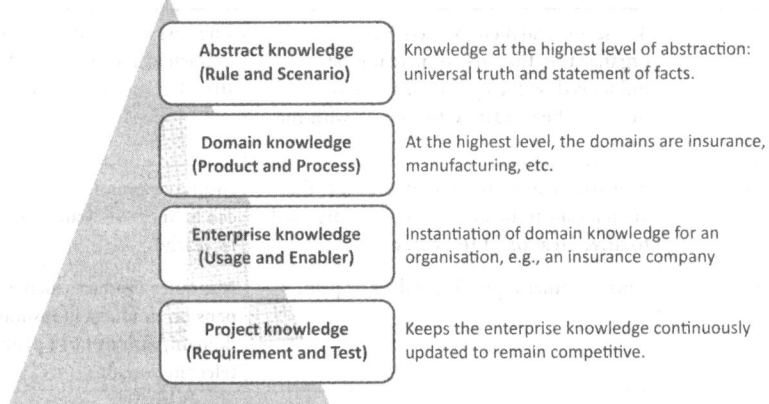

Figure 4.4 | Levels of knowledge

The number of building blocks required to capture a knowledge level will be the cumulative blocks of that level and the preceding levels. For example, to capture project knowledge completely, it requires a total of eight building blocks, two from the project knowledge building block and six from the previous knowledge levels. As we go down in the level, the granularity of information in the building blocks increases. For example, business rules and scenarios in project knowledge will be more detailed than in abstract knowledge.

It is worth noting that the definition of the four layers of knowledge are contextual. Project knowledge in one scenario can well be abstract knowledge in another scenario. Business rule at an abstract knowledge level may be manifested in vision and mission statements, whereas at project knowledge level it would be detailed and linked to the process steps. Let's take an example. In the wider context, the need to manage passwords effectively while accessing an IT system may be the project knowledge. But in the context of executing a project around password management, the same statement can be considered as an abstract knowledge. In the same context, the project knowledge can be 'the password must be eight characters long consisting of at least one special character'.

In Table 4.1, all the eight building blocks required to capture the project knowledge are defined.

Table 4.1 | Project knowledge building blocks

Building block name	Description	Examples
Rule	These are statement of facts for an organisation that may or may not be influenced by the local regulation. It includes the validation to comply with the rule.	The password must have 8 characters and should lock after 3 unsuccessful attempts.
Scenario	Scenario is an event or a set of events that are relevant to Business. Scenarios are used to drive creation of test cases.	Insurance premium frequency can be monthly, half yearly or yearly.
Product	This is domain specific product or plan.	Insurance products such as pension products in insurance domain, various tariff plans in telecom domain.

Contd.

Building block name	Description	Examples
Process	This is the lowest logical unit of work in business that can be specified in enough details for its implementation by an IT system.	Change of address, insurance claim notification.
Usage	Usage assists domain knowledge to be customised to an organisation. It is done primarily via user interface, reports and inbound and outbound communications.	A set of user interfaces of an insurance company to process death claim on a valid policy.
Enabler	The enterprise needs to keep working on improving its effectiveness continuously and Enabler, primarily via automation, helps in this regard. IT systems and their interfaces are examples of Enabler. Enabler implements usage primarily via IT applications.	Policy administration system brings sensible automation to servicing an insurance policy.
Requirement	These are the customer supplied requirements provided to initiate a project. These should be detailed enough to guide the solution design phase of the project.	There is a requirement to send an email to the user immediately after password is changed.
Test Case	These are test cases covering the entire project scope. They can be split into unit test, system test, system integration test, non-functional test and UAT.	To test that the change password confirmation message is received in the email address of the user.

4.3.2 | Software Project Knowledge Building Blocks

As defined earlier, project knowledge consists of eight building blocks. This is at a generic level and can be customised to domains. Customisation can be subjective and may vary, depending on the context and the person customising. I have come up with 18 building blocks of project knowledge, customised to software development. Figure 4.5 provides a mapping of 8 building blocks of Generic Knowledge Management Framework (GKMF) with 18 building blocks of software development.

As shown in Figure 4.5, the following customisation is made in the building blocks to suit IT project delivery:
- Process is split into 2 building blocks: process and process step.
- Usage is split into 7 building blocks as below:
    - Non-functional attribute
    - Business data

- Communication
- Report
- Screen
- Message
- Offline transaction
- Enabler is split into 4 building blocks as below:
  - IT application
  - Interface
  - Data
  - Logic

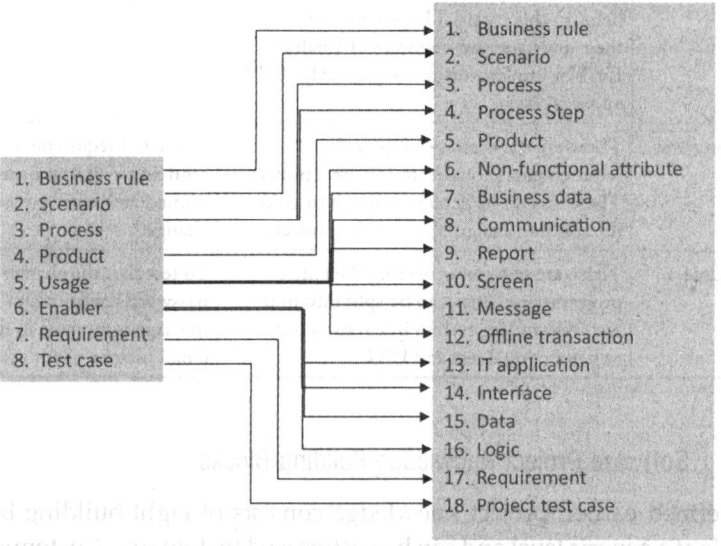

Figure 4.5 | Evolving 8 generic building blocks into 18 for software project delivery

Table 4.2 provides the rationale behind the evolution of the 8 building blocks of GKMF to the 18 building blocks of software project knowledge. In my experience, this is sufficient to provide fit-for-purpose representation of software project knowledge. However, it should be appreciated that scoping project knowledge will be subjective and context driven. For example, if it is a calculation oriented project, it may want to have 'calculation' as a separate building block rather than being accommodated in the 'business rule' building block.

Project Knowledge Model: Context and Definition

Table 4.2 | Rationale for evolution of software project knowledge into 18 building blocks

Building block: software development	Building block: Generic Knowledge Management Framework
Requirement	Requirement
Product	Product
Process	Process
Non-functional attributes	Usage: Non-functional attributes determine how appropriately the application behaves on the non-functional parameters such as performance, usability. Every enterprise may have their own standards for non-functional attributes.
Application	Enabler: IT applications are used to implement sensible automation in an enterprise.
Process step	Process: Process steps provide next level of details of a process via normal, alternate and exceptional path.
Business rules	Rule
Business data	Usage: Business data variation helps customising domain knowledge into enterprise knowledge.
Communication	Usage: Inbound and outbound communication helps customising domain knowledge into enterprise knowledge.
Interface	Enabler: IT application interfaces are important to understand how end-to-end processes are implemented via a set of IT applications.
Report	Usage: Report helps customising domain knowledge into enterprise knowledge.
Screen	Usage – Screen helps customizing domain knowledge into enterprise knowledge.
Message	Usage: Message helps customising domain knowledge into enterprise knowledge.
Offline transaction	Usage: Offline transaction helps customising domain knowledge into enterprise knowledge.
Scenario	Scenario
Data	Enabler: IT application consists of data and logic.
Logic	Enabler: IT application consists of data and logic.
Project test case	Test case

It is interesting to note that the list of eight generic building blocks of project knowledge can be customised to suit other industries as well. For example, a motor vehicle can be an enabler in the transport industry. I will leave it to readers to explore this further as this book is focused only on the IT industry.

Before proceeding further, let us define the building blocks not explained as a part of initial 8 building blocks of project knowledge. Table 4.3 provides the definitions, along with examples.

Table 4.3 | Building block definitions

Building block name	Definition	Example
Non-functional attributes	Non-functional attributes represent non-functional aspects of the software and generally relevant to all the processes. Examples of non-functional attributes are Security, Performance, Usability, Reliability, Maintainability and Portability. Non-functional aspects of Reporting, Customer Relationship, Workflow, Website and Information Technology should also be included.	In the entire application, the response time for the next screen to appear should be less than one second.
Process steps	This is a list of steps through which a process is completely specified. It includes happy path, alternate path and negative path scenarios. It is essentially a breakdown of 'Process' building block defined in Table 4.1.	For change in address the process steps may be: 1. Log in to the portal. 2. Request for change in address. 3. Change the address including post code. 4. Get a confirmation message from the portal that the address is changed.
Business data	Business data is normally screen fields and/or static data and flags that are easily understood by a business user. It is also known as logical data.	Name. Gender. Address.
Communication	The interaction of information between the organisation (e.g., insurance company) and customers or stakeholders of the organisation via various channels. It is also called inbound and outbound communication.	Bank annual statement (outbound communication). Letter request for death notification (inbound communication).

Contd.

Project Knowledge Model: Context and Definition

Building block name	Definition	Example
Interface	The interaction of data between the applications, either internal within the organisation or external.	Interface between policy administration system and payment system.
Report	The interaction between the application and user not via user interface but via a report that the user can go and analyse offline.	Channel usage report: For change of address, a monthly report that states the split of users per channel (e.g., portal, email request, call centre request, post letter request).
Screen	This is one of the most important components for user interface oriented applications as this is the best way to specify details of the requirement. For new applications, it is the placeholder for prototypes.	Login screen. Personal details screen. Change password screen.
IT application	A software developed primarily to automate business processes.	A Customer Relationship Management (CRM) application to automate relationship with customers.
Message	All the messages that a user of the application can see in the user interface (screen) or report or offline transaction logs.	'New password must contain at least one special character.'
Offline transaction	These are regular or one-off transactions that need to be executed outside of the normal real-time transactions. These are often scheduled or invoked by either service management team or business team. These are often known as batch transactions.	Generation of monthly mobile bill for a group of customers.
Data	This is also known as physical data and is part of the IT application.	The types of data may be: physical table, static data and spreadsheet. Audit fields are also examples of Data.
Logic	This is the physical inventory of an application related to processing and part of the IT application.	Some of the types of logic are: Online programme, Batch Programme.

The table above defines 12 building blocks of software project knowledge. The remaining 6 building blocks are defined in Table 4.1. From now onwards project knowledge will be used to indicate software project knowledge for simplicity.

4.3.3 | Project Knowledge Building Blocks Mapped to Knowledge-Intensive Phases

It is natural that the 18 building blocks must fit into the 4 knowledge-intensive phases, listed in Figure 4.2, of project delivery. Figure 4.6 has the mapping of phases to building blocks.

The 4 knowledge-intensive phases of software development are widely known and accepted. For the 18 building blocks of project knowledge and their mapping to these phases, there is nothing new in it; it is just an attempt to look at the same thing differently. Now that we delve deeper into the project knowledge, the knowledge aspects start becoming clear, indicating the viability of digitisation of project knowledge via the 18 building blocks.

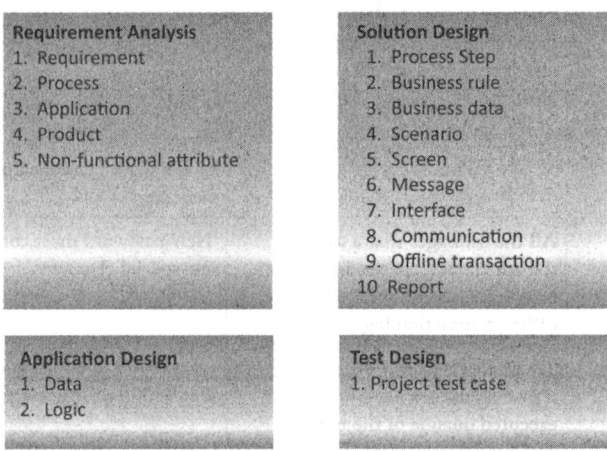

Figure 4.6 | Building blocks mapped to knowledge-intensive software development phases

4.3.4 | Project Knowledge: Away from Documents and towards a Model

In an attempt towards understanding the project delivery from the knowledge perspective, it is now easy to visualise the difference from the traditional approach: we have 18 building blocks instead of project documents. The identification of four instantiations of project knowledge that are complete in themselves and inter-related, helps us to explore a better mechanism to manage project knowledge than documents. Mapping the four instantiations of the project knowledge into 18 building blocks helps digitising the project knowledge. With this understanding, the Project Knowledge Model that manages project knowledge primarily with 18

Project Knowledge Model: Context and Definition

building blocks as listed above, starts taking shape. Let us first detail the relationship between these four instantiation of project knowledge that was briefly touched upon in section 4.2.3.

Relationship among Knowledge-Intensive Phases

The project knowledge is captured and maintained by PKM, covering the four knowledge-intensive phases of the project delivery as follows:
1. Requirement analysis
2. Solution design
3. Application design
4. Test design

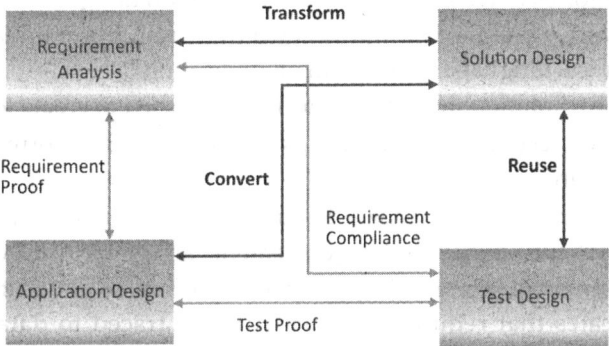

Figure 4.7 | Relationship between four forms of project knowledge

Each of these phases, on its own, represents fit-for-purpose knowledge of the project from the perspective of the business analyst (requirement analysis), business system analyst (solution design), system analyst (application design) and test analyst (test design). Assuming requirement project knowledge is complete (PKM assists in completeness of requirement via requirement review and mapping requirements with the inventories of the other four building blocks of requirement analysis project knowledge) the completeness of project knowledge of other phases can be achieved by the following mechanism:

1. Each requirement must be linked to one or more test cases, demonstrating the completeness of test project knowledge. To put it differently, if we know all the test cases of the project, there will be nothing new in the requirement to be learnt.
2. Each requirement must be linked to one or more solution design inventory, demonstrating the completeness of solution project knowledge.

3. Each requirement must be linked to one or more application design inventory, demonstrating the completeness of application project knowledge.

As detailed above, these four forms of project knowledge are similar, complete and can be mapped to each other. This indicates a possible relationship between these four forms of project knowledge. These four forms of project knowledge are related to each other by three primary and three secondary relationships as shown in Figure 4.7.

The three primary relationships between the four forms of project knowledge are:
1. Transform – Requirements are transformed into solution design via inventories of ten building blocks of solution design.
2. Convert – Solution design is converted from business language to technical language in the form of application design.
3. Reuse – Solution design inventories are reused to create test cases.

The three secondary relationships between the four forms of project knowledge are:
1. Requirement compliance – Requirement compliance of test design helps assuring that all the requirements are properly tested.
2. Requirement proof – Requirement proofing of application design indicates that requirements are directly traced to data and logic building blocks of application design. This exposes requirements directly to the application design and any gap can be easily identified.
3. Test proof – Test proofing of application design minimises the test defects as application data and logic are traced to test cases. This ensures that all the test cases are considered by the system analyst before even a single test case is executed.

Secondary relationships are less critical when compared to the primary relationships. Secondary relationships may not be maintained when the project budget does not allow or the project is of the nature where the accuracy of the specifications are not of utmost importance. For example, we can afford to leave the secondary relationships in a commercial product development, whereas it is not possible to leave it in a rocket launching project where accuracy of specifications is of utmost importance.

Having identified 18 building blocks of project knowledge and mapping them into the four instantiation of project knowledge, the next target is to devise a mechanism to specify fit-for-purpose information about them so that a suitable alternate to the documentation regime can be created.

Project Knowledge Model: Context and Definition

To completely specify the 18 building blocks, there is a need to:
   a. Determine attributes of each of the 18 building blocks.
   b. Create inventories of these building blocks by filling in their attributes.
   c. Establish the relationship between inventories of the same building block and inventories of different building blocks.
   Let us understand in detail.

Building Block Attributes

A building block can be defined by a set of attributes. For example, the list of attributes for requirement building block may be:
   a. Requirement ID
   b. Requirement name
   c. Requirement description
   d. Requirement owner
   e. Requirement rationale

For communication building block, the list of attributes may be:
   a. Communication id
   b. Communication name
   c. Direction (inbound or outbound)
   d. Communication description
   e. Communication channel

The attributes may be mandatory or optional. An agreed list of attributes for the building blocks can be arrived at by the relevant SME of the organisation. The attribute list is subjective and may vary, based on context and the personal preference of the SME.

One of the important attribute of the building blocks is 'usage mode'. It indicates the mode in which the inventory is used in the project. Its values may be: add, update, delete or regression. The meaning of regression is that the inventory is not impacted as a part of the project, but it needs to be included in the project for better understanding of the end-to-end process as it may result into better solutioning, effective test cases and better readability.

Attributes of a building block provides a platform to accommodate the latest thinking related to that building block. For example, attribute list of the requirement building block can be selected appropriately to match the user story format of capturing requirements.

Building Block Inventory

Once the attributes are known, the building blocks can be specified by creating their relevant inventories. A sample requirement inventory is specified via attribute list in Table 4.4.

Table 4.4 | Requirement inventory

Requirement Id	Name	Description	Owner	Rationale
R-001	Beneficiary update condition	Beneficiary of the insurance policy can only be changed if the request carries signature of the policyholder.	Customer Service	To avoid any future dispute on the change of beneficiary.

Minimum information required before an inventory is added – is ensured by the mandatory attributes of the building block. In the example above, the first three attributes of requirement (requirement id, name and description) may be considered as mandatory attributes. The objective is – when an information is added, it should not be incomplete. For example, a requirement without requirement name would look odd.

Inventory relationship

At a high level the project knowledge, instantiations are inter-related as explained earlier. At the lower level, inventories of building blocks across project knowledge instantiations are also related. There are two types of relationships. One type is between inventories of the same building block (intra relationship). For example, a requirement may be parent to another requirement. The other type is between inventories of different building blocks (inter relationship). For example, a requirement may be linked to a business rule. Relationships should also be specified by a set of attributes. An example of relationship is given in Table 4.5.

Table 4.5 | Relationship between requirement and communication

Requirement Id	Communication Id	Remarks
R-001	C-001	Beneficiary update needs policyholder's signed letter.

Relationships bind together all the information specified in the building block inventories and assist impact analysis. The total number of relationships across these 18 building blocks are 153 (calculated by $n*(n-1)/2$ algorithm where n=18). Additionally, there are 18 intra building block relationships. Taken together, the total number of relationship types is 153 + 18 = 171. It is worth noting that these are relationship types and not the actual number of relationships. For example, there is one relationship type between requirements and test cases. Assuming there are 10 requirements and 30 test cases, relationships between requirements and test cases may be 120 for example.

Information about a building block is complete when all its inventories are specified, and they are all related to the other inventories of the same or different building blocks appropriately. Project knowledge will be complete when information about all the building blocks relevant to the project is complete. The 18 building blocks and 171 relationships to completely specify the project knowledge certainly indicate digitisation of project knowledge. I would like to emphasise here again that 18 and 171 are not sacrosanct; they are subjective and may differ, based on context. These should just be treated as an illustration of the fact that project knowledge can be digitised.

The project knowledge tree, as illustrated in Figure 4.8, represents all the three aspects of specifying building blocks – building block attributes (of test case), inventories (instantiation of test case) and relationship (the way test case is related to all other building blocks via branches and root).

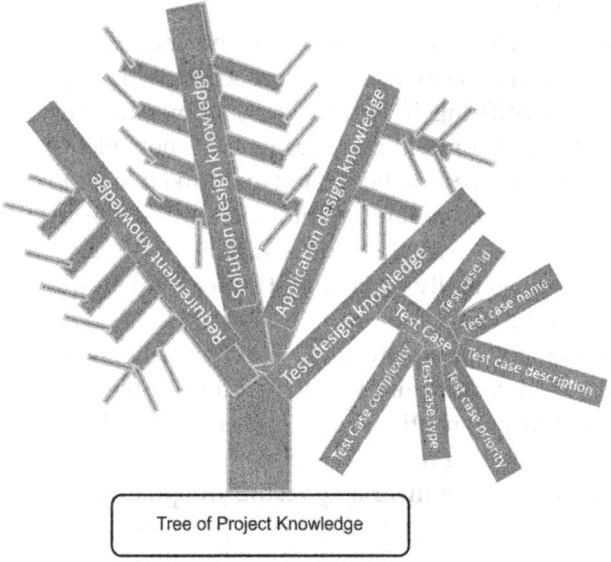

Figure 4.8 | Project knowledge tree

Having understood the mechanism to completely specify the project knowledge, the next important point is how to ensure this information is correct and to maintain its accuracy throughout the life of the project and, if possible, beyond.

Quality Assurance of the Project Knowledge

The project knowledge as discussed so far can be specified by 189 data points (18 building blocks and 171 relationships). The mechanism by which the information can be kept correct and updated throughout the project is as follows:
1. The information in the inventories of each of the 18 building blocks must be fit-for-purpose. Making an attribute of a building block mandatory or optional assists in maintaining data quality of the inventory. Inventory details must be under regular manual review to ensure it is fit-for-purpose.
2. Both positive and negative relationships must be reviewed. A positive relationship is an existing linkage such as requirement R-001 is related to communication C-001 in Table 4.5. This is more popularly named as 'traceability'. A negative relationship is when an inventory of a building block is not related to any of the inventories of the other building blocks. For example, requirement R-001 is not related to any business rule.

Traceability review ensures there are no incorrect linkages of the inventories. Negative relationship review serves two purposes:
1. It helps identifying if an inventory is missing from the project knowledge. For example, if a requirement is not linked to any test case, a new test case needs to be created and linked to that requirement.
2. It helps remove redundant inventory items. For example, if a business rule is not linked to any requirement, it must be analysed whether the business rule is really needed. If it is not needed, then the business rule should be deleted.

The mechanism to manage reviews effectively is via (static) defect management. A defect is raised as an outcome of the review and linked to related inventory or relationship. It is then analysed and the defect can either be fixed by taking remedial action or rejected if the defect is raised in error. Remedial action invariably results in updating inventory and/or relationship.

Tasks to Manage Project Knowledge and Its Quality

Project knowledge and its quality assurance have been fully quantified and digitised, as detailed earlier. That makes it easy to come up with a set number of tasks to cover all of it. Following is how tasks can evolve from higher to lower levels:

Project Knowledge Model: Context and Definition

- At the highest level, there is only one task: manage project knowledge.
- The next level can be three tasks: draft completion, review and rework of the project knowledge.
- The next level can be four tasks, managing the four instantiations of the project knowledge (requirement, solution design, application design and test design).
- The next level can be 12 tasks, managing draft completion, review and rework for the four instantiations of the project knowledge.
- The next level can be 24 tasks, 12 from the previous level and the remaining:
  - Six tasks: review and rework of requirement knowledge in solution design, application design and test design phase.
  - Four tasks: review and rework of solution design in application design and test design phase.
  - Two tasks: review and rework of test design in the application design phase.

At this level, there is an appreciation that building blocks of one project knowledge instantiation can be revisited in the review and rework mode in the subsequent project knowledge instantiation, e.g., requirement being reviewed in the solution design phase. Also review and rework in the subsequent phase is not applicable in application design as it is the last phase in the project knowledge capture exercise.

- The next level can be 54 tasks, representing draft completion, review and rework for the 18 building blocks of the project knowledge.
- The next level can be 126 tasks, 54 from the previous level and remaining from:
  - Thirty tasks: review and rework of five building blocks of requirement knowledge in solution design, application design and test design phase.
  - Forty tasks: review and rework of ten building blocks of solution design in application design and test design phase.
  - Two tasks: review and rework of test design in the application design phase.

The above evolution of tasks has demonstrated how the project knowledge management tasks can be digitised. Depending on the context, an appropriate level of tasks is chosen to work with.

These tasks are generally at a lower level of granularity than the traditional project delivery tasks and hence can be managed more effectively. For example, in the Waterfall methodology, a typical task will be to produce solution design document per process. Other tasks may be to review the document and update the document. Tasks here are at a lower level such as add, review and update business rule.

Reuse of Enterprise Knowledge

Out of 18 building blocks and 171 relationships that result in 189 data points of project knowledge, some are more reusable across the enterprise than others. Stable and less changeable data points are candidates for enterprise knowledge. Only 7 building blocks out of 11 building blocks categorised as enabler and usage building blocks, as detailed in Table 4.2, are considered as enterprise knowledge to be maintained in the enterprise. The selection is explained below.

- Application: Considered as they are the enablers of the enterprise knowledge and stable.
- Business data: Considered as they represent enterprise knowledge and are stable.
- Communication: Considered as they represent enterprise knowledge and are stable.
- Interface: Considered as they represent enterprise knowledge and bind the applications together.
- Report: Considered as they represent enterprise knowledge and are stable.
- Screen: Not considered. Although they represent enterprise knowledge, they are application dependent and change frequently.
- Message: Considered as they represent enterprise knowledge and there is a need to provide consistent messages across the enterprise.
- Offline transaction: Not considered as they are driven by tactical considerations and subject to frequent changes.
- Data: Not considered as it represents detailed physical knowledge (representing physical tables), it is application dependent and subject to frequent changes.
- Logic: Not considered as it is in technical language, it is application dependent and subject to frequent changes.
- Non-functional attributes: Considered as they are generic in nature and worth maintaining as enterprise knowledge.

The selection of the building blocks is subjective and prone to change to suit a particular circumstance or the subjectivity of SME's.

Project Knowledge Model: Context and Definition

The other five building blocks considered for enterprise knowledge are:
- Business rule of abstract knowledge
- Scenario of abstract knowledge
- Process of domain knowledge
- Process step of domain knowledge
- Product of domain knowledge

Requirements and project test cases being at the next level of details than the enterprise knowledge, are not considered. They are project specific and as such not stable enough to be considered as enterprise knowledge. As the enterprise knowledge matures with on-going and past projects, every subsequent project can directly reuse this information. These set of 12 building blocks and 10 relationships are worth maintaining for the enterprise knowledge. Figure 4.9 names these 22 data points (12 building blocks plus 10 relationships) of enterprise knowledge.

Considering tasks discussed earlier, reuse from enterprise knowledge is not a separate task, it is included in the draft completion task.

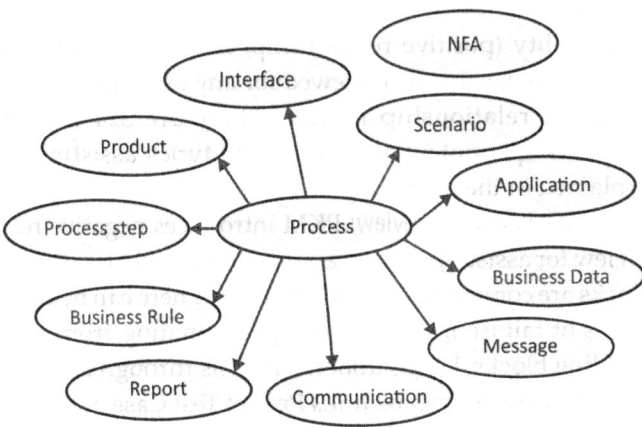

Figure 4.9 | Reusable enterprise knowledge

4.3.5 | Project Knowledge Model Defined

By now we can visualise a project knowledge management mechanism other than via project documents. As we know, this alternate mechanism is called the Project Knowledge Model. It completely scopes and manages the four instantiation of project knowledge and covers:

a. **Project Knowledge Specification:** In one instance, the fit-for-purpose project knowledge is specified by the inventories of 18 building blocks and their 171 relationships as discussed.
Figure 4.10 has 189 data points defining the project knowledge completely of a typical implementation.
As listed in Figure 4.10, the split of 189 data points is:
18 building blocks: from A1 (Process) to A18 (Project Test Case)
153 inter building block relationships: from B001 (relation between Application and Process) to B153 (relation between Project Test Case to Logic)
18 intra building block relationship: from B154 (relation between inventories of Process) to B171 (relation between inventories of Project Test Cases). The total number of relationship is 171 (153 + 18) that is in fact traceability.

b. **Quality Assurance around Project Knowledge:** Quality assurance is digitised and consists of:
- Inventory review: The review of the inventories of 18 building blocks.
- Traceability (positive relationship) review: 171 relationships of traceability need to be reviewed for any oversight.
- Negative relationship review: There are 324 (assuming 171 relationships) potential defect node types assisting quality as explained in the following:

Negative relationship review: PKM introduces negative relationship review for assisting quality assurance. Inventories of two building blocks are connected via a relationship. There can be two potential nodes of failure in a relationship, originating from either of the building blocks. Let us understand this through an example.
One of the relationships links Project Test Case and Requirement building blocks. This can give two potential nodes of failure:
1. A requirement that does not have an associated Project Test Case, which would have serious consequences including untested requirement promoted into the production environment.
2. A Project Test Case that has not stemmed from a requirement. Failure of such a test case should not prevent the system from going into production, unless the test case is correct and non-linkage to requirement itself is a defect.

Both these failure nodes should be analysed for potential defect. One relationship gives rise to 2 potential defect node types. The

189 Data points of project knowledge

		Process	Application	Product	NFA	Requirement	Process Step	Bus. Rule	Scenario	Business Data	Screen	Message	Report	Interface	Communication	Offline Txn.	Data	Logic	Proj. Test Case
A1	Process	B154																	
A2	Application	B001	B155																
A3	Product	B002	B018	B156															
A4	NFA	B003	B019	B034	B157														
A5	Requirement	B004	B020	B035	B049	B158													
A6	Process Step	B005	B021	B036	B050	B063	B159												
A7	Bus. Rule	B006	B022	B037	B051	B064	B076	B160											
A8	Scenario	B007	B023	B038	B052	B065	B077	B088	B161										
A9	Bus. Data	B008	B024	B039	B053	B066	B078	B089	B099	B162									
A10	Screen	B009	B025	B040	B054	B067	B079	B090	B100	B109	B163								
A11	Message	B010	B026	B041	B055	B068	B080	B091	B101	B110	B118	B164							
A12	Report	B011	B027	B042	B056	B069	B081	B092	B102	B111	B119	B126	B165						
A13	Interface	B012	B028	B043	B057	B070	B082	B093	B103	B112	B120	B127	B133	B166					
A14	Communication	B013	B029	B044	B058	B071	B083	B094	B104	B113	B121	B128	B134	B139	B167				
A15	Offline Txn.	B014	B030	B045	B059	B072	B084	B095	B105	B114	B122	B129	B135	B140	B144	B168			
A16	Data	B015	B031	B046	B060	B073	B085	B096	B106	B115	B123	B130	B136	B141	B145	B148	B169		
A17	Logic	B016	B032	B047	B061	B074	B086	B097	B107	B116	B124	B131	B137	B142	B146	B149	B151	B170	
A18	Proj. Test Case	B017	B033	B048	B062	B075	B087	B098	B108	B117	B125	B132	B138	B143	B147	B150	B152	B153	B171

Figure 4.10 Digitised project knowledge data points

153 relationships give rise to 2 * 153 = 306 potential defect node types. There are also 18 intra-relationships of building blocks (e.g., relationship between one requirement to another requirement) from which only one defect node can be derived that may, in many occasions, be theoretical. For example, the list of requirements not linked to any other requirement. This gives rise to 18 other failure nodes. This brings up the total potential defect nodes in the project knowledge to 324 (306 + 18).

The potential defect list from the negative relationships may not really be defects and hence a subjective assessment by the project team must be undertaken. For example, having a list of business rules not linked to any screen is a potential defect. It, however, may not really be a defect as some business rules may be linked to offline transactions and not to any screen.

The moment project team completes the positive relationship, it is easy to find out the negative relationship, that is, absence of relationship.

Figure 4.11 is a typical representation of PKM that includes inventory, relationship and quality assurance.

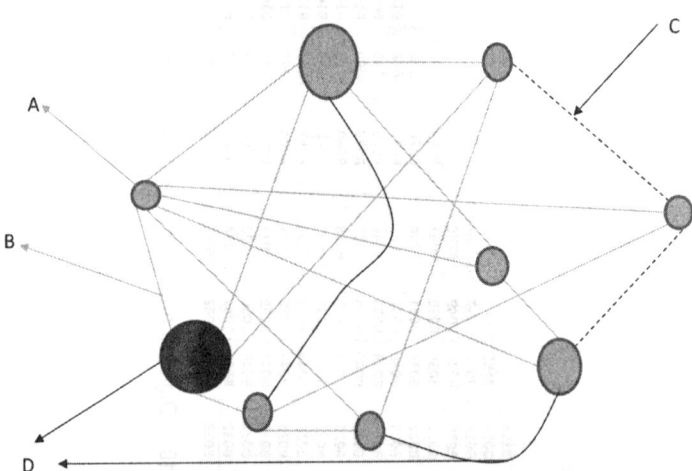

Notation (example):
A – Inventories of building blocks (Requirement-01)
B – Relationship types of inventories (Requirement-01 linked to Screen-01)
C – Negative relationship potential defect (Test Case-01 not linked to any requirement)
D – Manual defect (requirement related defect)

Figure 4.11 | Project Knowledge Model

Project Knowledge Model: Context and Definition

c. **Tasks to manage project knowledge:** Tasks must manage the project knowledge, its quality assurance and enterprise knowledge reuse that is:
   - 189 data points of project knowledge
   - 326 data points of potential defect node types and manual review of inventory and relationships
   - 22 data points of enterprise knowledge for reuse.

Evolution of tasks of project knowledge management from 1 to 126 is explained in the previous section. However, in most cases 24 tasks as depicted in Figure 4.12 are fit-for-purpose.

Tasks are of three types, draft to complete the work (draft), review and rework. These may be logically split into each instantiation of the project knowledge. Figure 4.12 is a schematic representation of the tasks to manage the project knowledge across all the four knowledge-intensive phases of project delivery.

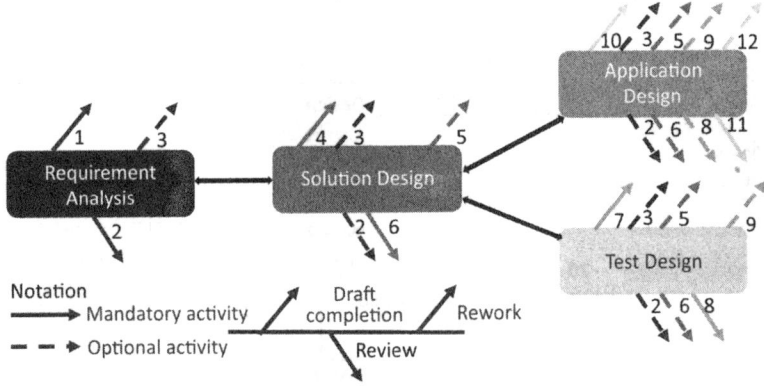

Figure 4.12 | Activities to manage project knowledge

As shown in the Figure 4.12, review and rework from the previous phase may continue as optional activity to ensure that the entire project knowledge is kept updated on a real-time basis. The project knowledge logically ends with application design and hence review and rework of test design phase is included in the application design phase. Each of the three types of activities is explained as follows:
   - *Draft activity*: All the inventories and relationships of in-scope building blocks are captured in the draft activity. It can be split into multiple activities.

- *Review activity*: All the inventories and relationships need to be reviewed for quality assurance. Relationships may be positive (traceability) or negative as explained earlier.
- *Rework activity*: Updating the inventory and relationship as a result of review activity constitutes rework activity.

In this manner, the tasks to manage the digital project knowledge are also digitised.

d. **Digital Project Knowledge Model:** The discussions so far provides a complete framework to manage project knowledge by digitising it. Together, it represents PKM. The actual model may vary as the number of data points of the project knowledge may be different depending on the company's needs. PKM provides an alternative to the document management regime.

In Figure 4.13, the digitisation of PKM is demonstrated. It should be noted, again, that this is a typical illustration and the numbers may vary depending on the preference of the SME and the context.

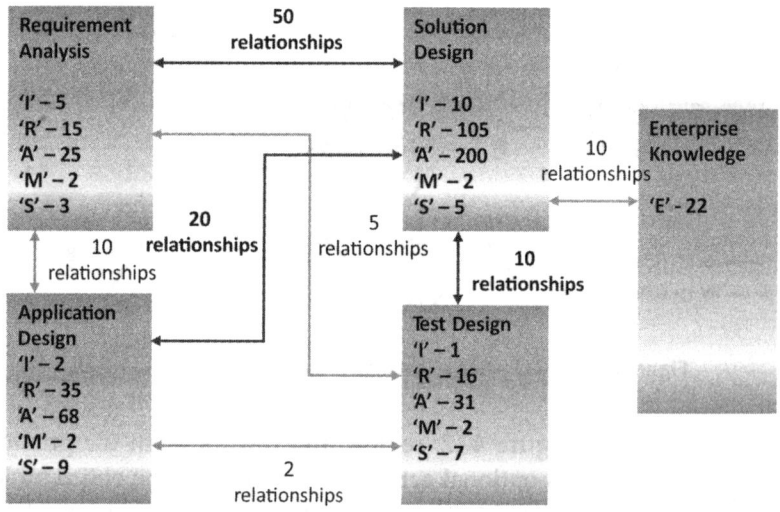

Figure 4.13 | Project Knowledge Model quantified

PKM manages project knowledge via 7 digitised constituents. For ease of reference, it is named 'PIRNMSE' and following is its expansion:

'P'roject knowledge-intensive phases that are 4 in number

'I'nventories of building blocks of project knowledge that are 18 in number. The split across phases are:
- Requirement analysis: 5 building blocks
- Solution design: 10 building blocks
- Application design: 2 building blocks
- Test design: 1 building block

'R'elationships between these inventories that are 171 in number. The split across phases are:
- Requirement analysis: 15 (5*4/2 = 10 inter plus 5 intra) relationships
- Solution design: 105 (10*9/2 = 45 inter plus 10 intra-relationships of solution design plus 10*5 = 50 relationships that bind 10 building blocks of solution design to 5 building blocks of requirement analysis)
- Application design: 35 (2*1/2 = 1 inter plus 2 intra-relationships of application design plus 10*2 = 20 relationships that bind 2 building blocks of application design with 10 building blocks of solution design plus 5*2 = 10 relationships that bind 2 building blocks of application design with 5 building blocks of requirement analysis plus 2*1 = 2 relationships that bind 2 building blocks of application design with 1 building block of test design)
- Test design: 16 (1 intra-relationship of test design plus 10*1 relationships that bind 10 building blocks of solution design to test cases plus 5*1 relationships that bind 5 building blocks of requirement analysis to test case)

'N'egative relationship review that results in 324 potential defect nodes. The split across phases are:
- Requirement analysis: 25 (10 relationship = 20 negative relationship plus 5 intra-relationships)
- Solution design: 200 (95 relationships = 190 negative relationship plus 10 intra-relationships)
- Application design: 68 (33 relationship = 66 negative relationship plus 2 intra-relationships)
- Test design: 31 (15 relationships = 30 negative relationship plus 1 intra-relationship)

'M'anual defects that are 2 in number (inventory and positive relationship, i.e., traceability review across all the phases)

'S'teps are activities that are 24 in number (phase split as per Figure 4.12)

'E'nterprise knowledge consisting of inventory and relationships that are 22 in number

PKM integrates the four instantiation of project knowledge via relationships as follows:
1. Requirements *transforming* into solution design driven by 50 relationships.
2. Solution design *converting* into application design driven by 20 relationships.
3. Solution design getting *reused* in test design driven by 10 relationships.
4. Requirements compliance into test cases driven by 5 relationships.
5. Requirements proofing into application design driven by 10 relationships.
6. Test proofing into application design driven by 2 relationships.

PKM clearly represents the entire project knowledge and it is well interconnected. It is easy to track the consequences of a change to an inventory item (such as requirement) or a relationship. Bringing this clarity to project knowledge is also termed as digitisation of the project knowledge. Compared to this, the project knowledge in documents is termed as analogue form of project knowledge. This movement from analogue to digital has the potential to revolutionise the project delivery environment and pave the way for a new generation of maturity into project delivery methodologies. This has the potential to tackle most of the problematic areas where the existing methodologies have limitations.

This model replaces the document production regime of project knowledge management completely and offers a viable alternate to it. PKM is domain agnostic and hence can fit into multiple domains (such as insurance, Banking). PKM can drive execution and management related activities better than the document production regime.

The project knowledge that is currently hidden in the paragraphs and sections of the document suddenly becomes transparent in the catalogued world of PKM. This gives the advantage of having a manageable source of information with the ability to analyse for inconsistencies, gaps and impact analysis.

e. **Enterprise Knowledge Reuse:** The 22 data points representing the enterprise knowledge have already been identified in the earlier sections. As the knowledge specification format is the same (digitised via list of attributes for specifying building blocks), the reuse from the enterprise knowledge to the project knowledge becomes easy. PKM facilitates the reuse. Figure 4.14 illustrates how enterprise knowledge is reused in the project and provides for continuous improvement in the project delivery environment.

Project Knowledge Model: Context and Definition 93

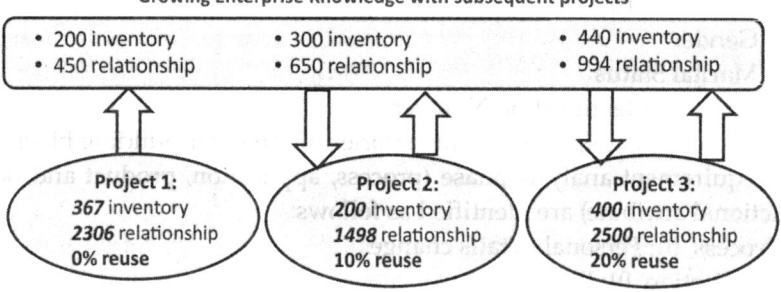

Figure 4.14 | Enterprise knowledge reuse: an example

It is worth noting that the enterprise knowledge area of the project knowledge model need not only be populated by the project deliveries. It should ideally be populated as a one-off exercise before start of any project and should keep growing with subsequent project deliveries.

4.4 | Project Knowledge Model: An Example

A specific requirement is chosen from the case study detailed in chapter 1 and inventories of all the relevant building blocks of PKM is listed. The objective is to visualise a simple version of PKM. To keep it simple, inventory relationships, quality assurance, reuse from the enterprise knowledge and project knowledge management activities are not detailed. Only one inventory of the relevant building blocks is detailed to convey the substance of PKM. The idea is that once we are clear about the constituents of the project knowledge (inventories of the relevant building blocks), understanding its other aspects should not be difficult.

Project Knowledge: Requirement Analysis Phase

As we know, requirements drive the project. There are five building blocks to specify the project knowledge in this phase. Sample inventory from each of the building blocks is listed below.

Requirement_01: The following personal details of a policyholder can be updated via the self-service portal.
1. Forename
2. Surname

3. Date of Birth
4. Gender
5. Marital Status
6. National Identification Number

Based on this requirement, inventories of the other building blocks of the requirement analysis phase (process, application, product and non-functional attribute) are identified as follows:

Process_01: Personal details change

Application_01: Portal

Product_01: Term Insurance

It is worth noting here that the requirement does not specify any non-functional aspects. This may be taken care of in the other requirements at the application level and not at individual transaction level.

Project Knowledge: Solution Design Phase

Via ten building blocks of solution design project knowledge, Requirement_01 is transformed into a detailed business solution, where all the information relevant to Business is captured. It should be noted that some of these inventories may have been identified in the requirement analysis phase while doing the requirement review. The inventories, one per building block, are listed as follows:

Business_Data_01: Gender: This is a mandatory field, one character long and can have three values, M: Male, F: Female and O: Other. Other is to include transgender and someone who does not wish to be identified as male or female.

Interface_01: Retrieve customer personal details: Personal details, as listed in Requirement_01, are stored in the CRM application. The portal will make a call to the CRM application to retrieve personal details, based on customer id of the logged in policyholder.

Screen_01: Personal details screen: This is the screen of the portal used for display and update of the personal details of the policyholder.

Message_01: Date of birth not updated: This is a screen message when the user clicks to update the date of birth but does not update it. This message is to remind the user that no update is detected when the user submits the request.

Process_Step_01: User clicks to change gender.

Business_Rule_01: National Identification Number, when being updated, must follow a specified format.

Scenario_01: For marital status, allowable values are:
- Single
- Married
- Divorced
- Live-in partner

It is worth noting that out of ten building blocks in the solution design, three are not impacted by the current requirement and they are:
- Communication: No inbound or outbound communication is related to this requirement, primarily as the transaction is happening in the portal. There may be separate requirements to address the communication aspects of Requirement_01 (such as documentary proof before the update can take place, for example, for update in surname) where the communication building block will be included.
- Report: There is no report directly related to this requirement.
- Offline transaction: There is no offline transaction visualised in this requirement.

Project Knowledge: Application Design Phase

Data and logic building blocks constitute application design project knowledge. Care should be taken to add only relevant data and logic inventories as adding the common infrastructural and environmental data and logic inventories will make PKM bulky and difficult to maintain. The main objective is to ensure that application design has considered all the other three compartments (requirement, solution design and test design) of the project knowledge.

Data_01: Personal details table of the CRM from which the portal retrieves the information.

Logic_01: The logic to load customer personal details screen.

Project Knowledge: Test Design Phase

Test case inventories are added in this phase so that the test cases can be traced to the other three compartments of the project knowledge. A sample test case is listed here:

Test_01: The user tries to update the national identification number but is unable to do so as the new value is not as per the specified format of the national identification number.

PKM will contain these inventories and move the IT industry away from the project documents. It should be noted that PKM is more digital than the example we have discussed. Let us understand this by using the example of Message_01. Message_01 is described by filling in the details of its constituent attributes as below:

Message id: Message_01

Message details: Date of birth not updated.

Message trigger: A screen message when the user is trying to update date of birth but does not update it.

Message remarks: This message is to remind the user that no update is detected when the user submits the request.

CHAPTER 5

Project Knowledge Model: A Differentiator

Having introduced PKM in chapter 4, this chapter presents its uniqueness in the project delivery environment.

Digitisation of the project knowledge is the core proposition of PKM. This chapter continues to identify and detail the differentiators provided by PKM that accelerate the project delivery with enhanced quality. This chapter identifies the reasons why this model could not be visualised much earlier. Finally, it summarises the benefits that project delivery would accrue from the model.

5.1 | Project Knowledge Model Characteristics: Traceability and Flexibility

Digitising project knowledge via traceability and in-built flexibility are the main characteristic of PKM.

The completeness of the project knowledge is ensured by:

1. Building block inventories (such as for requirement building bock, the inventory may be Requirement_01, Requirement_02) that can be completely specified by its mandatory and optional attributes (Requirement Id: mandatory field, Related department: optional field).
2. Exhaustive traceability (171 to be precise, for a typical implementation) capturing links between the two inventories keep the knowledge digitised and integrated in a single repository. In a traditional project there may be up-to ten relationships of traceability. PKM provides the capability to manage up-to 171 relationships (for example) of traceability in the project helping specify the project knowledge completely.

There is a significant difference between relationship of the Project Knowledge Model and traceability used in traditional sense. In PKM, the inventory that is traced, represents the lowest logical unit of information. Its completeness is to the extent that when inventories are combined with linkages, it represents complete project knowledge. In traditional traceability, it is a challenge to represent inventories at the lowest and logically complete information, as they are unstructured sentences and paragraphs in sections of the documents, difficult to be traced unambiguously.

In addition to being complete and fully traceable project knowledge, it is also flexible enough to cater for subjectivity as explained in the following:

1. The number of building blocks is subjective and can vary based on the context and subjectivity of the SME.
2. Attributes defining building blocks completely may be different for different organisations as they need to be evolved by the relevant SMEs.
3. Many of the 171 relationships may not have much practical usage and hence can be de-scoped for greater speed of project delivery by the project SMEs. One example may be the relationship between the building blocks 'Non-functional attributes' and 'Communication'.

5.2 | Advantages of the Project Knowledge Model

With PKM fully understood, its advantages are discussed in this section. Table 5.1 lists them out and then each advantage is further explained. The advantages listed are not in any priority order and are not grouped.

Table 5.1 | Advantages of the Project Knowledge Model

Sl. No.	Advantage
1.	Reduces communications overheads
2.	Digitises static test (review)
3.	A practical approach to address the quality of the project delivery
4.	Provides capability to replace traditional project documents
5.	Brings order to anarchy in project delivery
6.	Project management enablement through extreme quantification

Contd.

Project Knowledge Model: A Differentiator 99

Sl. No.	Advantage
7.	An optimal mix of parallel and sequential activities
8.	Supports natural evolution of knowledge
9.	Age old struggle between requirement and design simplified
10.	Enables reusability within the project knowledge phases
11.	Reuse from enterprise knowledge base facilitates continuous improvement in project delivery.
12.	Domain agnostic flavour
13.	Empowers the build team
14.	Focus on non-functional requirements
15.	Enables use of quantitative techniques in project delivery
16.	Creates an SME friendly environment
17.	Traceability enables impact analysis and maintains knowledge equilibrium
18.	Manages business and technical project knowledge optimally
19.	Separation of concern
20.	Enhances quality by maker-and-checker mechanism
21.	Effective requirement management
22.	Consolidated test case design

1. Reduces Communications Overheads: Let us assume that a project is run by a single member team, skilled and experienced in every aspect of project delivery. The person works at an average competency and completes the work in 100 units of effort. Efforts for communications overheads are added to this ideal effort due to the following reasons:

a. The project team consists of people with specialised skills and some effort is spent to make one team understand the work of the other team. In Waterfall, this primarily happens via project documents, the prime means of handover and takeover from one team to the other. It requires lots of effort to keep the documents updated with the changing requirements and design. A lot of effort also goes towards meetings, email exchanges and preparing reports.

b. Within the same team, if there are multiple members, it increases communications overheads as each member needs to be aware of the changes being made by the other members.

For a typical project, it is likely that communications overheads would cost another 100 units for a moderately sized team (5–8 members) and increases further with increase in team size.

PKM reduces this overhead by at least half as:

a. It creates a centralised knowledge repository in a digitised format that is easy to maintain and accessible to the entire project team. This reduces communications overhead and helps to develop a shared contextual knowledge across different stakeholders of the project.

b. PKM is predominantly in business language that can be understood by all in the project, reducing communications gap.

c. The repository is integrated and impact analysis for any change is greatly reduced, again helping to reduce communications gap.

2. Digitises Static Test (Review): Static test is all the reviews performed on the project artefacts. There is currently no integrated approach to static test in the Waterfall and Agile methodologies. This results in teams spending time to identify the same defect that someone else has already identified in past. In Agile, the issue is not that obvious as the team is co-located and their interaction is more frequent than in Waterfall. In PKM, the defects are linked to the inventory or relationship and therefore they can be easily identified to prevent someone discovering the same defect while reviewing inventory or relationship. Figure 5.1 illustrates this.

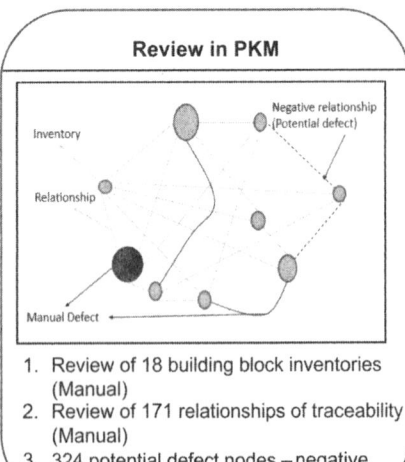

Figure 5.1 | Traditional review and review in PKM

Project Knowledge Model: A Differentiator

We have seen that the project knowledge is digitised in 189 data points (in a particular implementation), replacing the project documents. Therefore, review of the project knowledge can also be digitised. This is achieved in the following manner:

1. All the inventories of the 18 building blocks should be manually reviewed for correctness and completeness.
2. All the 171 relationships established should be manually reviewed for correctness and completeness.
3. PKM can read the current relationships and indicate an inventory with no related relationship (negative relationship) to inventories of a specific building block. This is easy to do so as the existing relationships for an inventory are already digitised.

Some of the examples of negative relationship are:
a. Requirement_01 is not linked to any test case.
b. Business Rule_01 is not linked to any requirement.

Negative relationship review covers an important aspect of review. It helps in finding out the missing elements preventing the correctness and completeness of the project knowledge. For a reviewer, it is always easy to comment on existing information, but it is difficult to find out what is missing. This review helps finding out missing relationships which can be corrected to complete the project knowledge. Negative relationship review should be completed before manual review by SME, as in that case the SME receives a better quality information to review.

3. A Practical Approach to Address Quality of the Project Delivery: To err is human. Everyone in the project team is prone to make mistakes: only the extent may vary. However, there is an expectation that the software produced should be free from defects. The following points highlight the factors that impact quality of the software as people often make mistakes:

1. As not everyone in the team is fully skilled, their work introduces bugs which need significant quality effort to be identified and corrected.
2. Even if a person is skilled, doing 100% correct work the first time is almost impossible except for trivial cases.
3. Communications gaps add to lower quality work.
4. Testing effort is needed to certify the quality of the software.
5. Traditional document reviews need costly SME effort. Also, it is difficult to review free-form text and paragraphs.

PKM can reduce the *As Is* quality effort almost by half. The following points explain how:

1. Reusability of the existing information is easy as the knowledge base is digitised and information can be easily extracted. This is difficult in the document regime where the information is not digitised. Ability to reuse also reduces inconsistency and therefore reduces the probability to make an error.
2. Detectability of an error increases as the information is in a single repository and more transparent than project documents.
3. PKM is bound by the exhaustive traceability mechanism and has 324 potential nodes of failure (negative relationships) that can be retrieved by the model. It takes care of a significant portion of the review effort. These potential errors are clerical in nature, saving costly SME review effort.
4. There are three manual reviews that we foresee for the optimised project delivery:
    a. *Requirement review*: As requirements form the base of the software being developed and generally come from the customer, they need to have a manual SME review.
    b. *Traceability and inventory review*: All the traceability links that have been created in the project must be manually reviewed to address the oversight of the person who created the links. This is done across all the phases of the project. Additionally, inventories need to be reviewed manually to ensure they are specified completely and correctly. As the information is digitised, its review is faster than the traditional manual document review.
    c. *Document review*: For various reasons, even if the project knowledge is digitised, there is a need to produce documents. PKM can extract the documents using the information available in its inventory and relationships (Chapter 6 has details of it). The documents can then be distributed to parties who may not have access to the digitised PKM. Besides, many people in the project may be more comfortable reviewing documents rather than reviewing knowledge in its digital form. The document review may not detect significant errors as the 'Traceability and inventory' review would already have detected the majority of the errors.

These three manual review data points replace the two manual review (inventory and relationship review) data points discussed chapter 4.

The total number of quality assurance data points stand updated to 327 (3 manual and 324 of negative relationship) from 326.

This is an optimal combination of manual and negative relationship review that facilitates quality in the project delivery.

Traditional project knowledge has two sets of artefacts, business and technical, making it difficult for technical and non-technical people to understand the entire set of artefacts. This is a challenge for quality assurance of the project knowledge. PKM addresses this challenge to a significant extent. PKM contains four forms of project knowledge. Three of them represent its business component (requirement, solution and test design) and one of them (application design) represents its technical component. The business component of the project knowledge can be understood by the entire project team. However, technical knowledge is usually only understood by technologists. Technical knowledge is derived knowledge from business knowledge. PKM concentrates on focusing on business knowledge so that it is in a language for all to understand and comment on. At the same time, PKM has also been prescriptive that the technical specialists prove that their technical solution (through 'Data' and 'Logic' building blocks) traces all the elements of business knowledge. Now, even non-technical people can look into the related technical solution. Since the technical solution is to-the-point, there is a good chance even for non-technical persons to detect any issues, which is very difficult in the traditional project delivery.

As per PKM, one of the first activities in project delivery is to select the relevant project knowledge data points from the set of 189 data points. Proactive digital scoping (in the form of 'yes' and 'no') at the initial stage of the project sets the focus of the project right and reduces oversights in the initial phase, reducing potential rework in the later phases. If the initial scoping itself has an oversight, PKM provides a better mechanism to add or delete the project knowledge data points than what is required to update project documents.

PKM ensures the project knowledge scope remains fit-for-purpose. If the knowledge can be specified by 18 building blocks, then 189 data points represent the project knowledge. If the project knowledge can be specified in 17 building blocks, then 153, that is, $(n*(n-1)/2 + n)$ data points represent the project knowledge. The number of building blocks needed is contextual and organisation specific. This sense of completeness of the project knowledge scope is less apparent in other methodologies – making PKM more relevant for maintaining quality of the project knowledge.

4. Provides Capability to Replace Traditional Project Documents: The digitisation framework of PKM gives enormous power to the project team as the knowledge now can be easily managed in a digital format rather than writing documents which are relatively less structured. Any output can be extracted from PKM via standard and ad-hoc reports, reducing significant effort in the project. Integrity of the project knowledge in PKM can be maintained with ease when compared to the documents.

This topic is dealt with in more detail in chapter 6.

5. Brings Order to Anarchy in the Project Delivery: The effort spent on building and testing the software costs about 40% of the total project delivery effort. Almost 60% of the effort goes towards requirement gathering and business, technical and test solutioning (as derived from Figure 13.2 of Chapter 13). The software development is predominantly project delivery methodology agnostic and it is a set of pure coding and unit testing activities, based on a plan. Software development (build) requires specialised technical skills and the output will heavily depend on the competency and experience of the build team involved. Test execution and defect management is also relatively standard across methodologies.

It is the remaining 60% effort area, where chaos can rule, is what the existing methodologies struggle to address. The main reason for struggling is that the logical unit of output in this area is documents (business, technical and test solutioning) and it becomes difficult to create and maintain the documents in real-time and ensure quality across the document set.

There is an interesting point to note in the area of 40%. In 'build', if it is not correctly coded, it will not execute and the code must be corrected for it to work. Test cases will also clearly either fail or pass. This gives a confidence to the team about whether they are making progress in the right direction or not. However, in the 60% area, where the documents are the equivalent of code, there is no readily available mechanism to ensure what is written in the documents is correct. Many times, requirements are found to be incorrect only during the testing phase, thereby creating a huge amount of rework, invalidating the existing estimates of effort and costs.

The following is a common sense approach to bring order to this 60% area:

Project knowledge maintenance, which predominantly forms this 60% effort area, is split into two areas: business and technical. Whereas business knowledge can be understood and commented by anyone in the project, technical knowledge is in the purview of the few technology skilled members of the project.

Managing project knowledge via PKM is structured, transparent and effective. It starts with capturing the core business project knowledge by adding information to the data points of requirement analysis phase. It then expands the business knowledge to its completeness by adding

Project Knowledge Model: A Differentiator

information to the data points of solution design phase. From this point onwards two parallel streams of project knowledge are captured. One is, again, business project knowledge by adding information to the data points of the test design phase. The other is technical project knowledge by adding information to the data points of the application design phase.

End-to-end traceability mechanism of the model helps keeping the business and technical project knowledge integrated with each other, helping to maintain its quality in real-time. Through traceability, the technical project knowledge is linked to one or more building blocks of the business project knowledge, depending on the project budget and nature of the project. This assists the quality of the build. Traceability also helps understanding negative relationship potential defects and reducing effort for impact analysis.

The project knowledge is managed by the relevant SMEs in the project. This helps building a self-managed team and reduces management overheads to a significant extent. Working in this culture, therefore, has significant advantage over the document regime and face-to-face interaction regime of Waterfall and Agile methodologies. We lose transparency of the project progress in the document regime as the document creation can take weeks and months before anyone can review it. Agile has no scientific way of knowledge management (it relies on face-to-face interaction), hence its progress is difficult to measure. However, as the Sprint duration is a couple of weeks, the work is exposed sooner than the Waterfall methodology. In contrast, project knowledge progress as per PKM is transparent and the team knows about it in real-time.

6. Project Management Enablement through Extreme Quantification: The 189 constituents of project knowledge (22 of them being reusable from enterprise knowledge) are quality assured by 327 data points and all of them are to be managed by 24 generic activities of project delivery. This increases the transparency of information significantly, something which is not usually seen in the project documentation regime.

Build and test execution activities can similarly be digitised as they are closely related to application design and test design activities.

This level of quantification is unheard of in the current project delivery environment. The lowest logical unit of project knowledge output in the Waterfall and Agile methodologies is a document. The typical tasks in these methodologies are: create a document, review a document and so on. In PKM, the digitised data points drive the project knowledge and its quality assurance, and the examples would be: add inventory of business rule, establish business rule relationship, review negative relationship of business rule and so on. This takes project delivery transparency to a new level.

All the activities are primarily related to a phase. Depending on circumstances, they may be executed in the subsequent phase as well. This helps in calculation of rework and phase containment effectiveness. For example, if requirement is updated in solution design phase, it is probably indicating rework.

Due to transparency provided in PKM, the status of the project is known with more accuracy. Let us understand this through an example. In the traditional project delivery, the project manager checks with test team about the status of the completion of test case design. He or she must believe what test team communicates. If the progress is not as desired, all that he or she can say is to work extra hours and try to complete the work in time. In contrast, PKM itself can calculate the progress of test design based on the information it has. And it is much more reliable and accurate as it is derived from the actual work on project knowledge rather than just believing anyone.

Exposing the project knowledge via digitisation ensures that it is read significantly more by the project team when compared to it being written in documents. This increases the probability of the detection of wrong information faster.

There are suggestions to spend half of the project schedule on different forms of testing [9]. This is driven from the assumption that IT is a knowledge driven industry and it is difficult to structure the knowledge quickly: it evolves. Through PKM, knowledge can be created and maintained much better, giving a more structured approach than project documentation. This helps in implementing the much coveted aim of the project delivery: doing things right the first time. This creates an environment where quality is in-built and then we may not have to spend half of the project effort trying to test it from different perspectives (as there will be less defects).

7. An Optimal Mix of Parallel and Sequential Activities: PKM has been able to find the fine balance in managing the knowledge-intensive phases of project delivery. Between requirement gathering and solution design, the relationship is sequential. Unless requirements are defined to a sufficient level, solution design should not be started. Also, the relationship between solution design and application design and between solution design and test design is sequential.

However, these two relationships (Solution design-Application design and Solution design-Test design) itself are parallel in nature. This is possible since we specify the details in solution design to its completeness (fit-for-purpose for the project delivery). All the details coming from Business are specified in the solution design. For example, all the error messages are specified in the solution design. This makes it possible for application and test design to start in parallel. This poses an interesting question - which phase should be the last one, application design or test design? The point to note here is whereas system analyst can understand test cases, test analysts will have difficulty in understanding inventories of application design. This naturally makes application design the last phase to be completed as in that case system analyst can ensure all the test cases are traced to the inventories of application design.

The above activity relationship creates a fine balance between Waterfall and Agile methodologies.

8. Supports Natural Evolution of Knowledge: In the set of charts shown in Figure 5.2, an attempt has been made to understand how knowledge matures naturally and how it matures under various methodologies. The chart has analysed one portion of the project knowledge, i.e., requirement and follows its maturity through different phases of project delivery.

Evolution and maturity of knowledge follows a pattern that is shown in the first graph. It is clear from the other set of graphs that Waterfall and Agile methodologies differ from the natural evolution of project knowledge. Waterfall assumes requirements can be written correctly the first time and leaves little space for them to mature during subsequent phases of the project. Agile assumes requirements evolve continuously. Natural evolution assumes they evolve at a rapid state initially; in the subsequent phases the speed of change stabilises and reduces to a large extent.

PKM on which KDD is based on, closely follows the natural evolution of requirement as explained in the following:
1. Requirements mature sufficiently in the Requirement Analysis phase via its linking with the other four building blocks of the phase, digitised manual and negative relationship review and also via requirement transformation (to solution design) mechanism.
2. The traceability with subsequent phases ensures that any gap in requirements is addressed appropriately and thus requirements mature naturally and scientifically.

In summary, to take knowledge to perfection, it evolves during the phase it belongs to and then through traceability matrix it keeps maturing in the subsequent phases. Both are important as roughly 80% of the evolution should happen during the main phase and the remaining 20% in the subsequent phases. Other knowledge constituents follow similar pattern like requirement in PKM.

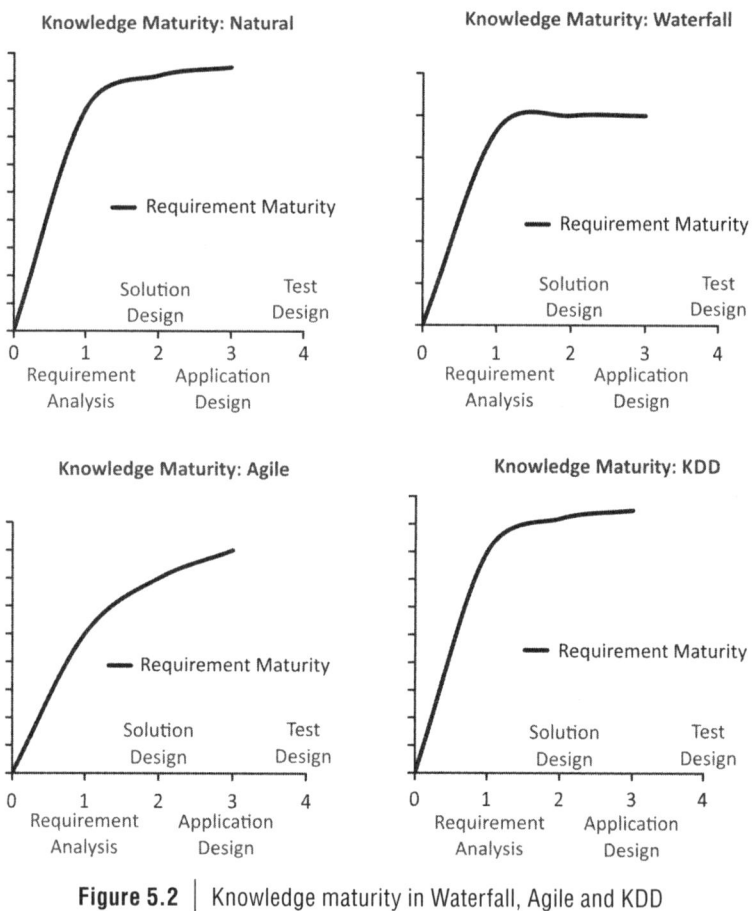

Figure 5.2 | Knowledge maturity in Waterfall, Agile and KDD

9. Age Old Struggle between Requirement and Design Simplified: It is natural for requirements and solutioning to mature from each other. However, in a typical customer-vendor relationship, this natural maturing is restricted as vendors demand fixed requirements and customers many times claim the new piece of information as design details and not new requirement. Providing fixed requirements at the beginning of the project is not practical and that is a perpetual issue between the customer and the vendor.

In PKM, transformation of requirements into solution has eased this area of conflict significantly. The usual discussion whether a piece of information is requirement or solution gets less prominence. The model is based on 18 well-defined building blocks. Whatever information is received from the customer, is added into PKM as requirements. Requirements are then analysed. There are two outcomes of the requirement analysis. One is transformation of the requirement into skeletal solutioning inventory. The other is a list of queries where the requirement seems to be inconsistent and/or not understood. These two outcomes help to develop the contract between the vendor and customer, greatly simplifying any area of contention. Any new requirement thereafter would obviously need the contract to be amended.

10. Enables Reusability within the Project Knowledge Phases: Holding the knowledge in PKM rather than documents greatly increases its reusability. Reusability is in-built into the model.

Solution development reuses requirement knowledge to its best. Solution inventories are created from the requirement statements. Test cases are created by reusing solution inventories.

11. Reuse from Enterprise Knowledge Base Facilitates Continuous Improvement in Project Delivery: Out of 189 project knowledge data points, some are more reusable than others and can act as an enterprise knowledge base for an organisation. An example of such data point is 'Application', as it lists all the applications that the enterprise has. An example of a data point not reusable to a large extent is 'Requirement', as it is contextual to the project and transformed subsequently to other, more stable building blocks. However, coming up with the list of reusable data points is subjective and different organisations may have a different set of data points constituting their enterprise knowledge base. In chapter 4, there is a list of 22 building blocks and relationships as one typical set of the enterprise knowledge base. The enterprise knowledge base is domain agnostic and hence can be used for any domain. Table 5.2 lists the building block and relationships and the related delivery phase.

When a project is complete, a portion of the project knowledge should be moved to the enterprise knowledge. The enterprise knowledge can also be enriched by spending dedicated efforts to review and add information into it.

The enterprise knowledge base helps to improve the reuse culture in project delivery. As the format and structure of the enterprise knowledge is the same as the project knowledge, the reuse is intuitive. The inventory and relationships available in the enterprise can be directly reused in the project delivery environment.

Table 5.2 | Enterprise knowledge building blocks and relationships

Building Block / Relationship	Delivery Phase
Process	Requirement analysis
Application	Requirement analysis
Product	Requirement analysis
Non-functional attribute	Requirement analysis
Relationship between process and product	Requirement analysis
Relationship between process and application	Requirement analysis
Interface	Solution design
Business data	Solution design
Scenario	Solution design
Communication	Solution design
Report	Solution design
Business rule	Solution design
Process steps	Solution design
Message	Solution design
Relationship between process and interface	Solution design
Relationship between process and business data	Solution design
Relationship between process and communication	Solution design
Relationship between process and report	Solution design
Relationship between process and business rule	Solution design
Relationship between process and scenario	Solution design
Relationship between process and process step	Solution design
Relationship between process and message	Solution design

The advantage of this mechanism can be better understood when we compare it with the traditional approach for reuse. The traditional approach is to read the project documentation of the previous projects and extract the reusable sentence or paragraphs or sections from those documents. It is difficult to ascertain that the information contained in these documents are up-to-date or not. Often, documents are hardly reusable for subsequent projects even if they are related.

The enterprise knowledge, thus maintained, can help the future projects significantly. Quantification of reuse can be determined easily, which is a major limitation in the projects following the Waterfall and Agile methodologies. In the PKM, it is easy to make a statement that x% of the project knowledge is reused from the enterprise knowledge base as both the project and the enterprise knowledge is in the format of inventory and relationships.

At the start of a project, there may be significant knowledge available in the enterprise knowledge base that can be easily reused. And with each project delivered, the information available in the enterprise knowledge increases. This facilitates the culture of continuous improvement in the project delivery environment, something which has always been desired, but the implementation of which has been a concern of the industry.

As software development is the main objective of the project delivery, asset creation, if it does not directly benefit the current project, is not seen as a useful thing to do and it remains in the wish list of the company. However, PKM, by invoking bidirectional interaction between project knowledge and enterprise knowledge, has shown a practical way to create enterprise knowledge without the company incurring too much cost in doing so.

12. Domain Agnostic Flavour: The building blocks of PKM are not specific to any domain and cover process-intensive domains such as banking, retail and insurance. Necessary customisation may be required, based on the terminology adopted by the domain. For example, in insurance, 'product' (such as life insurance product, which is a project knowledge building block) is commonly understood, but in telecom, it is better understood as a 'plan' (such as 999 monthly plan with free calls up to 120 minutes).

One of the important reasons why Waterfall and Agile methodologies could not be prescriptive while detailing knowledge-intensive phases such as requirement analysis is because they assume that domain related project knowledge is different for different domains and better managed by domain SMEs such as business analysts. All that the methodologies can do is to have activities of producing, reviewing and agreeing with the documents that capture knowledge in that phase. One of the examples of documents is Business Requirement Specification (BRS). PKM has domain agnostic project knowledge. Let us understand it clearly that the framework (i.e., of 189 data points of project knowledge) alone is domain agnostic, but the information contained in the framework will be specific to the domain. This allows the model to be prescriptive while detailing knowledge-intensive phases, making it different from the other methodologies.

13. Empowers the Build Team: Build teams are the creators of the software and no matter how well the requirement and solutioning are done, if it does not find appropriate place in build, software quality is going to suffer. The build team is generally not exposed to requirements and test cases. They primarily work from solution documents. Exposing them to the requirements and test cases via PKM enables them to broaden their perspective, bringing additional quality to the project. Confidence of the build team increases significantly when it traces the application design inventories to project test cases. In a way, the build teams tests the application design before a single test case is executed, thereby reducing test execution defects significantly.

Build team benefits significantly from the three forms of project knowledge in the business language (Requirement, Solution and Test) in a catalogued format. This improves the understanding of what needs to be done as a developer, which is significantly superior compared to the document set. Many times, they find requirements to be clearer than the solution statements and the project thus saves potential rework.

14. Focus on Non-Functional Requirements: Non-functional requirements are generally neglected and picked up late in the project delivery and might need significant rework. In PKM, we have a superset of non-functional attributes from which the ones relevant to the project are chosen in the requirement analysis phase. A sample list of non-functional attributes is provided in Appendix A. The selected non-functional attributes are then elaborated in the solution design phase. Thus, build and test teams are aware of the non-functional requirements when the project reaches application design and test design and hence the risk of omission of a non-functional attribute is reduced significantly.

15. Enables Use of Quantitative Techniques in Project Delivery: As PKM digitises the project knowledge, techniques relying on quantification of project knowledge are easily enabled. Progress of the project knowledge completion is transparent and can be easily calculated. The reason is that the model can keep a tab on the 189 data points of project knowledge, whereas other methodologies can measure the progress via production of the project documents. Project progress indicators can be retrieved by PKM, reducing the need to take inputs from the project team for project management purposes.

Orthogonal Array Test Strategy (OATS), a test design optimisation technique relies on the business scenario value that is one of the building blocks in the project knowledge. OATS can be easily implemented via PKM.

16. Creates an SME Friendly Environment: In the Waterfall methodology, SMEs are in great demand and they need to drive the show. In Agile, the basic assumption is the team members should be the SME in their own area. PKM assists SMEs as can be understood from the following examples:

1. Scoping the project at the initial stages is a major challenge for an SME. Three levels of scoping in PKM (as explained in section 9.2.1 of Chapter 9) and having a superset of project knowledge in 189 data points make things simple for an SME. As the constituents of the project knowledge are known at the start of the project, any information, if known, can be added to the model even if the information belongs to a phase different from the phase the project is currently in. If the information is related to a phase the project has already crossed, it might be a candidate for change control. If the information is for a phase that the project has not yet reached, it ensures the information is not lost in transit. For example, if in the project initiation workshop the team comes to know of additional information relevant to the testing phase, it may not remain in the notebook of the project team waiting for it to be documented after a couple of months when testing phase commences. The model allows entering this information in real-time, creating an unlinked inventory, waiting for the testing phase to detail the information further.

2. Structured data entry with mandatory and optional fields helps in capturing the information with the same quality. If a person responsible for the information addition does not know some of the mandatory attributes, he needs to find the information out from various stakeholders, including the SME, if needed. This helps maintaining the quality of the information to the same level. In the document production regime, the author can easily skip information and it would take significant review and rework to get the information to the same level.

3. Potential defects via negative relationships helps the SMEs as they will no longer have to spend any extra effort to find defects of clerical nature. The defects can come from the model itself. An example is a requirement not linked to any test case.

17. Traceability Enables Impact Analysis and Maintains Knowledge Equilibrium: Probability of change in the requirement or solutioning is the biggest threat to in-time project delivery as it invalidates the current plan and estimates. Impact analysis is done to estimate the probable change, to enable the management to decide whether to implement the change or not. PKM has 171 relationships of traceability that makes the impact analysis simple to perform as the project knowledge is catalogued and integrated. Any requirement or solutioning inventory has other related inventories across the project knowledge in the model. In the traditional project delivery, the impact analysis is done by SMEs of different teams (e.g., business analyst, system analyst) and the project artefacts also need to be updated. As not more than ten relationships of traceability are available in the traditional project delivery, it needs heavy involvement and more effort from the SME to do the impact analysis.

Traceability also assists in maintaining knowledge in PKM in an equilibrium (complete, saturated) state - without any defect. The moment a defect is introduced in the project knowledge eco system, the knowledge equilibrium is lost. However, the defect can be quickly linked to one or more inventory and or relationship due to exhaustive traceability mechanism of the model. This helps in knowing the reason of losing the knowledge equilibrium. By updating related inventory and or relationship, the knowledge equilibrium is regained in PKM. This is a beautiful feature of PKM, difficult to find elsewhere with respect to project delivery. An analogy can be – in a calm pond when a pebble is dropped, it creates disturbance and there is a sudden spurt of waves in the water. It however, gradually dies down with time by sheer inertia regaining the equilibrium state.

18. Manages Business and Technical Project Knowledge Optimally: Application design output is in technical language and not everyone in the project will be able to understand it. However, requirement analysis, solution design and test design outputs represent business knowledge and are understandable to all in the project. PKM digitises the three business knowledge and challenges the build team to trace the business knowledge to technical knowledge so that the quality of the software can be positively influenced. This is a simple, sensible and accurate approach to manage project delivery. Tracing technical project knowledge to the three forms of business project knowledge minimises the defects in the test execution phase. This is because all the test cases, solution design and requirement analysis inventories are traced to the 'data' and 'logic' building blocks of application design. Hence, theoretically, there will be no defect in executing the test cases. The approach taken in the application design is to capture only enough 'data' and logic' inventories that can prove its direct linkages with the business knowledge. If an attempt is made to capture exhaustive list of 'data' and 'logic' including the framework related and common utility inventories, it might increase the inventory volume significantly making it difficult to maintain. Hence this pragmatic approach is taken to balance the business and technical knowledge optimally in the PKM.

Doing something similar by following the traditional methodologies depending on the documents for the project knowledge is difficult.

19. Separation of Concern: One of the ways of managing things (including knowledge) better is to utilise the concept of 'separation of concern' where we identify different concerns within the scope and separate them out so that they becomes loosely coupled instead of tightly coupled when they are together. And then manage these concerns by focusing on each of them separately. Looking at these concerns separately also helps in understanding the linkages of these concerns (as all concerns are within the scope). This provides a basic framework for managing things better.

There are multiple usages of the separation of concern concept in PKM. It starts with the three categories of activities, i.e., knowledge, execution and management related. From the task accomplishment perspective, activities can also belong to one of draft, review and rework type. There are four blocks of project knowledge: requirement analysis, solution design, application design and test design. Also, separation of business knowledge and technical knowledge helps. Adding project knowledge in PKM and then looking at the result of that via document by-products (as explained in Chapter 6) rather than trying to create the document from scratch may also fall under separation of concern.

Through the attributes of process step building block, PKM creates three pools to place the process steps. Process step is the lowest logical unit of work that is understandable in business and suitable to be understood by IT in technical terms. The first pool represents user actions, the second one represents activities in the front-end IT applications and the third one represents activities in the back-end IT systems. This provides a mechanism for separation of process steps for IT and Business. It complies with separation of concern and brings IT and Business together. Whereas Business is mostly in the user action and front end IT application pool, IT is mostly in the front end and back end IT application pool making the front end IT applications as a common pool for better interaction between Business and IT teams.

Another good example of separation of concern is the parallel execution of application design and test design activities. After detailed specification of the software as a part of solution design, test design is concerned with 'what' is expected out of the software and application design is concerned about 'how' to implement the software specifications. The target of both test design and application design is the same software, but the considerations are different. There is a benefit in both the phases working almost independently post solution design, and any anomaly between the two can be detected while tracing the inventories of both the test cases and application design knowledge.

One of the best usages of separation of concern, however, is the concept of building block and relationships. When defining a building block inventory, it does not need to know anything about the relationships. For example, when defining a requirement, we do not have to worry about which application the requirement is related to. All we need to do is to capture all the attributes that define the requirement, such as requirement id, requirement description. When defining the relationship, we only need to worry about the linkages of various inventories and its rationale. We do not need to worry about adding any further information to the inventory. For example, Requirement_01 is linked to Scenario_02. Capturing inventory and relationships separately is facilitated by PKM. Inventory and relationships can easily get mixed in the Waterfall and Agile methodologies. For example, while defining requirements, it may also link the requirement to the relevant application. There is nothing wrong in it, but separating the inventory and relationship brings in more effectiveness and improves maintainability of the information. For example, if we need to change the relationship, we may be able to do it without changing the details of the inventory in the model.

20. Enhances Quality by Maker-and-Checker Mechanism: For an output to be of quality, the maker-and-checker concept provides a supporting environment. The output is first created by the maker function and then the checker function checks the output to make sure it is of quality. Quality is built into the four portions of project knowledge via this concept as illustrated in Table 5.3.

The maker-and-checker mechanism ensures the project knowledge evolves in the most scientific manner. An independent checker function is more effective in bringing quality to the output. The exhaustive traceability of PKM helps implementing the maker and checker concept.

Project Knowledge Model: A Differentiator

Table 5.3 | Maker-and-checker mechanism across the four portions of project knowledge

Project knowledge portion	Maker	Checker
Requirement analysis	Built by mapping requirements with process, NFA, application and product: Executed by business analyst	Checked by tracing requirements against solution design: Executed by business system analyst
Solution design	Built by transforming requirements: Executed by business system analyst	Checked by tracing solution design against application design: Executed by system analyst
Application design	Built by converting solution design: Executed by system analyst	Checked by tracing application design against test cases: Executed by system analyst
Test design	Built by reusing solution design: Executed by test analyst	Checked by tracing test design against requirement: Executed by test analyst

21. Effective Requirement Management: Requirement is the only building block that comes from outside of the project team (it comes from the customer) and is input to the remaining building blocks of project knowledge. Therefore, it needs to be managed better than other building blocks. PKM ensures the requirements are appropriately linked to the remaining building blocks of project knowledge via traceability.

PKM helps in reviewing requirements via manual and negative relationships review mechanism. Creating the skeletal solution design inventories as part of manual requirement review (transforming requirement into solution design) is an interesting feature of the model. Once the requirements start their journey in the requirement analysis phase of the project delivery, they can change only due to two reasons: the requirement is wrong or incomplete or if there is a change introduced in the requirements by the customer. Wrong and incomplete requirements, hopefully, should be addressed via requirement review as prescribed by the model. Change request caters to change of requirement coming from the customer. Change request can also be influenced by the requirements review done by the project team. Exhaustive traceability mechanism of PKM helps in implementing change request through easier impact analysis. PKM provides full clarity to evolving requirements by storing the first version of the requirement to the current version along with the reason of change at each version, assisting in effective requirement management.

22. Consolidated Test Case Design: As per PKM, solution design contains the complete information that is required to produce the software to the lowest level of details understood in the business community. This provides a great platform to create all types of test cases ranging from unit test to UAT in one format which are sourced from the same information base of solution design. In the traditional methodologies, test cases are created at different points in time by different teams, such as development team creating unit test case from High Level Design (HLD) document, test team creating system and system integration test cases from Functional Specification Document (FSD) document, user acceptance team creating UAT cases from Business Requirement Specification (BRS) document. It should be noted that unit test case consists of low level business testing and it is not intended to cover technical unit test case. There is no need for the project team to go into the details of a technical unit test. This is either done by the programming tool itself or left to the discretion of the development team. An example of business unit test is to check for the display of an error message and an example of technical unit test to ensure all the paths are travelled in a 'for' loop.

This mechanism of creating test cases at all levels at one go in the same format results in significant saving of efforts compared to doing it in the traditional way. Quality and coverage of the test cases are assisted by exhaustive traceability mechanism of PKM.

This compares well with the methodologies based on testing. It redefines V-Model methodology as it uses only solution design knowledge to design test cases at all the levels. Test Driven Development (TDD) emphasises on test by developers and Behaviour Driven Development (BDD) emphasises test by users. KDD has an overall approach for end-to-end test cases combining developer, tester and user perspective and, in that way, can be seen as combining the approach taken by TDD and BDD.

5.3 | Reason for Delay in Discovering Project Knowledge Model

Having gone through the PKM details, there is hardly anything that appears to be new. The model is just arranging and combining things that are either well known in the IT industry or can be easily appreciated as a good idea. The question now is, why did it take so long to discover the model in its entirety? Following are some of the reasons:
  1. Development of tools to assist project delivery is almost always driven by technologists who have only a basic knowledge of domain and its

complexity. The result is that the tools are very good in the technology aspects such as work flow, auditability and collaboration features. But when it comes to domain understanding, it is less matured. The tools predominantly remain in requirements and test areas and leave the majority of solution and application design areas as a black box.

This has hampered the original thinking around project knowledge.

2. The IT industry has seen a huge investment in research on the technology side. As a result, it has seen exponential improvements in storage capacity, processing speed, database maturity and user friendly programming languages. It has, however, not invested enough around domain knowledge which could have covered the project knowledge as defined in this book. With all the ingredients of project knowledge available for decades, it should not have taken us so long to evolve this Project Knowledge Model or something very similar to it with appropriate investments.
3. The advent and popularisation of processes and use cases have also hindered the fundamental research around project knowledge. Use case generally accompanies 7–9 building blocks of PKM and with heavy reliance on use cases, serious attempts were not made to look beyond. I looked beyond use cases and came to realise that there are 18 building blocks that, taken together, drive the entire knowledge in the project, creating a robust and complete specification of the software, assisting in its development.
4. Discovery of Agile, in a way, is responsible for slowing the research around project knowledge. Agile gave a feeling that anything other than coding was a waste of effort and shrunk the scope of documentation significantly. At the same time, it did not provide any alternative knowledge base that could specify the software completely, leaving a big gap.
5. The business analysts, who are best placed to discover exhaustiveness of the project knowledge, usually do not have the same level of maturity in solution design, application design and test design. Therefore, they are not able to see the end-to-end picture and visualise the project knowledge completely.

5.4 | What Does it Really Mean for Project Delivery?

PKM and its digitisation accelerate project delivery. The main benefits are:
1. It results in consolidated digitised project knowledge that can be referred by anyone in the project with equal ease.

2. Significant review effort is saved by negative relationships potential defect nodes contained in PKM.
3. Exhaustive traceability with 171 relationships is provided, thus simplifying impact analysis.
4. Significant test design effort is saved as it reuses information from the solution design knowledge base.
5. Moving project knowledge to enterprise knowledge takes it to the path of continuous improvement, where subsequent projects can reuse the knowledge from previously executed projects.

CHAPTER 6

Project Knowledge Model *vs* Project Documents

Although this topic is touched upon in the previous chapters, this chapter concentrates on comparing PKM against project documents with respect to the creation and maintenance of project knowledge. It introduces both the mechanisms and provides an exhaustive comparison of the two from different perspectives. An example is provided for both document extract and PKM extract to aid understanding of their differences. It also details the artefact sets that can be extracted from PKM.

6.1 | Project Knowledge Model and Project Documents

Figure 6.1 depicts how knowledge is managed in a typical project delivery from the perspectives of PKM and document production regime. Document production regime is based on Waterfall (structured) methodology. Agile methodology have a sleeker version of the document production regime.

Any methodology of software development starts from gathering requirements and ends with the working software and the related specifications of the software. The traditional methodologies have been relying on document production regime for capturing specifications of the software from solution, technical and test perspective. In the Waterfall methodology, emphasis is given on rigorous maintenance of the documents during different phases of the project delivery. Agile methodology go for 'fit-for-purpose' documentation and documents are kept at high level so that they do not need frequent changes.

As mentioned earlier, keeping the documents updated in real-time is a challenging task in project delivery and that causes a lot of gaps in communication, ultimately delaying the project. This is one reason the Agile methodology only go for high level documentation that does not need frequent updates.

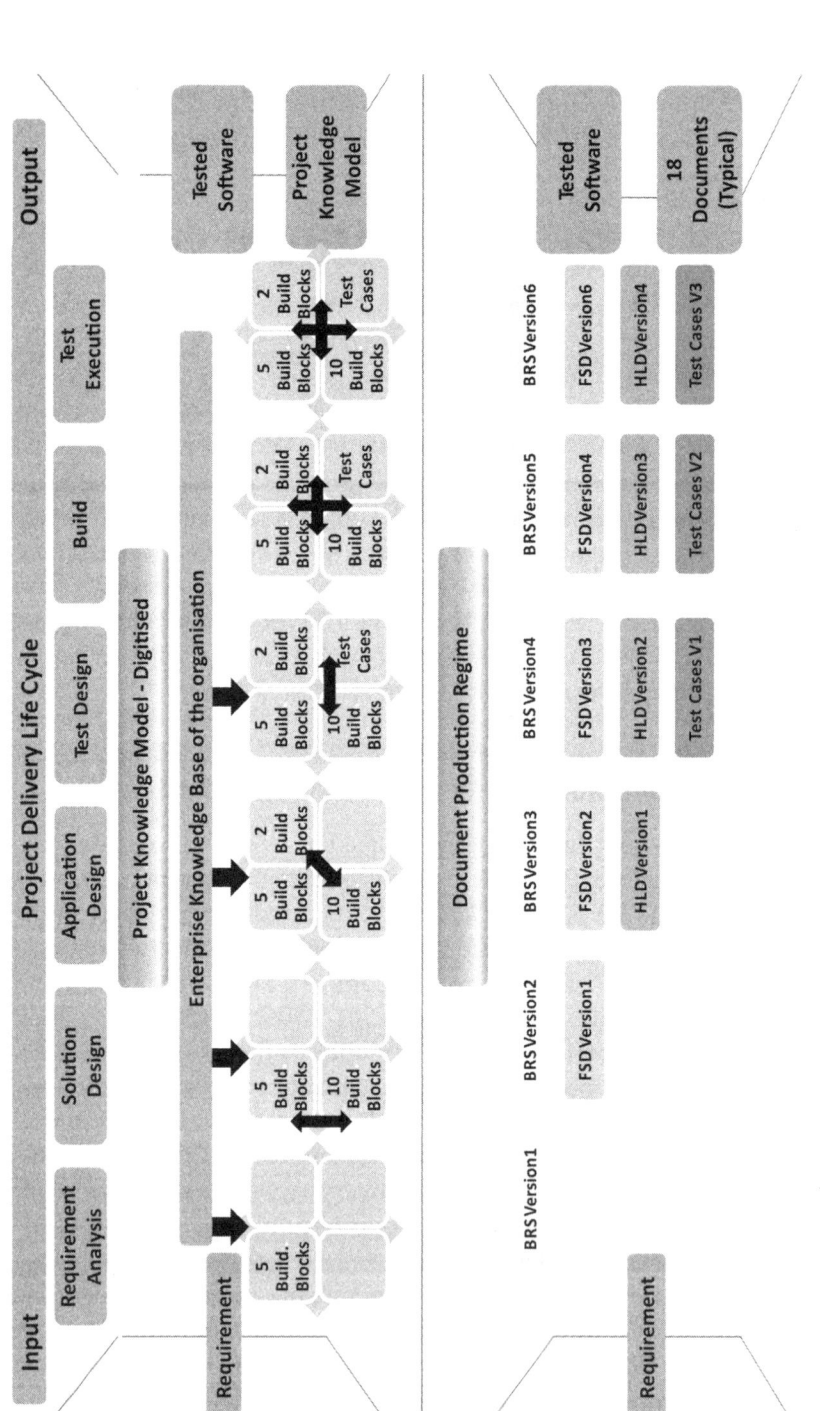

Figure 6.1 | Project knowledge management in project delivery

Project Knowledge Model vs Project Documents　　　　　　　　　　　　　　123

The main issue with the document production regime is that there is a need to update the contents of the documents regularly as the project progresses through different phases. But the problem is the before the updated document can be issued, it needs to be approved by the relevant stakeholders. The revised version of the documents is mostly issued on reaching selected milestones. For example, in Figure 6.1, six versions of BRS (Business Requirement Specification) are visualised over the course of the project delivery lifecycle. Let us say there is a gap of two months before the next version of the BRS is scheduled to be released. From the couple of days of release of the last version, the information contained in the document may not be the latest. And over the next two months the gap between the knowledge in the project team and in the project document will keep getting bigger. Also, everyone in the project may not be aware of this updated project knowledge as the medium of circulating project knowledge is still the document. Even if the next version of the document is released, what is the surety that it will have all the updates that it should have and everyone in the project team go through the document to appreciate the changes? This limits the effectiveness of the working of the project team and the main reason for the reduced usage of the Waterfall methodology.

In contrast the book details PKM which can replace the document production regime. Through 18 building blocks, the model scopes the entire project knowledge and clubs the building blocks together in the four knowledge containers representing the four knowledge-intensive phases of project delivery (i.e., requirement analysis, solution design, application design and test design). The model helps adding information to these building blocks for the respective phases. The model also helps in keeping all the information consistent and integrated by enabling information interaction between different knowledge intensive phases. Any change of information in any phase can easily be propagated to other phases to ensure the information remains consistent. Figure 6.1 represents this.

Let's look at PKM from a different perspective. We know that 18 building blocks of project knowledge gives rise to 189 data points of project knowledge. There will be inventories for each of the 18 building blocks and altogether 171 types of relationships between these inventories. Figure 6.2 makes it easier to visualise this. The spider-web of the figure represents PKM. Circles in the spider-web indicate inventories of building blocks. Examples may be: Requirement_01, Business Rule_02, Scenario_03, Screen_04 and so on. The lines connecting two circles represent relationship between the two inventories. Examples may be: Requirement_01 is related to Scenario_03 and Business Rule_02 is related to Screen_04.

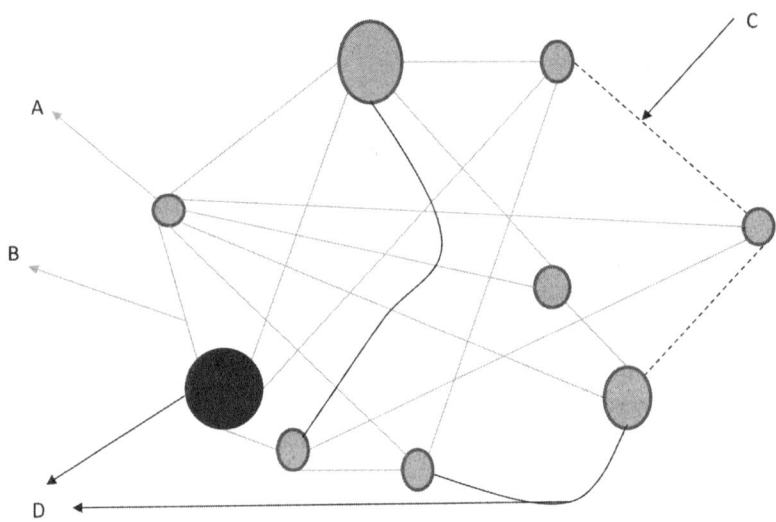

Notation (example):
A – Inventories of building blocks (Requirement_01)
B – Relationship types of inventories (Requirement_01 linked to Screen_01)
C – Negative relationship potential defect (Test Case_01 not linked to any requirement)
D – Manual defect (requirement related defect)

Figure 6.2 | Project Knowledge Model

PKM integrates the inventory and its relationships in a transparent manner, replacing the need of a document to capture the project knowledge. Another important characteristic is the quality assurance mechanism around PKM. Reviewing inventories and relationships are relatively easier than reviewing documents.

The model has a self-healing mechanism as well, i.e., there is a mechanism to retrieve and detect potential errors due to negative relationship, as explained earlier. If an inventory is not related to the inventories of a different building block, the model can retrieve the information. For example, the model can detect if a test case is not related to any requirement inventory, helping to assure the quality of the information contained in PKM. There are 324 potential defect nodes (as detailed in Chapter 4) that the model can identify.

The model digitises the whole project knowledge via 189 data points integrated with each other, resulting in a mesh that is much easier to create and maintain. When needed, this model produces documents, extracting the information from the different data points of the model.

6.2 | Comparison of Project Knowledge Model and Project Documents

Table 6.1 lists out the main attributes of project delivery related to project knowledge and compares PKM with document production regime.

Table 6.1 | Comparison of Project Knowledge Model and project document

Attribute	Definition	Document Production Regime	Project Knowledge Model	Remarks
Structure	The structure and framework under which the project knowledge is managed.	Not scientific	Scientific	At the best, document will have a template to structure the project knowledge, whereas PKM has integrated 189 data points to manage the project knowledge. The model is scientific. Following is an example to illustrate this: In the requirement capturing template of the document regime, it is not uncommon to see a column for related business rules. In PKM, while capturing details about the requirements, business rules are not listed, everything is captured only as a requirement. Business rules are listed separately and then, via traceability, the requirements and business rules are linked.
Redundancy	Same information repeated at multiple sections of a document or in multiple documents.	Quite prevalent	Minimal	PKM has the inventory specifications and relationship framework that helps reusing the information where needed, rather than duplicating it across project delivery.

Contd.

Attribute	Definition	Document Production Regime	Project Knowledge Model	Remarks
Consistency	Information in one section does not contradict information in other section of the same document or across various documents.	Quite prevalent	Maximum	Logical compartmentalisation of project knowledge into 189 constituents with unambiguous scope is the specialty of PKM. This assists in greater consistency of the project knowledge. This sophistication is not there in the document production regime where the knowledge is captured in free-form text and it is difficult to ensure consistency across sections and documents. Also, provision of reusing information from previous phase of the project and from enterprise knowledge base helps keeping the information consistent in the model. Digitisation of the project knowledge via PKM helps in detecting any inconsistency early.
Integrity	Changing information at one place should also result in changing information at all the other related places.	Needs to be manually ensured	Maximum	The building block and traceability mechanism helps in keeping the project knowledge integrated. It helps in identifying the information that must be changed because of change in related information as all the related information is linked via traceability. Let us understand it with an example. SMEs found out that the Requirement_01 needs to be changed. The model allows the requirement to be changed. From that point onwards, it will get reflected in all the reports and project documents extracted from the model as it will always extract Requirement_01 from the same source.

Contd.

Project Knowledge Model vs Project Documents

Attribute	Definition	Document Production Regime	Project Knowledge Model	Remarks
				Due to change in Requirement_01, there is also a need to make sure if any other information needs to be changed. This is done easily in PKM. All the linked inventories of other building blocks are analysed for any change and, if needed, are changed. Also, other requirements linked to Requirement_01 are also analysed to see if they need to change. Reduced redundancy also helps in keeping the project knowledge integrated. Document generation regime lack this level of sophistication.
Auditability	This determines how updates to the original information are version controlled, tracking who changed the information and when, for audit purposes.	Difficult to comply	Fit-for-purpose	In the document production regime, auditability is enabled manually by adding track changes, version control and revision list. It is easier to include standard audit features in PKM. Even without the standard audit feature, PKM can achieve auditability partly via the following mechanism: Project artefacts from the model should be extracted at different milestones so that the difference in information can be tracked easily. Also, any change in information should be linked to a defect, giving the change a complete transparency.

Contd.

Attribute	Definition	Document Production Regime	Project Knowledge Model	Remarks
Completeness	To specify the information that is fit-for-purpose in a project delivery environment.	Difficult to comply	Fit-for-purpose	The 189 data points of PKM provide a superset of information that is fit-for-purpose for a project in a typical implementation. The number can vary depending on the organisation and the type of project, but can be predicted accurately in each of the scenarios. It is domain agnostic. When a project is started, scoping the data points ensures there is minimal oversight. Also, there is a fit-for-purpose list of attributes for each of the data points that helps capturing the complete information. This rigour is not present in the document production regime.
Reuse	If the information is available in the project, do not create it again but reuse it.	Difficult to comply	Fit-for-purpose	In the document production regime, when the same information is to be referred again, many times it is copied and pasted. This reuse is unscientific as any change in the original information is difficult to be updated in the reused information. In PKM, through the inventory and relationship mechanism, reuse has been optimised. For example, solution design reuses requirement knowledge and test design reuses solution design knowledge. Project knowledge also reuses enterprise knowledge that keeps growing with subsequent projects.

Contd.

Attribute	Definition	Document Production Regime	Project Knowledge Model	Remarks
Rework	If the information is not captured correctly the first time, rework is required.	Prevalent	Optimised	The inventory cataloguing and relationship mechanism of the model ensures relevant information is considered at the correct point in time and reduces the chances of making a mistake. Structured information entry while specifying the inventory also helps in capturing the information correctly the first time itself, reducing the need for rework. Provision of mandatory and optional attributes while adding inventories also help in capturing complete information. If at all rework is needed, the cost of rework is less in the model due to its effective impact analysis mechanism driven by exhaustive traceability. Documents undergo significant rework due to their unscientific structure and particularly if the author is not experienced enough.
Oversight	Probability of missing out some information.	Prevalent	Optimised	The superset of project knowledge constituents and attribute list specifying an inventory, reduces the probability of oversight in PKM. A combination of mandatory and optional attributes defining a building block achieves a fine balance between what is too much of information and what is incomplete information.

Contd.

Attribute	Definition	Document Production Regime	Project Knowledge Model	Remarks
				This also helps in reducing oversight. Potential defects due to negative relationship extracted from the model detect oversight in traceability. Scoping of data points at the beginning of the project also reduces the probability of oversight. Scientific evolution of knowledge via the model assists, too. In the absence of all of these, the document production regime is primarily dependent on expensive manual review by SME to detect oversight.
Detectability of an error	If the information is captured incorrectly, the probability of it getting detected early.	Difficult to comply	Fit-for-purpose	In PKM, the information is structured, integrated and catalogued. It increases the transparency of information when compared to documents and makes it easier to read, understand and review. As it becomes a single source of knowledge, the information is traversed multiple times more when compared to documents that are read only when necessary. It is relatively difficult to detect an error from free-form text of a document when compared to the structured information of PKM.

Contd.

Project Knowledge Model vs Project Documents

Attribute	Definition	Document Production Regime	Project Knowledge Model	Remarks
Review	Reviewing the project knowledge.	Difficult to comply	Fit-for-purpose	Whereas document production regime is dependent on the costly manual SME review, PKM can retrieve potential defects through negative relationships, whose detection is clerical in nature (e.g., a test case is not linked to any requirement). There are 324 such potential defect nodes that can be extracted from the model. Additionally, manual SME review in the model is better organised as it may result in raising a defect linking to one or more inventory and/or relationships.
Change Management	Complying with changes in the information across project knowledge.	Difficult to comply	Fit-for-purpose	Accommodating change of information is manual in the document production regime and different authors of different documents need to perform impact analysis to change their document to comply with the requirement. Through 189 data points of inventory and relationship mechanism, the impact analysis for any change in project knowledge becomes easy in the model. The model can retrieve inventories related to the impacted inventory easily, that otherwise is left to the discretion of the SME.

Contd.

Attribute	Definition	Document Production Regime	Project Knowledge Model	Remarks
Document Production	Ability to produce documents to specify project knowledge.	Manual	Extractable	Different members of the team create documents manually in the document production regime. Documents extracted from the information existing in PKM are free from many of the ills of the document production regime. For example, a piece of information may be repeated in the document or a set of documents many times, but the information will be consistent as it is extracted from the same source in PKM.

6.3 | Document Excerpt and Equivalent Project Knowledge as per the Project Knowledge Model

We will take an excerpt from the Functional Specification Document (FSD). We will then demonstrate that every single piece of information in the excerpt is the inventory/relationship of related solution design building blocks of PKM.

Excerpt of the FSD (the example discussed is illustrative) is provided in the following text. It relates to setting up security questions and answers while completing user registration. The security questions and answers are needed when performing critical transactions online.

Document Excerpt for Setting Up Security Question and Answer While Doing User Registration

The following is the document excerpt:

"As part of the user registration process, answers to three security questions must be provided. Questions can be selected from the following list:

- Place of birth
- Mother's maiden name
- Name of your first school
- Name of your best teacher
- Name of your favourite colour

Additionally, the user must have the ability to create their own questions for any of the three questions required to be set up.

All the three questions must be different, whether selected or created. In other words, it must not be possible to select the same question again. There is no constraint on answers, i.e., all the three answers may be the same. Once a question is selected or created, the data entry field must be activated to allow for inputting the answer. The answer must be at least 4 characters long.

The system must display an appropriate message whenever the validation fails."

Let us now look at the equivalent project knowledge as per PKM. As it is the FSD extract, let us restrict to the solution design building blocks.

Equivalent project knowledge as per PKM for Setting Up Security Question and Answer While Doing User Registration

Equivalent project knowledge in terms of inventories of related building blocks are listed below. For completeness and for interested readers, inventory relationships are given in the Appendix D.

Inventory of Process Step Building Block:

Process_Step_01: The user selects / creates three questions and answers.
Process_Step_02: System validates the questions / answers.
Process_Step_03: System displays error message.
Process_Step_04: System stores three questions and their answers.

Inventory of Business Data Building Block:

Business_Data_01: Security question–01. selectable or enterable. When enterable, the minimum length is 20 characters and the maximum length is 40 characters.

Business_Data_02: Security question–02, selectable or enterable. When enterable, the minimum length is 20 characters and the maximum length is 40 characters.

Business_Data_03: Security question–03, selectable or enterable. When enterable, the minimum length is 20 characters and the maximum length is 40 characters.

Business_Data_04: Security answer–01, enterable. Minimum length is 4 characters and maximum length is 10 characters.

Business_Data_05: Security answer–02, enterable. Minimum length is 4 characters and maximum length is 10 characters.

Business_Data_06: Security answer–03, enterable. Minimum length is 4 characters and maximum length is 10 characters.

Business_Data_07: Security question–01, indicator whether it is selected or created.

Business_Data_08: Security question–02, indicator whether it is selected or created.

Business_Data_09: Security question–03, indicator whether it is selected or created.

Inventory of Business Rule Building Block:

Business_Rule_01: Security question setup will be complete when all the three questions and answers have been added correctly. It will not be possible to complete one or two questions and leave the rest to be completed later.

Business_Rule_02: There is no validation around number of questions selectable or enterable. All the three questions can be selected. However, it is also possible to have all the three questions created by the user.

Business_Rule_03: All the three questions must be different. It is not possible to create a question which is already a selectable question. The system in this case should prompt the user to select the question instead of creating the same again.

Business_Rule_04: There is no validation on the answer being same or different. All the three answers can be the same.

Business_Rule_05: Once a question is selected or created, the data entry field must be activated to allow for inputting the answer.

Inventory of Scenario Building Block:

Scenario_01: Questions can be selected from the following list:
- Place of birth
- Mother's maiden name
- Name of your first school
- Name of your best teacher
- Name of your favourite colour

Scenario_02: Questions can be of two types

- Selectable
- Created

Scenario_03: Enterable and selectable question scenarios are:
- All three questions selected
- Only two questions selected
- Only one question selected
- No question selected

Inventory of Message Building Block:
Message_01: (Error): Same question cannot be added again.
Message_02: (Error): Question must be at least 20 characters long.
Message_03: (Error): Answer must be at least 4 characters long.
Message_04: (Error): Question already exists as selectable question, create a different question or reuse the selectable question.

Inventory of Screen Building Block:
Screen_01: Security question setup screen: The three security questions are selectable (via a list box) but will have a flag (against each question) to indicate that the user wants to create the question. For enterable question and answer, the length of the field will be fixed, 40 for the question and 10 for the answer. The user will, therefore, not be able to input the question or answer more than the length allowed. The error message will be displayed only when the length of the question or the answer is less than the minimum length required. When the question is selected or created, there will be a flag to indicate the same so that the answer field will become editable.

It is worth noting that the FSD extract about the security question and answer setup has covered 6 of 10 building blocks of solution design and has no information about the remaining four building blocks listed below:
- Communication
- Report
- Offline transaction
- Interface

It is obvious that the project knowledge in PKM is digitised and hence easily retrievable and reusable. Three paragraphs of the FSD extract are replaced by 26 inventories and 140 relationships of the solution design project knowledge, a portion of PKM. The format of inventory and relationships of the model encourages a structured approach towards capturing the project knowledge, which is difficult to achieve via the traditional project documents.

6.4 | Output of Project Knowledge Model

When it comes to the traditional outputs of project knowledge, inventory and relationships format of PKM may not always work. The model should have an ability to convert the information it has into the traditional project knowledge documents.

Requirements are fed into PKM. Requirements are then analysed via the model which ensures that the requirements evolve scientifically and help creating a complete specification of the software from business, technology and test perspective.

I have come up with a list of 20 project artefacts that should cover end-to-end project knowledge. The model should be able to produce them as it contains the project knowledge and its progress. Figure 6.3 lists them.

Model created project artefacts simulate the *As Is* and the traditional situation. The project documentation now can be supplied to stakeholders who may not have access to PKM, such as customers. This also helps the project team members who are not well-versed in project knowledge in the inventory and relationship format and would prefer the project knowledge in document format for better understanding and review. Document review can be treated as another way of ensuring inventories and linkages are correct and help to improve the quality of the information contained in the model.

Model created project artefacts accomplish one important task. As the artefacts are produced from the same consolidated knowledge, information contained in the artefacts does not have any inconsistency or contradiction. As the progress reports are based on the information available, they are realistic and not prone to be tampered by the team members for reporting status or progress.

Another point for the model created project artefacts is that the entire artefact set can be extracted at any point of time. Taking these outputs at important milestones (or as specified by the project management) of the project will give a fair indication of how the project delivery is progressing. Any difference of information between two milestone outputs should be explainable by the negative relationships and manual review mechanism of PKM, thus providing full clarity about the evolution of the project knowledge.

Table 6.2 describes these outputs.

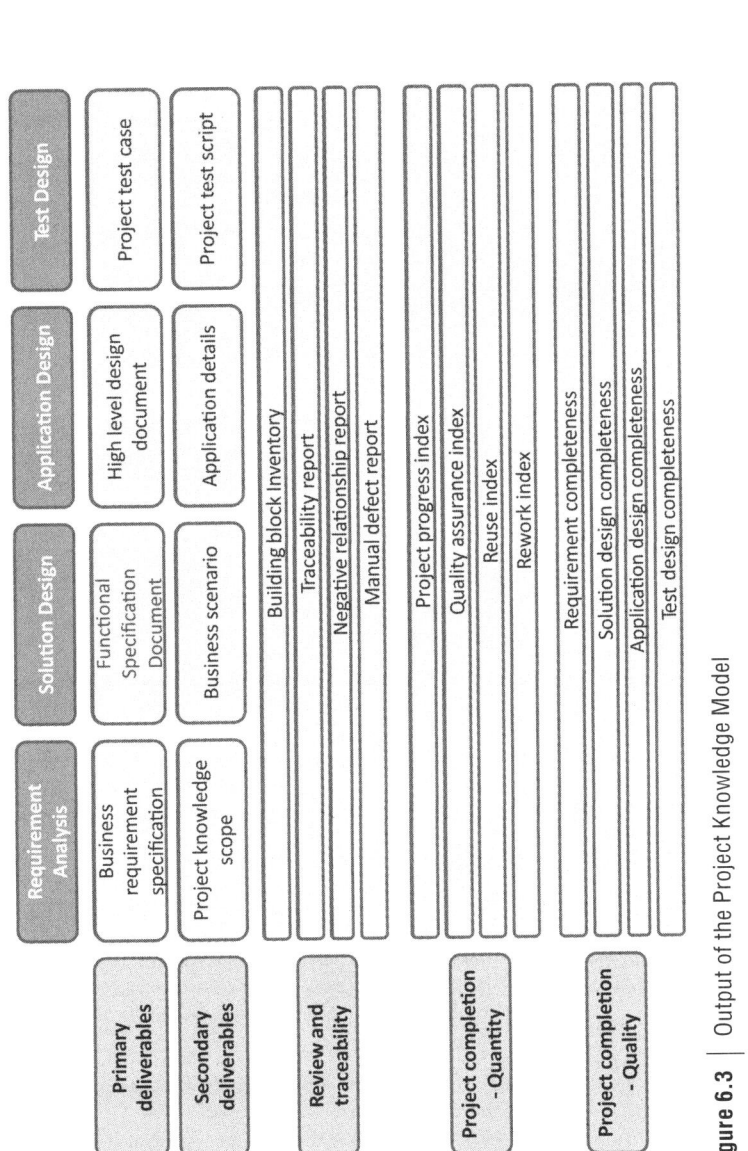

Figure 6.3 | Output of the Project Knowledge Model

Table 6.2 | **Output of the Project Knowledge Model**

Output Type	Output Name	Description	Delivery Phase
Primary deliverables	Business Requirement Specification	This is the refined requirement catalogue at the end of requirement analysis phase. The refinement from the customer supplied requirements are due to two main factors: 1. Requirement review. 2. Requirement transformation into solution design inventory.	Requirement analysis
Primary deliverables	Functional Specification Document	This document specifies the solution at Business level completely. Details are at a level that does not require any further input from Business. For example, all the screen messages are specified in Functional Specification Document.	Solution design
Primary deliverables	High Level Design document	This document specifies technical inventories and traces them with FSD, Requirements and Project Test Cases.	Application design
Primary deliverables	Project Test Case	This consists of test cases covering the entire project from Unit Test (UT) to User Acceptance Test (UAT).	Test design
Secondary deliverables	Project knowledge scope	It scopes the building blocks and positive and negative relationships. It needs to be done carefully as any oversight here may prove to be costly in the later phases of the project.	Requirement analysis
Secondary deliverables–	Business scenario	This document specifies all the business scenario and business rules related to the project that drive test design and application design.	Solution design
Secondary deliverables	Application details	This gives an exhaustive list of solution design inventory per application, bringing absolute clarity about what to do in the build phase.	Application design
Secondary deliverables	Project test script	For the test cases which are more complex in nature, test scripts will be used so that each of the steps of the test case is explained clearly.	Test design
Review and Traceability	Building block inventory	It consists of inventories of up to 18 building blocks of the project knowledge.	All phases

Contd.

Project Knowledge Model vs Project Documents

Output Type	Output Name	Description	Delivery Phase
Review and Traceability	Traceability report	It consists of up to 171 relationship types of inventories of the 18 building blocks of project knowledge.	All phases
Review and Traceability	Negative relationship report	It lists out up to 324 potential nodes of defect (negative relationships).	All phases
Review and Traceability	Manual defect report	It lists out defects of inventory and relationship of the project knowledge. Together with negative relationship report, it provides a consolidated list of static review of the project.	All phases
Project Completion: Quantity	Project progress indicator	It provides information about how much progress has been made and how much is left to be completed.	All phases
Project Completion: Quantity	Quality assurance indicator	It indicates the total number of negative relationship reviews and manual reviews and their status.	All phases
Project Completion – Quantity	Reuse index	It gives reuse index from the enterprise knowledge base.	All phases
Project Completion: Quantity	Rework index	It compares the phase (e.g., requirement) effort with the effort related to this phase in the later phases (e.g., effort related to requirement in the solution design, application design and test design phases).	All phases
Project Completion: Quality	Requirement completeness indicator	Requirement and Process coverage indicators measure requirement phase completeness.	Requirement analysis
Project Completion: Quality	Solution design completeness indicator	Requirement and Process step coverage indicators measure solution design phase completeness.	Solution design
Project Completion: Quality	Application design completeness indicator	Test case and solution design coverage indicators measure application design phase completeness.	Application design
Project Completion: Quality	Test design completeness indicator	Requirement and solution design coverage indicators measure test phase completeness.	Test design

CHAPTER 7

Extending Project Knowledge Model to Cover End-to-End Project Delivery – KDD

This chapter shows how PKM drives project delivery. PKM is expanded to Extended PKM (EPKM) to include majority of execution and management related activities so that it can cover end-to-end project delivery. It gives rise to Knowledge Driven Development (KDD) – a new project delivery methodology.

The chapter starts with understanding the broad scope of KDD in project delivery. Concepts important to appreciate KDD are detailed. The end-to-end project delivery phases are traversed using KDD via the standard quality gate approach. Other aspects of project delivery such as quality are also considered. Relevance of KDD across domain and types of projects are discussed. At the end, the chapter lists out differentiators that KDD is trying to bring in.

7.1 | Introduction

As discussed in chapter 4, there are three types of activities in project delivery, i.e., relating to knowledge, execution and management. The project knowledge related activities are the most important and covered by PKM. PKM digitises the project knowledge to an extent that makes it possible to bring in similar digitisation in the activities related to execution and management. PKM can be extended to cover a majority of the execution and management related activities and a new project delivery method can be conceived. This has resulted in the evolution of Knowledge Driven Development or KDD.

As discussed in chapter 2, there are three basic characteristics on which project delivery methodologies are based upon:
  a. Structured or empirical

Extending Project Knowledge Model to Cover End-to-End Project Delivery 141

    b. Sequential or iterative

    c. Full delivery or delivery in increments

Waterfall is structured, sequential and typically full delivery in one go and Agile is empirical, iterative and incremental delivery. KDD can be categorised as:

    a. Mix of structured (with its 189 data points of project knowledge) and empirical (evolved over the years based on experience, research and interaction with experts). The ideas may be intuitive but they are not proven yet and hence empirical.

    b. Mix of sequential (solution design does not start before requirements are matured to a significant extent), non-sequential (test design and application design start in parallel after solution design) and iterative (once the project knowledge is specified completely, it becomes easy to create build and test execution into logical units, suitable for iteration).

    c. It has the flexibility of full delivery and incremental delivery depending on need. Due to digital knowledge management, increments can be managed effectively. It is now easy to visualise that KDD is inspired by both Waterfall and Agile methodologies with PKM as differentiator.

7.2 | KDD Focus Area

Every project delivery methodology owes its existence to some important reason. Waterfall methodology came to give a structure to the ad hoc ways to deliver projects. Agile methodology evolved as a revolt against the limitation to keep the project documents updated in real-time and strict sequential nature of different phases in the Waterfall methodology. Agile took a pragmatic approach towards knowledge management and almost got rid of the elaborate documentation. KDD felt that it is better to analyse the root cause of why the project documents cannot be kept updated in real-time and provide an alternative solution. It came up with a digitised framework of managing project knowledge via PKM. KDD focus areas are explained as follows:

Core Focus: PKM is the core focus of KDD that eliminates the need to produce and maintain documents throughout the four knowledge-intensive phases (requirement analysis, solution design, application design and test design) of project delivery.

Moderate Focus: KDD drives the other important areas of project delivery through the core area. For example, test cases produced during the test design phase drive the execution and defect management during test execution phase. Technical inventories created during the application design drive the build phase of the project. Quality assurance becomes easy as the project knowledge is digitised. Project management is primarily driven by the execution of catalogued project knowledge and the quality assurance framework around it by a set number of activities. It takes a pragmatic approach about enterprise knowledge, primarily focusing on reusability.

Low Focus: Areas such as procurement of software and hardware required for project delivery and selection of vendors are not the focus area of this methodology. Feasibility study and cost-benefit analysis are also not the focus area of KDD. KDD starts with requirement gathering. Training and competency development is a low focus area; it is assumed that the team members follow the current prevailing standards. Project financials, inducting the team and managing their leave plans are also low focus area of KDD and it is better done in the current, standard way.

7.3 | KDD Core Values

Following are the five core values KDD is based upon:

1. Structured Knowledge Capture via Traceability: Figure 7.1 is a sample representation of PKM on which the KDD is based. Project knowledge in the document (analogue knowledge) has been structured and simplified via the inventory and relationship mechanism (digital knowledge). Digital project knowledge increases the transparency of the project knowledge, making it easier for the project team to review and identify any error faster. Let us understand the figure better through Table 7.1.

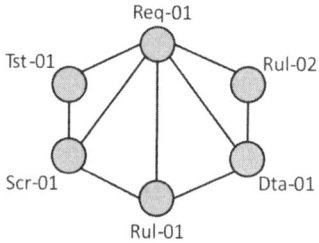

Figure 7.1 | Inventory and relationship driven project knowledge

As clear from Table 7.1, it is easy to visualise that creating the project knowledge and its subsequent maintenance due to review or requirement changes is more efficient in PKM than in the document production regime as the knowledge is split there over multiple documents. One of the biggest simplification that is brought in by PKM is to separate the linkage from the inventory specification. For example, the traceability mesh in Figure

Extending Project Knowledge Model to Cover End-to-End Project Delivery

7.1 gives the big picture of the project knowledge and can be reviewed quickly for correctness of the linkage without going into the details of the inventories. At the same time, when individual inventories are reviewed, they can be reviewed in completeness without worrying about the linkages each inventory contains.

Table 7.1 | Understanding project knowledge via inventory and relationship

Inventory / Relationship	Remarks
Req_01	An inventory of requirement. This is where the requirement is specified via mandatory and optional attributes such as requirement id, requirement name. While specifying requirements there is no need to worry about the linkage considerations such as to which business rule it is linked.
Tst_01	An inventory of test case specified completely. Reviewing the Tst_01 might indicate that it also tests Rul_01 and in that case Tst_01 is linked to Rul_01.
Scr_01	An inventory of user interface specified completely. Review of Scr_01 might indicate an interface that needs to be added as a separate interface inventory.
Rul_01	An inventory of business rule specified completely.
Dta_01	An inventory of physical data specified completely.
Rul_02	An inventory of business rule specified completely.
Req_01-Tst_01	Relationship between Req_01 and Tst_01. It indicates that Tst_01 is linked to Req-01. From the figure above, it becomes clear that the Req-01 is not completely tested by the Tst_01 as Rul_01, Rul_02 and Dta_01 are not tested by Tst_01.
Tst_01-Scr_01	Relationship between Tst_01 and Scr_01.
Scr_01-Rul_01	Relationship between Scr_01 and Rul_01. Review might indicate that Scr_01 is linked to Rul_02 and not to Rul_01.
Rul_01-Dta_01	Relationship between Rul_01 and Dta_01.
Rul_02-Dta_01	Relationship between Rul_02 and Dta_01
Rul_01-Req_01	Relationship between Rul_01 and Req_01
Req_01- Scr_01	Relationship between Req_01 and Scr_01. It becomes clear that Scr_01 is not converted in application design as no data or logic building block is linked to Scr_01. This is a defect that needs to be addressed by system analyst.
Req_01-Rul_02	Relationship between Req_01 and Rul_02
Req_01-Dta_01	Relationship between Req_01 and Dta_01

144 Knowledge Driven Development

2. Digitising End-to-End Project Delivery Driven by Extending the Project Knowledge Model: Let us recollect the figure from chapter 2, where we understood end-to-end project delivery at a generic level. We will look into the same figure, repeated as Figure 7.2, and relate it with KDD.

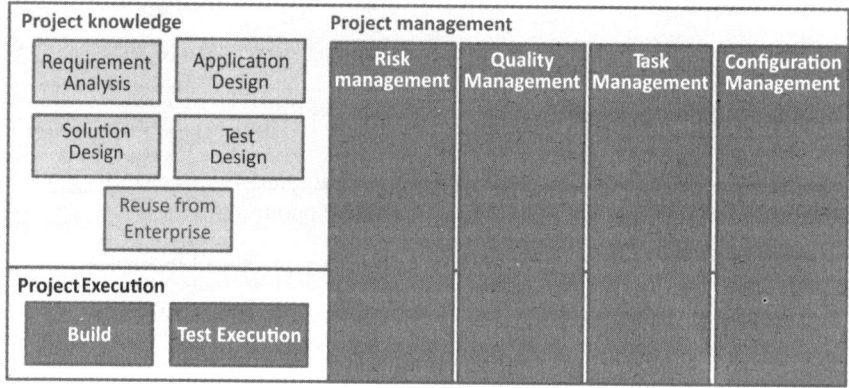

Figure 7.2 | End-to-end project delivery activities

PKM covers the project knowledge related activities completely, as explained earlier. Table 7.2 explains how KDD copes with end-to-end project delivery. Softer aspects, such as training and competency, are excluded as they are not the focus area of KDD.

Table 7.2 | End-to-end project delivery activities

Aspects	Remarks
Requirement analysis	KDD prescribes how exactly the requirement should be analysed and managed. The differentiator here is the concept of treating output of the requirement analysis phase as complete project knowledge from the requirement perspective. At this level project knowledge includes not only the list of requirements, but also the list of 'in-scope' non-functional attributes, product, applications and processes. The mechanism of transforming requirements into solution design, explained earlier, enables smooth transitioning to the solution design phase. This is a scientific approach not seen in other methodologies.
Solution design	KDD prescribes how exactly solution is designed to the lowest level, primarily via inventories and relationships, replacing the need to create project documents. As the solution evolves naturally and scientifically from requirements, there is less probability of any oversight.

Contd.

Aspects	Remarks
Application design	Knowledge about application design is currently limited to the development team of the project. KDD takes a pragmatic approach for application design, where technical specifications are produced. From technical project knowledge perspective, KDD believes that having all the detailed technical information in PKM may not be required. All that is required is the confidence provided by the development team that application design caters to the entire requirement, solution design and test design related knowledge available in PKM. KDD takes a balanced approach. Flooding PKM with too much of technical knowledge might impact its readability and hence its use by the entire project team. The reason is technical information can only be understood and reviewed by the development team. Other teams such as business analyst, test analyst and project manager will not understand the technical information to be able to comment on its quality. Also, leaving the entire technical information out of PKM will limit its effectiveness as in that case it will not have any scientific way of proving that the development team has considered all the requirements. The balanced approach of KDD is that – it visualises the entire application set as consisting of some data (such as xml, table, file object) and some logic (method, routine, procedure). These become two building blocks of the application design portion of the project knowledge and the inventory relationship mechanism can be utilised to capture the application design knowledge. Only relevant data or logic inventories that are a direct conversion of the solution design inventories are added. This helps in maintaining traceability. Common subroutine and infrastructure related data or logic inventories are not added as it will make the application design inventory unnecessarily bulky. This enables KDD to ensure that every single inventory of other knowledge-intensive phases such as solution design can be traced to one or more inventories of application design. This provides a scientific way of proving that the knowledge contained in the different knowledge-intensive phases is implemented via application design.
Test design	KDD prescribes how exactly test cases are designed to the lowest level. It enables test cases to be traced scientifically to the inventories of requirement analysis, solution design and application design building blocks. Any change to any of the other phase knowledge can be easily analysed for its impact on test cases via the traceability mechanism. The traceability mechanism reduces the chance of gap in test coverage. Test cases in KDD are created for the entire project, from unit test to UAT, in one format, minimising duplication and therefore named as Project Test Case.
Reuse from Enterprise	PKM has two compartments of knowledge: one for the project and the other for the enterprise. Both are in the same format, thereby increasing the reusability between them. Information in the enterprise knowledge can be added in two ways. One is standalone, for example, adding the list of applications of the enterprise. The other way is from the outputs of project delivery. At the end of a project, the relevant portions of project knowledge are moved to the enterprise knowledge area of PKM.

Contd.

Aspects	Remarks
	Reuse from enterprise for the project delivery becomes simple. Before any inventory in the project knowledge is added, relevant inventories from the enterprise knowledge area are made known, to exploit the reuse opportunity. The enterprise knowledge can be reused either directly or with customisation. This mechanism of recharging enterprise knowledge continuously enables continuous improvement in project delivery quality. This is because with every project completed, the enterprise knowledge portion is enriched, which increases its capability for reuse for the next project creating a continuous improvement environment.
Build	Application design inventories can be tracked for the completeness or progress of the build phase. If the build work can be split based on any criteria, such as functionality, it can be completed in increments, making it easier to manage build.
Test execution	Project Test Cases can be tracked for the completeness or progress of test execution phase. Defect management will be made simpler as the defects raised can be linked to a test case as well as the related inventories of requirement, solution design and test design.
Risk management	Risk items can be linked to project knowledge and therefore risk is easier to manage. It should be noted that not all risks can be linked to project knowledge.
Quality management	Via 324 negative relationships and 3 manual data points of quality assurance, KDD is prescriptive about quality management of the project knowledge. Digitisation of the project knowledge has helped digitising its quality assurance as well. KDD takes a scientific approach on quality management, by giving importance to quality assurance (review management) in the project knowledge and quality control (defect management) in execution of the project knowledge to build the software.
Task management	KDD has a good influence on the following aspects of task management: Estimation: As it has a catalogue of project knowledge, estimation becomes easy. Planning and tracking: KDD has 56 generic steps of project delivery that can be customised and tracked as a standard and reliable plan. Tasks are of three types: draft, review and rework. Efforts measured against them help in calculating review, rework and phase containment effectiveness.
Configuration management	It consists of: Audit control: KDD enables auditability for crucial knowledge constituents. Change Management: Traceability makes change easier to manage. Release management: At requirement level, release management is facilitated. Requirements can be split to facilitate multiple releases if required. This includes version control of project knowledge for release. Code versioning is not with PKM.

Let us define an Extended Project Knowledge Model (EPKM) which makes it convenient to manage end-to-end project delivery. The objective will be to facilitate as much execution and management related activities as possible. Some of the examples may be:

Extending Project Knowledge Model to Cover End-to-End Project Delivery 147

- Test defect and risk can be added to the model as new building blocks.
- Execution and management related activities are added to the existing list of activities.
- Standard release management, including version control (not of code, but of the project knowledge), audit features, collaboration features and workflow features may be added to PKM.

It should be kept in mind that EPKM and KDD are not exactly the same. Whereas EPKM drives most of KDD, as KDD is a methodology, KDD would also use other implements such as code versioning tool to cover end to end project delivery. The EPKM would assist executing KDD activities that are explained via quality gates in the next section.

3. Ability to Visualise the Project Activities from Project Delivery and Task Accomplishment Perspective: From the project delivery perspective, any activity in a project can be mapped to one of three categories: Management, Execution and Knowledge. Sample activities under these categories are:
  a. Management activity: Tracking the progress of the team against a set target.
  b. Execution activity: Build a piece of software by the development team.
  c. Knowledge activity: Prepare a Business Requirement Specification document.

This division of work helps to gain clarity of thought by which we can visualise how a project can be delivered more effectively.

Let's understand these activities from value addition perspective. Knowledge and execution related activities result in specific outputs in a project. Knowledge related activities produce specifications of requirement, solution (business and technical) design and test cases. Execution related activities produce the software itself. Both activities have their own importance. If the knowledge related activities are not done with quality, they may produce wrong specifications for the software. In that case, it does not matter how good the execution related activities are: they will produce lower quality software because of the wrong specifications.

Execution related activities have their own importance. If the quality of the execution related activities is not good, the software quality will suffer, no matter how good the specifications are. Management activities do not produce any output directly contributing to software or its specification, however they are key to managing the activities of knowledge and execution.

In Waterfall methodology, the management drives the project, but it generally does not have the in-depth understanding of the knowledge and execution related activities. In Agile methodology, the system analysts, who are implementing execution related work, drive the project, with assistance from business analysts, who are implementing knowledge related activities and management. In the Agile methodology, however, business analysts do not get enough time for exhaustive specifications of requirements. They work with the system analyst in an ad hoc and unstructured manner (with significant pressure of time to deliver) to make them understand what the requirements are.

It seems there are inherent issues with both the methodologies of project delivery. Going by the three activities and their value addition in the project delivery environment, the KDD methodology adopts a more scientific approach. Here the project delivery is driven by people managing the knowledge related work and assisted by people managing execution related and management related activities. KDD ensures that the people who know about the project most (i.e., have specified the project requirements) drive the project.

There are three types of activities to accomplish a task of the project delivery: draft completion, review and rework, as explained in chapter 4.

These two perspectives (project delivery and task accomplishment), when combined together, provide a mechanism to manage end-to-end project delivery. Figure 7.3 extends project knowledge activities (24 generic activities) from Figure 4.12 to cover the execution and management related activities.

For a specific phase, a mandatory activity is one that must be executed, e.g., build review in build phase. An optional activity is one that may or may not be executed in that phase, e.g., if no test design related defect is identified in the build phase, the activity test design rework may not be executed and therefore is tagged as optional activity for that phase. The execution related activities are generic and can be repeated in the project if delivered in chunks. The project management activities are listed separately to indicate that the majority of the activities are performed across phases.

The total number of generic activities to manage end-to-end project delivery now stands at 56 and consist of:
- A total of 24 activities of project knowledge management
- A total of 32 activities of execution and management related activities as listed in the Figure 7.3

Transparency of project delivery increases by introducing specific activities of review and rework type of the previous phase (e.g., test design

Extending Project Knowledge Model to Cover End-to-End Project Delivery 149

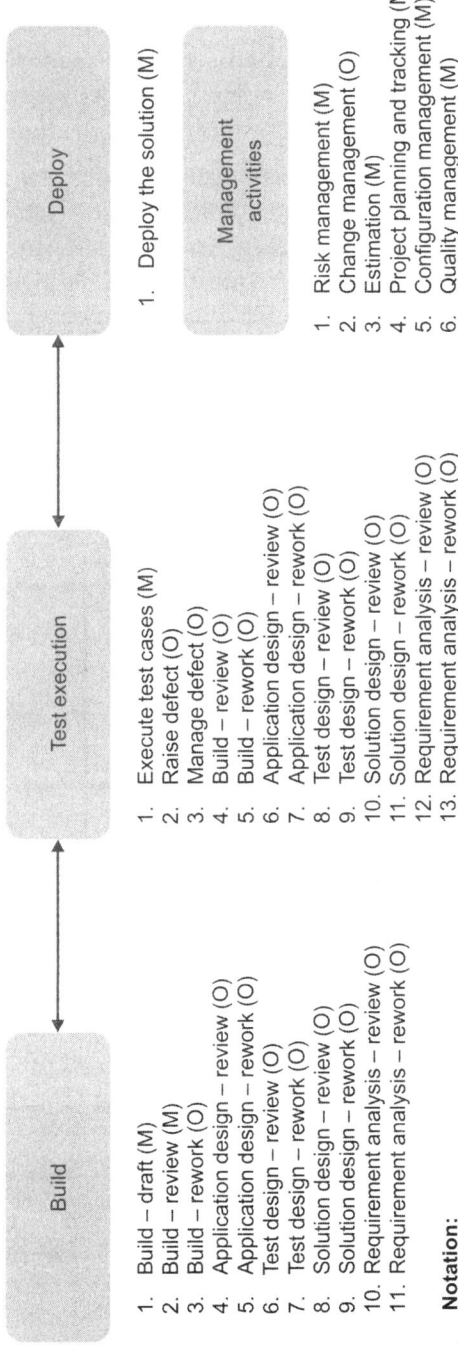

Figure 7.3 | Execution and management related activities

review in build phase). This helps in quantification of the review and rework activities which, in turn, provide a good indicator of the project progress and effectiveness of the project team. It now becomes easy to provide a more realistic, revised end-to-end estimate during the project delivery phases by extrapolating the current experience of review and rework efforts.

4. A Combination of Sequential, Parallel and Iterative Activities for Maximum Effectiveness: Different phases of project delivery are related to one another in terms of running them in sequence or in parallel. In Waterfall methodology, the relationship is primarily sequential. In Agile methodology the relationship is primarily parallel and delivered in chunks via iteration, where all the phases from requirement to test are repeated for each iteration.

KDD has taken a knowledge-based approach and visualises the relationship between different phases of the project as indicated in Figure 7.4. This is different from a typical Waterfall or Agile method. It is an optimal mix of parallel and sequential phases.

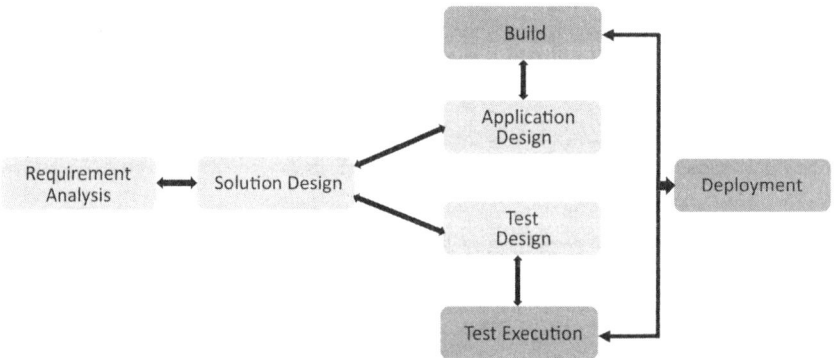

Figure 7.4 | Relationship between project delivery phases in KDD

Different phases and the combinations of phases are related to one another via sequential and parallel relationship as given in Table 7.3.

Table 7.3 | Relationship between different phases of project delivery

Phases / Combination of phases	Relationship	Remarks
Requirement analysis and solution design	Sequential	Solution design cannot start before a significant proportion of requirements have been detailed, to an extent that is considered fit-for-purpose.

Contd.

Phases / Combination of phases	Relationship	Remarks
Solution design and application design	Sequential	Application design cannot start before a significant proportion of solution design has been detailed, to an extent that is considered fit-for-purpose.
Solution design and test design	Sequential	Test design cannot start before a significant proportion of solution design has been detailed, to an extent that is considered fit-for-purpose.
Application design and test design	Parallel in the beginning	Solution design captures all the details that are ever needed by the build and the test teams. This ensures the application design by the build team and test design by the test team can be started in parallel. Starting test design need not wait for application design to complete.
Application design and test design	Sequential at the end	Test design is completed first; inventories of application design can then be traced to the test cases and any resulting gap can be addressed. This has a potential to reduce the number of defects during test execution as all the test cases have already been traced by the application design inventories. The reason for test design to complete first is that whereas a system analyst can understand test cases and relate them easily to the application design inventory, it will be difficult for a test analyst to understand application design inventory to be able to trace it to the test cases.
Build and application design	Sequential	Build should not start unless the application design is stabilised, indicating its sequential nature.
Test and test design	Sequential	Test cases can be executed only when the related test case is detailed completely.
Build and test	Sequential	Test cases cannot be executed before the relevant build is complete.
Solution design-test design and Solution design-application design	Parallel	Once solution design is complete, application design and test design can start in parallel.

Let's discuss iteration in KDD. The digital structure of KDD makes it possible to do iterations at three levels.

- Once the requirement analysis phase is complete, we may decide to split the total work in chunks, primarily based on functionality, and deliver it chunk-wise in iterations. Each iteration would need performing the activities of solution design to test execution for the selected chunks in the iteration. PKM will help in seamless integration of later chunks with the chunks already implemented.
- Often we may decide to complete the requirement analysis and solution design phase and then split the total work in chunks to be delivered in iterations. In this case, the steps right from application design up to test execution would be repeated for each iteration for the related chunk.
- We can even complete application design and test design, in addition to requirement analysis and solution design, before we go for iteration. In this case, iteration will consist of build and test execution.

The iterations go into various releases of the same project as in Waterfall and Agile projects. The decision about when to iterate depends on the nature and size of the project, to be decided by the project SMEs. It is interesting to note here that the version control of the project knowledge in PKM will greatly assist in managing iterations and releases.

The unique relationship described between different phases is an optimal balance between what is professed in the Waterfall and Agile methodologies.

5. Appreciation that Doing Things First-Time-Correct Is Not Realistic: Had project delivery team done the work correctly the first time itself, it would have saved almost half of the project effort (20% on reviews and 30% on test: my guess). Project delivery methodologies find it difficult to handle the reality that work cannot be done right the first time. Waterfall methodology assumes that requirements can be completely specified in the requirement analysis phase. Then onwards if there is a change, it needs to be handled by the change management process. Agile methodology does not believe in freezing the requirements and keeps them maturing in build and test, resulting in significant rework many times.

KDD aims to handle the fact that things cannot be done first-time-correct in a different way. Let's understand this from requirement management perspective, but the approach is similar in other areas as well. KDD aims to complete at least 80% of the requirements for the project in the requirement analysis phase. In the solution design phase, it aims to grow the requirements by 10%, taking the total requirements to 90% of the project requirement. From the remaining 10%, 5% is added in the application design and test design phases and the last 5% is added in the build and test phases of the project. Figure 7.5 illustrates this.

Extending Project Knowledge Model to Cover End-to-End Project Delivery   153

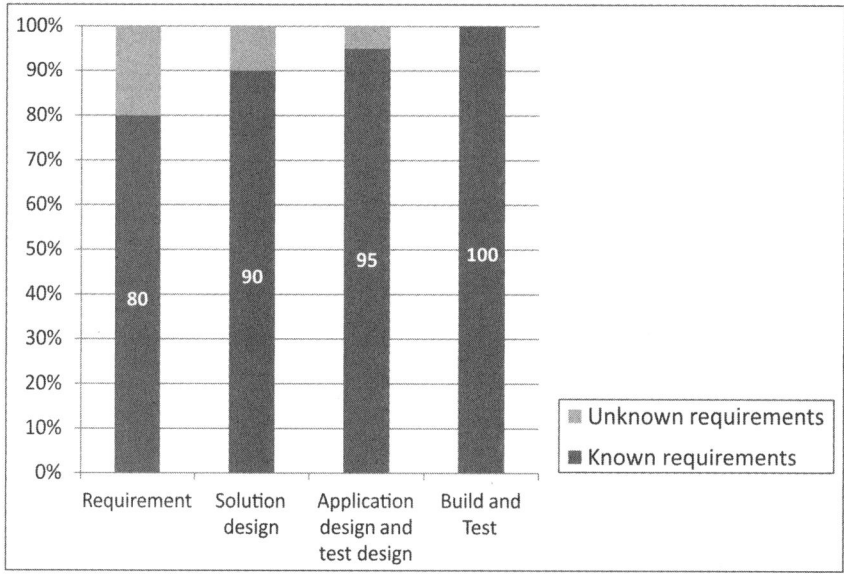

Figure 7.5 | Fault tolerant evolution of knowledge

KDD has an in-built mechanism in the form of PKM to implement these objectives. All the four knowledge-intensive phases are related to one another as explained earlier. The completion of a phase and its traceability with the previous phase gives much more confidence on the completeness of the previous phase. It aims for 90% completeness of the previous phase knowledge. The rate of change in the previous phase decreases significantly post that, covering the remaining 10% of the phase knowledge in all the other, subsequent phases. The progress can be quantifiably measured as the knowledge is in the form of inventories and relationships. This quantification helps in identifying the skill gap if the project progress significantly differs from the KDD objectives of phase knowledge completeness.

7.4 | End-to-End Project Delivery Using Quality Gate

KDD visualises end-to-end project delivery via ten quality gates and eight phases as per Figure 7.6. It is interesting to note that in the Figure 7.4, there are seven phases in KDD whereas here there are eight. 'Deployment' phase in the Figure 7.4 is split into two phases 'Project Implementation' and 'Project Closure' in Figure 7.6. A separate treatment to project closure activities seem

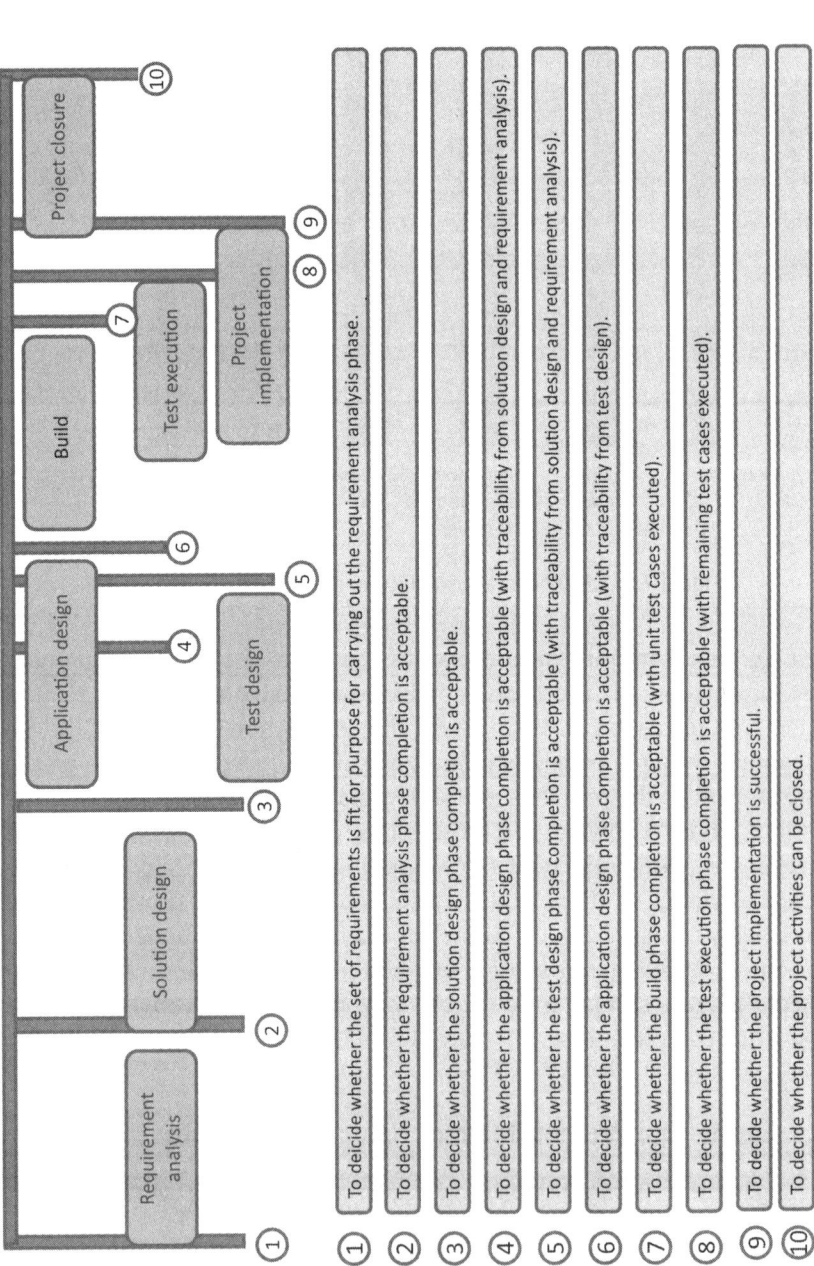

Figure 7.6 | KDD project delivery governance: quality gate approach

Extending Project Knowledge Model to Cover End-to-End Project Delivery

natural where we are defining KDD from quality gate perspective. This is a typical visualisation and a project working with KDD may choose to customise it, based on the need.

It is relevant to mention here that there are no prerequisites to be fulfilled before starting a project following KDD. If there is enterprise knowledge available in the KDD format, it can be directly reused in the project delivery. If there is no enterprise knowledge to reuse (such as the first project to start following KDD), the necessary inventories of the relevant building block are created as a part of the project and later moved to the enterprise knowledge for reuse by subsequent projects.

Now let us understand the details of the KDD quality gates.

Gate 1 – To Decide Whether the Set of Requirements Is Fit-for-Purpose for Carrying Out the Requirement Analysis Phase

A. *Start and end point for the gate:* It starts when the customer supplies the requirement and ends when the project team considers it fit-for-purpose to proceed to the requirement analysis phase.
B. *Input:* Customer supplied requirements: draft.
C. *Activities to reach the gate from the previous gate:*
Analyse requirements with a view to start the requirement analysis phase. This phase is to arrest any obvious major gap in requirements. It has sense check activities and does not need elaborate requirement analysis that is the aim of the 'requirement analysis' phase. KDD in general accepts customer supplied requirements AS IS, to do proper requirement analysis in the 'requirement analysis' phase. Performed by: project business analyst.
D. *Activity validations:* If one business analyst does it, to be validated by another business analyst (from another project if needed).
E. *Outputs:* Customer supplied requirement – sense checked.
F. *Gate exit criteria:* Requirements found to be fit-for-purpose for executing requirement analysis phase of the project.

Gate 2 – To Decide Whether the Requirement Analysis Phase Completion Is Acceptable

A. *Start and end point for the gate:* It starts with the analysing and reviewing requirements and ends when information entry into the five building blocks, including requirements of the requirement analysis phase, is treated as complete by the project business analyst.

B. *Input:* Customer supplied requirements are sense-checked by project business analyst.
C. *Activities to reach the gate from the previous gate:*
   1. Add requirements to PKM.
   2. Perform project scoping by adding relevant inventories via the following set of three evolving layers:
      a. Project knowledge scoping: Select building blocks and their relationships relevant to the project from the 189 data points representing the complete project knowledge. This customises PKM to a specific project.
      b. Project knowledge quality scoping: Select negative relationships (out of 324 nodes) and manual review (out of 3) data points relevant to the project. This helps in customising the quality assurance aspects of PKM to suit the project needs.
      c. Project scoping: Scope non-functional attributes, process, application and product inventories. This is where a definitive list (inventories) of these building blocks is arrived at for the project. Inventories may either be new or reused from the enterprise knowledge base of PKM.
   3. Create relationships amongst these inventories including requirement inventories. An example can be Requirement_01 is linked to Process_04. Intra building block inventories are also linked, such as Requirement_01 is linked to Requirement_02 in parent-child relationship.
   4. Create the solution design inventories that can be directly derived from requirement inventories. In this exercise, each of the requirements is analysed and equivalent inventories of solution design are identified. For example, one requirement may give rise to one screen, one business rule and five business data. These solution design inventories are identified at a basic level of details so that they can be completely specified in the solution design phase. This is called 'requirement transformation into solution design'. This helps in building the core solution design knowledge in the requirement analysis phase which gets completed in the solution design phase, encouraging natural evolution of project knowledge. This also acts as a powerful technique for requirement review.

5. Tag all the inventories and relationships moving to the next gate as a part of version control. The remaining inventories and relationships may move later, or pushed to the next release.
D. *Activity validations:*
   1. Review requirements.
   2. Review negative relationship potential defect nodes.
   3. Review existing inventories, traceability linkages and scoping data manually.
E. *Outputs:* PKM consisting of:
   1. Analysed and agreed requirements, subject to outstanding reviews.
   2. Non-functional attribute list, process list, application list and product list and their traceability.
   3. Log of review including risks, if relevant.
F. *Gate exit criteria:*
   1. Not more than 15% outstanding requirements review.
   2. A total of 90% of the inventories of the four building blocks of requirement analysis phase must be linked to one or more requirements.
   3. A total of 90% of the inventories of the four building blocks of requirement analysis phase must be linked to one or more processes.
   4. All the negative relationship reviews analysed and not more than 15% actionable review comments remain open.
   5. Not more than 15% outstanding manual review comments.
   6. Efforts are captured for all the activities in the phase tagged as draft/review/rework (updating information post review).

Gate 3 – To Decide Whether the Solution Design Phase Completion Is Acceptable

A. *Start and end point for the gate:* It starts with expanding on the core solution design inventory and ends when fit-for-purpose information related to solution design building blocks is added into PKM.
B. *Input:* PKM consisting of the output of the requirement analysis phase.
C. *Activities to reach the gate from the previous gate:*
   1. Expand on the inventories of the ten building blocks of solution design that exist in an incomplete status, which were a by-product of the requirement analysis phase.
   2. Add inventories of the solution design building blocks, where relevant, during solution design analysis.

3. Link these inventories together and with inventories of requirement analysis phase (both inter and intra-relationship).
4. Elaborate the non-functional attributes captured during the requirement analysis phase.
5. Tag all the inventories and relationships moving to the next gate as a part of version control. The remaining inventories and relationships may move later or pushed to the next release.

D. *Activity validations:*
1. Review Functional Specification Document (FSD) that can be extracted from PKM.
2. Review negative relationship potential defect nodes.
3. Review traceability and inventory specifications.

E. *Outputs:*
PKM: knowledge added, which is equivalent to the knowledge contained in the FSD.

F. *Gate exit criteria:*
1. Not more than 15% outstanding review comments on FSD.
2. A total of 90% of the inventories of the solution design building blocks must be linked to one or more requirements.
3. A total of 90% of the inventories of the 14 (9 of solution design and 5 of requirement analysis) building blocks must be linked to one or more process steps. The tenth building block of solution design is the process step itself.
4. All the negative relationship reviews analysed and not more than 15% actionable review comments are open.
5. Not more than 15% outstanding traceability and inventory specification review defects.
6. Efforts are captured for all the activities tagged as draft/review/rework. Review and rework may be for the current phase or for the previous phase knowledge. This is to ensure review and rework are quantified appropriately.

Gate 4 – To Decide Whether the Application Design Phase Completion Is Acceptable: Part 1

A. *Start and end point for the gate:* It starts with adding data or logic inventories and ends when application design phase is treated as

complete (with traceability with solution design and requirement analysis inventories).
B. *Input:* PKM consisting of the output of the solution design phase.
C. *Activities to reach the gate from the previous gate:*
   1. Add inventories of data/logic.
   2. Link these inventories together, and with inventories of solution design and requirement analysis phases (both inter and intra-relationship).
   3. Tag all the inventories and relationships moving to the next gate as a part of version control. The remaining inventories and relationships may move later or pushed to the next release.
D. *Activity validations:*
   1. Review High level Design (HLD) document that is extracted from the model.
   2. Review negative relationship potential defect nodes.
   3. Review traceability and inventory specifications.
E. *Outputs:*
   PKM: knowledge added, which is equivalent to the knowledge contained in HLD.
F. *Gate exit criteria:*
   1. Not more than 15% outstanding review comments on HLD.
   2. A total of 90% of the inventories of data/logic must be linked to one or more of the solution design Inventory.
   3. A total of 90% of the inventories of data/logic must be linked to one or more requirements.
   4. All the negative relationship reviews analysed and not more than 15% actionable review comments are open.
   5. Not more than 15% outstanding traceability and inventory specification reviews.
   6. Efforts are captured for all the activities tagged as draft/review/rework. Review and rework may be for the current phase or for the previous phase knowledge. This is to ensure review and rework are quantified appropriately.

Gate 5 – To Decide Whether the Test Design Phase Completion Is Acceptable

A. *Start and end point for the gate:* It starts with creating test cases and ends when the test design phase is treated as complete by the test analyst.
B. *Input:* PKM consisting of the output of the solution design phase.

C. *Activities to reach the gate from the previous gate:*
   1. Add inventories of Project Test Cases.
   2. Link these inventories together and with inventories of solution design phase and with requirement analysis phase (both inter and intra-relationship).
   3. Tag Project Test Cases as unit test, integration test, functional test, non-functional test and UAT.
   4. Prepare test data and link it to test cases.
   5. Prepare test schedule and link test cases.
   6. Tag all the inventories and relationships moving to the next gate as a part of version control. The remaining inventories and relationships may move later or pushed to the next release.
D. *Activity validations:*
   1. Review negative relationship potential defect nodes.
   2. Review traceability and Project Test Case specifications.
E. *Outputs:*
   PKM: knowledge added which is equivalent to the knowledge contained in the Project Test Cases.
F. *Gate exit criteria:*
   1. A total of 90% of the Project Test Cases must be linked to one or more of the solution design Inventory.
   2. A total of 90% of the inventories of Project Test Cases must be linked to one or more requirement analysis inventories.
   3. All the negative relationship reviews analysed and not more than 15% actionable review are open.
   4. Not more than 15% outstanding traceability and inventory specification reviews.
   5. Efforts are captured for all the activities tagged as draft/review/rework (updating information because of review). Review and rework may be for the current phase or for the previous phase project knowledge. This is to ensure review and rework are quantified appropriately.

Gate 6 – To Decide Whether the Application Design Phase Completion Is Acceptable: Part 2

A. *Start and end point for the gate:* It starts with the completion of the test design phase and ends when the application design phase is treated as complete (with traceability to Project Test Cases).

B. *Input:* PKM consisting of the output of the solution design and test design phase and application design phase without traceability to Project Test Cases.
C. *Activities to reach the gate from the previous gate:* Link data/logic with inventories of the Project Test Cases. This ensures the application team has statically tested all the test cases even before a single test case is executed. This reduces rework in the project to a significant extent. Tag all the inventories and relationships moving to the next gate as a part of version control. The remaining inventories and relationships may move later or pushed to the next release.
D. Activity validations:
  1. Review negative relationship potential defect nodes.
  2. Review data/logic linkage with Project Test Case.
E. *Outputs:*
  PKM: knowledge added which is equivalent to the knowledge contained in HLD enhanced with traceability to the Project Test Case.
F. *Gate exit criteria:*
  1. A total of 90% of the inventories of data/logic must be linked to one or more Project Test Cases.
  2. All the negative relationship review analysed and not more than 15% actionable review comments are open.
  3. Not more than 15% outstanding traceability reviews.
  4. Efforts are captured for all the activities tagged as draft/review/rework. Review and rework may be for the current phase or for the previous phase project knowledge. This is to ensure review and rework are quantified appropriately.

Gate 7 – To Decide Whether the Build Phase Completion Is Acceptable

A. *Start and end point for the gate:* It starts with coding and ends when build phase is treated as complete.
B. *Input:* PKM consisting of the entire project knowledge.
C. *Activities to reach the gate from the previous gate:*
  1. Code against data/logic.
  2. Unit Test data/logic.
  If the entire build can be logically split into chunks, the above activities can be repeated for each of the chunk to complete the build.
D. *Activity validations:*
  1. Code Review.
  2. Defect management and updating PKM, where relevant.

E. *Outputs:*
   1. PKM consisting of the entire project knowledge updated with the changes in the build phase.
   2. Draft Software.
F. *Gate exit criteria:*
   1. Code Review passed.
   2. A total of 90% of the defects raised are resolved.
   3. Efforts are captured for all the activities tagged as normal/review/rework. Review and rework may be for the current phase or for the previous phase knowledge. This is to ensure review and rework are quantified appropriately.

Gate 8 – To decide whether the test execution phase completion is acceptable
A. *Start and end point for the gate:* It starts with the completion of the build phase and ends when test execution (including UAT) phase is treated as complete.
   In case where build can be split in multiple chunks, test execution can start as soon as the build of the first chunk is complete.
B. *Input:* PKM consisting of the entire project knowledge updated until the build phase.
C. *Activities to reach the gate from the previous gate:*
   1. Execute Test Cases.
   2. Defect management and updating the PKM, where relevant.
   If the entire build can be logically split into chunks, these activities can be repeated for each of the chunk to complete the test execution.
D. *Activity validations:* Raise Defect.
E. *Outputs:*
   1. Final Software.
   2. Test completion report.
F. *Gate exit criteria:* There is no critical outstanding defect. Efforts are captured for all the activities tagged as normal/review/ rework. Review and rework may be for the current phase or for the previous phase knowledge. This is to ensure review and rework are quantified appropriately.

Gate 9 – To Decide Whether the Project Implementation Is Successful
A. *Start and end point for the gate:* It starts with the completion of the test execution phase and ends when the software is released to production.
   In case where build can be split in multiple chunks, implementation can be gradual, and the first chunk can be in implementation as soon as it is built and test execution of the chunk is complete.

B. *Input:* PKM consisting of the entire project knowledge updated until the project has completed the test execution phase.
C. *Activities to reach the gate from the previous gate:*
   1. Release of the software to production.
   2. Tag the inventories and relationships that represent the software deployed.
D. *Activity validations:* Operational tests to have a quick sense-check that the software works.
E. *Outputs:* Final software running in production.
F. *Gate exit criteria:* Operational test is successful and there is no major defect outstanding or a decision is taken to move to production with the existing defects.

Gate 10 – To Decide Whether the Project Activities Can Be Closed
A. *Start and end point for the gate:* It starts with the completion of the project implementation phase and ends when all the project activities are closed. For chunked delivery it may start before the implementation of the last chunk.
B. *Input:* PKM consisting of the entire project knowledge updated until the project is implemented.
C. *Activities to reach the gate from the previous gate:*
   1. Move relevant project knowledge into the enterprise knowledge area of PKM. This ensures the knowledge in the digitised format keeps growing with every project.
   2. The updated PKM is handed over to the service management team.
   3. All the agreed inventories and relationships are deployed in the software.
   4. Create project completion report that includes sections on lessons learnt and suggestions for future.
D. *Activity validations:* Review the latest addition to the enterprise knowledge.
E. *Outputs:* Enriched enterprise knowledge in PKM.
F. *Gate exit criteria:*
   1. Service management team accepts the handover from the project team.
   2. Enterprise knowledge is updated.

The gated approach is taken to prove that the KDD has considered end-to-end project delivery and is not just restricting itself to project knowledge management. This provides a broad framework against which a project can be delivered under KDD. This is not similar to the quality gates of the Waterfall methodology that follow a sequential path. Quality gates in KDD are open both sides and traversing between the gates in case of major updates due to review or change in requirements is made easier, faster and transparent via PKM. The ability to adapt itself to any change is a major differentiator of KDD when compared to the other methodologies.

The sign-off mechanism of document production regime is replaced with the gating mechanism in KDD. KDD has the latest combined view of the project knowledge at any point of time and the gating mechanism ensures its evolution during different phases of project delivery.

If there is a need and the project can be split into smaller functionalities, usually called chunks, chunks-wise delivery may be opted for. Depending on the comfort of the project team, the project can go for chunks delivery mode either post requirement analysis or post solution design or post application design, as discussed in the previous section.

Figure 7.6 assumes no iteration up to application design. In build and test execution, some sort of parallelism or iteration is assumed, which is realistic, although it will vary based on the nature and size of the project.

7.5 Tracking Project Delivery Quality via Key Performance Indicators (KPI)

For the first time in the history of project delivery, PKM has digitised the project knowledge. Project knowledge fulfils the requirements of knowledge related activities of the project and helps in execution related activities of the project as well. It is not difficult for the Project Knowledge Model to accommodate execution related activities and therefore cover the end-to-end of project delivery. It then allows PKM to extract various key performance indicators (KPI) to track the quality of project delivery in real-time which eases the load project management to a significant extent.

Table 7.4 lists the important KPIs of project delivery, an algorithm to derive it and how PKM helps in deriving it.

Table 7.4 | KPIs to monitor project delivery quality

Sl. No.	KPI	Derivation	Assisted by PKM
1	Tracking against the estimate	The % work done against the estimate. To be calculated at any point of time of the project.	In-scope inventories help in estimating as this is objective. During project delivery, efforts are captured against the activities. This helps in calculating the percentage work done against the estimate.

Contd.

Sl. No.	KPI	Derivation	Assisted by PKM
2	Defect density	Number of defects (review as well as testing defects) across all the phases per requirement. To be calculated at the end of the project delivery.	Review log is available in PKM and testing defect log is available in the Extended Project Knowledge Model (EPKM).
3	Review effectiveness	Static review log / (Static review log + Test defect log). To be calculated at the end of the project delivery.	Information to calculate review effectiveness is available in the EPKM.
4	Cost of quality	Test (design + execution) effort + Review effort + Rework effort / Total effort. To be calculated at the end of the project delivery.	Information to calculate cost of quality is available in the EPKM.
5	Test coverage against requirement	Requirements traced to test cases / Total number of requirements. To be calculated at the end of test design phase.	Information to calculate test coverage against requirement is available in PKM.
6	Test coverage against solution design	Solution design inventory traced to test cases / total number of solution design inventory. To be calculated at the end of the test design phase	Information to calculate test coverage against solution design is available in PKM.
7	Test coverage against application design	Application design inventory traced to test cases / total number of application design inventory. To be calculated at the end of test design phase.	Information to calculate test coverage against application design is available in PKM.
8	Requirement phase containment effectiveness	Total no. of defects related to requirement in the requirement phase / Total number of requirement defects in the requirement phase + subsequent phases. Can be calculated at the end of each phase post requirement phase.	Information to calculate requirement phase containment effectiveness is available in the EPKM.
9	Solution design phase containment effectiveness	Total no. of defects related to solution in the solution design phase / Total number of solution defects in the solution design phase + subsequent phases. Can be calculated at the end of each phase post solution design phase.	Information to calculate solution design phase containment effectiveness is available in the EPKM.

Contd.

Sl. No.	KPI	Derivation	Assisted by PKM
10	Application design phase containment effectiveness	Total no. of defects related to application in the application design phase / Total number of application defects in the application design phase + subsequent phases. Can be calculated at the end of each phase post application design phase.	Information to calculate application design phase containment effectiveness is available in the EPKM.
11	Test design effectiveness	Total number of defects in Unit Test + System test + System integration test / (Total number of defects in Unit Test + System test + System integration test) + Total number of defects in UAT. To be calculated at the end of UAT.	Information to calculate test design effectiveness is available in the EPKM assuming Business uses it for UAT.
12	Total defect containment effectiveness	Total number of defect and review log before release / Total number of defect and review log before release + Total number of defect post release. To be calculated post release at an agreed point in time during service delivery.	Information to calculate total defect containment effectiveness is available in the EPKM if it is continued to be used in the service management environment.
13	Rework percentage	Rework effort / Rework effort + Review effort + Draft effort. To be calculated at the end of each phase.	Information to calculate rework percentage is available in the EPKM. Draft activity is only relevant for the phase where it naturally belongs to. In the next phase, it is counted as part of rework activity. For example, updating requirement in the solution design phase will count towards rework in the requirement phase.
14	Review percentage	Review effort / Rework effort + Review effort + Draft effort. To be calculated at the end of each phase.	Information to calculate review percentage is available in the PKM.
15	Reuse percentage	Project knowledge inventories reused from the enterprise knowledge / Total number of project knowledge inventories.	Information to calculate reuse percentage is available in PKM.

7.6 | Fitment for Different Types of Domains and Projects

7.6.1 | Domain Relevance

KDD is based on knowledge and knowledge in its true form should be independent of the industry (domain). At the same time, it should be customisable for a particular industry. The building blocks of project knowledge are relevant for most of the industries. And they are customisable as well. Let us understand this with an example. Product is one of the building blocks in PKM. This would mean insurance products such as term insurance in the insurance industry. In telecom industry, it will represent various monthly or yearly plans that a typical telecom company provides.

In my view, KDD can be applied to all the domains except for research oriented domains such as chip design.

7.6.2 | Project Type Relevance

KDD is intended to be used for development, maintenance, enhancement and support projects. KDD is relevant for platform rationalisation, portal, finance, workflow related, CRM related projects. It may not be relevant for infrastructure projects.

KDD can work for software product manufacturing and customisation where knowledge of the product is first digitised and then maintained during the product lifecycle.

7.7 | KDD differentiators

1. KDD supplements Agile with project knowledge management and speeds up Waterfall by providing a better (structured) way of managing project knowledge as an alternative to document production regime.
2. Managing project knowledge via digitisation has enabled real-time updates to KDD, which is difficult to achieve via project documents.
3. PKM assists in extending digitisation to build, test execution and project management.
4. In the test design, KDD proposes a new concept which, in a way, has combined the propositions of TDD (Test Driven Development) and BDD (Behaviour Driven Development). TDD is closer to the

development team and BDD is closer to the test team. KDD proposes the creation of Project Test Cases at one go (from unit test cases to UAT cases) and then distribute them to different stakeholders (such as build, test and user teams) for execution and defect management. This may appear to take more effort in test design activities than the traditional methodologies, but if we combine the test design effort of the build, test and user acceptance team, we realise test design is not more in KDD. Also, due to the additional quality and coverage via PKM, we actually reduce the test execution effort as there are fewer defects (one of the reasons being the test cases statically tested by the development team before a single test case is executed).
5. KDD empowers the project team, particularly the build team, and eliminates waste of effort caused mainly due to communication gaps.
6. Through negative relationship, KDD assists significantly in the review effort.
7. Reuse is facilitated mainly via test case creation. Test cases are created by mixing and matching the inventories of solution design.
8. Reuse and maintenance of the enterprise knowledge provides the ability for continuous improvement, as every subsequent project can reuse relevant knowledge from enterprise knowledge.

It is not difficult to visualise that PKM, which is core to KDD, brings in a fresh accelerator in project delivery which increases the quality, with reduced effort, by maximising reuse and minimising rework.

In summary, KDD is a new methodology and, as such, there will be many apprehensions to it. I have addressed some of the concerns about KDD in Appendix E.

CHAPTER 8

Extended KDD: Pre-Requirement and Post Delivery

In this chapter, we look at the product lifecycle rather than project lifecycle. Before a project starts via defined requirements, a business case must be established. Also, once the product is delivered, it is supported by the service management for support and maintenance until it is decommissioned. These two phases of the product delivery should also get the benefit from the concept of digital Project Knowledge Model. This chapter discusses the relevance of PKM in these two phases of the product delivery that can be covered by the Extended KDD.

8.1 | Business Case (Pre-Requirement)

Cost of delivering software must be significantly less than the benefit it can deliver within a specified period, as determined by the customer. This makes the business case for the delivery of a software. A software delivery project usually passes through the business case before the requirement analysis phase of the project can start. Monetary considerations are always the key, either directly or indirectly. Indirect monetary considerations are obvious in regulatory and technology upgrade projects. Non-compliance with regulatory requirements might incur a heavy penalty, and technology upgrades, if not done, can result in unpredictable interruptions of services.

There are usually two identifiable phases in the product delivery before the requirement analysis phase begins. They are:
1. Initiation phase where an idea is generated and assessed for feasibility and cost-benefit. It goes through the scrutiny of the senior management to ensure it is as per the goals of the company and fit to go to the next phase.

2. Concept phase, where *As Is* and *To Be* are detailed and, if needed, multiple solution options are arrived at. Out of them, one solution option is chosen, to be detailed further. There will always be a default option of not to do anything. For choosing a solution option, cost-benefit considerations are the key. Once a solution option is chosen, high level requirements are created, which become the input to the requirement analysis phase, which is the first phase of project delivery as detailed in the earlier chapters.

One of the biggest challenges in these early phases of product delivery is determining the size of the work. This is where the enterprise knowledge base of PKM comes to help. For each of these initial phases of initiation and concept, enterprise knowledge base can be used to size the work. The level of information available will be more in the concept phase than in the initiation phase. The total number of selected inventories of enterprise knowledge base, based on scoping the project, broadly determine the size of the work.

PKM can be used for specifying high level requirement and high level solutioning. There can be multiple throw-away PKMs, one for each solution option, to decide which one to go for, if at all. This may contain fit-for-purpose information to be able to estimate the size of the project.

8.2 | Service Management (Post Delivery)

Once the project is delivered, the software starts its life and keeps running for a period of time until it is decommissioned for various reasons. There is a need to keep it running, fix any production defects and accomplish any maintenance and enhancement needs of the software. The Service Management function of the organisation is responsible for this.

The biggest pain area in service management is lack of an effective knowledge management framework. In the handover process, the project team hands over the software product to the service management team. Along with the software, they should also hand over all the underlying knowledge that was used to create the software so that it helps the service management team to continue to support, maintain and enhance the software.

In the Waterfall methodology, the entire project documentation is handed over, which ideally should contain the complete project knowledge. However, in a majority of the cases, these documents are plagued with incompleteness, inconsistency, redundancies and are not kept updated with the latest software delivered, as in the later phases the team's priority is to deliver the software rather than updating the documents. Even if the documents are 80% correct, once the service management team loses confidence on the quality of the documents, they rarely use them for any practical purpose.

In Agile methodology the situation is even worse. The entire project knowledge is contained in a few documents that are produced at high level and lack any practical utility to the service management team. These documents can only give an overall picture of the project, but not any detailed view that is present in the Waterfall methodology. Most of the time, the service management team needs to understand the code to gain project knowledge, which is a slow and costly process.

This has prompted the service management team to create its own knowledge management framework, resulting in huge investment that, ideally, should not be required as this entire knowledge was available with the project team in the first place.

KDD has an answer to the challenge around project knowledge management. The output of the project delivery in KDD is the software as well as PKM that specifies the software completely from the requirement, solution, technology and test perspective. As it is digitised, it is more usable when compared to the project documents.

The service management team can use PKM to satisfy all their needs of understanding the details of the software, without going through the code. The project knowledge is integrated together by an exhaustive traceability mechanism greatly assisting impact analysis for any maintenance and enhancement work. This helps the service management team to keep the project knowledge updated in real-time, until the software is decommissioned.

A close interaction of the enterprise knowledge with the project knowledge creates an environment of continuous improvement in quality of delivery and service management teams.

To help the service management team further, PKM can be integrated with the ticket management system and snippets of knowledge that exist in the service management team. Snippets help resolving the known and standard issues.

Extended KDD (EKDD) is a variation of KDD that fulfils the needs of the initiation and service management teams in addition to the project delivery team.

CHAPTER 9

KDD Compliance with Standards of Project Delivery

Without going into too much complexity, KDD concentrates on core project delivery and brings simplicity into it. In this chapter, we will look into six standards and frameworks of different disciplines in software engineering and demonstrate that KDD is compliant with them as long as they come in direct area of influence of what KDD is trying to accomplish. The core proposition of KDD is based on PKM. Figure 9.1 names the six standards and frameworks of project delivery that will be detailed in this chapter with respect to the compliance of KDD with them.

Figure 9.1 | Standards of project delivery

9.1 | Quality Assurance Framework

As mentioned earlier, digitising the project knowledge has helped KDD implement a better quality implementation than the other methodologies of IT project delivery.

In this section we will see, through two known quality frameworks, how KDD has enabled quality in project delivery. The quality frameworks are Six Sigma and CMMI.

9.1.1 | Six Sigma

Six Sigma is a disciplined, data-driven approach and methodology for eliminating defects in any process. It can be applied from manufacturing to transactional and from product to service industries. It improves business processes by defining, measuring and analysing workflows in order to reduce defects in an organisation's products and services. In Six Sigma, outputs within six times standard deviation on either side of the mean are considered normal and outside of it are treated as defects. In Six Sigma, 3.4 defects or less are expected per million occurrences.

Six Sigma can be applied to the domain of IT project delivery since IT project delivery consists of business processes and workflows to be implemented and managed by the different teams of the project. There are numerous project delivery methodologies listed earlier in Table 2.1 in chapter 2 that provide their own way of implementing the business processes and workflows in a project. In KDD, we go back to the generic business processes and workflows and visualise end-to-end project delivery from the project knowledge perspective. Table 9.1 illustrates how KDD complies with the six themes [10] of Six Sigma and reduces defects to the minimum while executing end-to-end project delivery business processes.

Table 9.1 | KDD compliance with Six Sigma

Six sigma theme	Description	KDD compliance	Explanation
Genuine focus on the customer	In Six Sigma, customer focus becomes the top priority. Six Sigma improvements are measured by their impact on customer satisfaction and value.	High	For project delivery, customers are in focus through their requirements. KDD always keeps the requirements in focus via its traceability with 17 other building blocks that penetrate into solution design, application design and test design. Visibility of requirements across the SDLC is not so transparent in other methodologies.

Contd.

Six sigma theme	Description	KDD compliance	Explanation
Data and fact driven management	Despite the fact that we live in the digital age, a majority of the decisions are still based on opinions and assumptions. Six Sigma takes the concept of 'management by fact' to a more powerful level as it is based on quantification.	High	KDD brings extreme quantification in project delivery by: 1. Digitising the project knowledge in 18 building blocks and 189 relationships between them. 2. Quality assuring the project knowledge via 327 data points of quality assurance; most of them are via the negative relationship mechanism of PKM. 3. Enabling reuse in the project delivery via the enterprise knowledge contained in the 22 data points. 4. End-to-end project delivery is managed by 56 generic activities and 10 quality gates.
Processes are where action is	Six Sigma positions the processes as the key vehicle of success.	High	Managing project delivery via 56 generic and well-defined activities is one of the key propositions of KDD. Different activity types help calculating normal, review and rework efforts that make monitoring and control of the project delivery transparent.
Proactive management	Proactive means acting in advance of events rather than reacting to them. Six sigma relies on proactive management.	High	One of the major bottlenecks of the traditional methodologies is the subjectivity around the area of project knowledge management. As KDD digitises it, the management is able to influence this area proactively. Progress reports of different phases, negative relationship review and exhaustive traceability, as extracted from PKM, help in proactive management of the project delivery.

Contd.

Six sigma theme	Description	KDD compliance	Explanation
Boundaryless collaboration	Six Sigma stresses on boundaryless collaboration to cut costs to a great extent.	High	Different teams (such as development team, test team) of the project need to refer to the same PKM to meet their project knowledge requirements, as well as to keep themselves aware and updated with the project knowledge of the other teams. With exhaustive traceability, this is done in a seamless manner, facilitating close collaboration between the project teams.
Drive for perfection and tolerate failure	These two ideas are complementary and not contradictory.	High	KDD is based on matured thinking on project knowledge management. It assumes that many times a person cannot do things right the first time and it needs some iteration to reach perfection. This is done via its exhaustive traceability mechanism in KDD. Whereas it digitises the entire project knowledge in 189 data points, it also provides for flexibility in the number of data points depending on context and subjectivity of the SME.

9.1.2 | CMMI

CMMI (Capability Maturity Model Integration) is a structured and systematic collection of best practices for process-improvement. It is administered by the CMMI Institute (http://cmmiinstitute.com), 100%-controlled subsidiary of Carnegie Innovations, Carnegie Mellon University's technology commercialisation enterprise.

CMMI mentions five levels of maturity which an organisation may have, from delivery perspective. There are process areas relevant for each of these levels. The concept of KDD is clearly in alignment with CMMI concepts. Table 9.2 demonstrates how KDD complies with the process areas of CMMI [11] under various levels of maturity.

Table 9.2 | KDD compliance with CMMI

Sl. No.	Process Area	Maturity Level	KDD compliance	Explanation
1	Requirement Management	2	High	Requirement change management, along with impact analysis, requirement transformation to solution, requirement review (manual and via negative relationship), requirement traceability to test and application design provide a robust framework for requirement management.
2	Project Planning	2	Medium	Extreme quantification of the project knowledge and its quality assurance help in determining the size of the project, which is the key to planning. A total of 56 generic project delivery activities form the key to project planning. These activities are at the level of adding inventory and relationship and their quality assurance, which is more transparent than a typical project planning in Waterfall methodology. Reduction of rework, greater reuse and reduction of test execution defects, which are key features of KDD, help in creating a reliable plan which is less prone to change.
3	Project Monitoring and Control	2	High	Through 20 project artefacts covering the end-to-end project delivery, the project status in KDD is more transparent than any other methodology. These artefacts can be extracted at any point of time from PKM and are typically taken at the quality gates to help crossing the gates. The combination of project artefacts and quality gates helps in project monitoring and control. The 15 KPIs, as defined earlier, also contribute towards project monitoring and control in KDD.
4	Measurement and Analysis	2	High	In a typical KDD implementation, the end-to-end project delivery is covered in 56 generic activities with 189 data points of project knowledge and 327 data points of quality assurance mechanism around the project knowledge. The data points are integrated with each other and maintained by PKM in a digitised manner. Measurement and analysis at any point in the project journey is facilitated by PKM.

Contd.

KDD Compliance with Standards of Project Delivery

Sl. No.	Process Area	Maturity Level	KDD compliance	Explanation
5	Configuration Management	2	Medium	KDD visualises Extended Project Knowledge Model as a configuration management mechanism for maintaining knowledge about the project. For code configuration management, there no view of KDD and it relies on the latest configuration management tools available in the market.
6	Process and Product Quality Assurance	2	High	Using the negative relationships and manual defect mechanism with exhaustive traceability, KDD ensures process quality assurance, resulting in product quality assurance.
7	Supplier Agreement Management	2	Not Applicable	Not directly related to what KDD focus areas are in project delivery.
8	Decision Analysis and Resolution (DAR)	3	Medium	The purpose of DAR is to analyse possible decisions using a formal evaluation process that evaluates identified alternatives against established criteria. The digitised knowledge of the project and enterprise of KDD assists in the evaluation process.
9	Integrated Project Management	3	High	KDD complies with features of Integrated Project Management such as reuse of knowledge, collaboration and extreme quantification of the project knowledge as explained earlier. This is enabled via Extended Project Knowledge Model.
10	Organisational Process Definition (OPD)	3	Medium	OPD establishes a usable and maintainable set of organisational processes and work environment standards. It is stored in process asset library. KDD, having digitised project and enterprise knowledge, helps standardising organisational processes but is limited to project delivery.
11	Organisational Process Focus (OPF)	3	Medium	OPF follows thorough analysis of the strengths and weaknesses of existing processes within an organisation. OPF is the planning, implementing and deploying of process improvements. KDD features are: • Exhaustive traceability • Project knowledge management

Contd.

Sl. No.	Process Area	Maturity Level	KDD compliance	Explanation
				• Enterprise knowledge management • Negative relationship and manual reviews • Prescriptive steps for effective project delivery These help in process improvement initiatives to increase reuse and reduce rework in the area of project delivery.
12	Organisational Training	3	Not Applicable	Skill-set building is not the focus of KDD.
13	Product Integration	3	High	Product integration is the assembling of the product from the products components, ensuring that the product, as integrated, functions properly and delivers the results. All the necessary information for product integration resides in PKM. Inter-component interfaces are catered for at business (through interface building block) and technical (through data and logic building block) levels.
14	Requirements Development	3	High	User Story format can be chosen for requirement definition by accommodating it in the requirement building block attributes in PKM. The elaborate review, traceability and requirement transformation mechanism ensures that requirements are developed and matured faster than the other methodologies.
15	Risk Management	3	High	Risk management can be a part of the manual review process that links it to appropriate inventory or relationship, if relevant. If needed, risk management can be added as a separate building block.
16	Technical Solution	3	High	PKM has technical solution as one of the four compartments of the project knowledge. It is fully traced with the other compartments, namely, requirement, solutioning and test design knowledge.
17	Validation	3	High	The objective of validation is to make sure that the product meets the user's requirements, irrespective of what is written in the specifications. Through the Project Test Case building block of PKM and its traceability with requirement, solution and application knowledge, KDD provides an optimal validation environment in project delivery.

Contd.

KDD Compliance with Standards of Project Delivery

Sl. No.	Process Area	Maturity Level	KDD compliance	Explanation
18	Verification	3	High	Verification ensures that the products deliver their specified requirements. Through exhaustive traceability mechanism of KDD, the requirements move to solution design, application design and test design with full transparency assisting in requirement verification. Negative relationships and manual review, with linkage to relevant inventory also assists in the verification process. This is a better way to verify the specifications when compared to verifying them in the traditional way against a document set.
19	Organisational Process Performance (OPP)	4	High	Following process implementation, the process performance is measured using actual results of the process improvement. Process performance is measured by both process and product indicators. Process indicators are measures such as efficiency gains, cycle times and defect removal. Product indicators are measures such as reliability, capacity, response time and cost. KDD digitises the project knowledge and its quality assurance which helps measuring process performance, primarily via 15 KPIs, as defined in chapter 7.
20	Quantitative Project Management	4	High	KDD enables extreme quantification of project as the focus changes from project documentation to management of 189 project knowledge data points via 327 negative relationship and manual review data points of its quality assurance. A total of 56 generic activities manage it. This helps managing the project more quantifiably than other methodologies.
21	Causal Analysis and Resolution (CAR)	5	High	The purpose of CAR is to identify causes of defects and other problems and act to prevent them from occurring in the future. KDD, through its digitised project knowledge, makes finding root cause of the defect more transparent than the other methodologies. The provision for linking a defect to one or more inventory or relationship helps detecting a known defect without the chance of rediscovering it again.

Contd.

Sl. No.	Process Area	Maturity Level	KDD compliance	Explanation
22	Organisational Performance Management (OPM)	5	Medium	OPM helps in achieving the business goals by proactive management of organisational performance. Elaborate framework of digitised project knowledge and its quality assurance simplifies the project delivery. Close interaction of the project knowledge with the enterprise knowledge helps keeping the performance of an organisation on a continuous growth path. KDD is more at the project delivery level than at the enterprise level.

9.2 | Project Management Framework

PMP and PRINCE2 are two of the popular project management frameworks adopted across the world for project management practice. PRINCE2 takes a different approach from PMP, but both aim to improve the project performance and, eventually, its success rate. In the following sections, relevance of KDD in both the frameworks is discussed.

9.2.1 | PMP

PMBOK (Project Management Body of Knowledge) is the de facto standard in project management. It is published by Project Management Institute (PMI) which conducts the PMP certificate programme. In Table 9.3, knowledge areas [12] of PMBOK and KDD compliance with it are discussed.

Table 9.3 | KDD compliance with PMP

Knowledge Area	KDD compliance	Explanation
Integration	High	Integration deals with integrating other knowledge areas. It creates project management plan and monitors and controls it. In KDD, there are 56 generic activities that cover end to end project delivery and become the basis of project management plan.

Contd.

KDD Compliance with Standards of Project Delivery

Knowledge Area	KDD compliance	Explanation
		Table 7.4 of Chapter 7 lists 15 KPI's that can be extracted via the PKM. These KPI's bring transparency to the project delivery status making it easy to direct and manage project execution. These KPI's are based on the well-defined activities categorised as normal, review and rework taking them to the smallest unit that can be measured effectively in terms of effort and therefore can be easily tracked. This is more granular than traditional activities used in other methodologies such as producing a document and reviewing a document. An important distinction between the 15 KPI's extracted in KDD and collected manually in other methodologies is their objectivity. KDD calculates KPI's based on the information it has in PKM. In other methodologies, they are collected primarily from different project teams. There may be several reasons why the KPIs may not be accurate as the team may not have a good idea of the progress or, more importantly, sometimes the team may not want to give the true picture of the progress. Additionally, there are 8 project completion indicators (as detailed in Table 6.2 of chapter 6) that can be extracted from PKM to guide the project across all their phases.
Scope	High	Scope relates to collecting requirements, defining and controlling scope and creating Work Breakdown Structure (WBS) to brake the project into manageable component. WBS generally comprises of deliverables (such as FSD) and activities to accomplish these deliverables. KDD allows for requirement capture in a structured manner. The requirement is then reviewed, updated if relevant and transformed to solution design ensuring it is fit-for-purpose. In KDD, project scoping is accomplished at three levels as explained in section 4 of chapter 7. This rigour brings more science to the scoping process and reduces the chances of oversight. 171 relationships of traceability, negative relationship and manual review help in verifying and controlling scope.

Contd.

Knowledge Area	KDD compliance	Explanation
Time	High	Time knowledge area deals with creating activities, scheduling and estimating them. In KDD, there are 24 generic activities to manage 516 (189 + 327) data points of project knowledge and its quality. There are 32 more activities to manage execution and management related activities. The activities are pre-sequenced. Review and rework activities of the previous phase are invoked only when a defect of the previous phase is detected in the current phase. Data point approach helps in estimating and managing activities. For the initial projects, the project team can come up with a sensible guess for estimating the activity. Gradually it can be standardised for an organisation. Activities are based on data points that makes estimation and tracking objective and easily measurable. Key performance indicators listed in Table 7.4 of Chapter 7, help in controlling the schedule effectively.
Cost	Medium	It deals with project cost and budget. The PKM helps in the project estimate. Converting that into cost can be done easily. KDD helps controlling the project delivery via 8 phases, 10 quality gates, 15 KPI's and 20 project artefacts and, therefore, helps controlling costs.
Quality	High	It deals with project quality – both the quality assurance and quality control aspects of it. KDD has in-built quality as follows: 1. A total of 324 negative relationships are extracted from PKM. This assists in finding out potential defects in the project knowledge. 2. Capability to manage manual reviews of digitised project knowledge, in the format of inventory / relationship. 3. Test design via the concept of reuse of solution design. 4. Facilitating reuse from the enterprise knowledge.

Contd.

Knowledge Area	KDD compliance	Explanation
		Quality assurance focusses on preventing testing defects. Quality assurance must be completed before quality control. Negative relationship and manual review mechanism assists in quality assurance. Exhaustive traceability also assists. Quality control focusses on identifying testing defects. Quality control is a reactive process. Creating unit test to user acceptance test in one format with exhaustive traceability assists in quality control. It covers the test cases against requirement, business and technical solution in a single repository, i.e. PKM.
Human resources	NA	It deals with human resources aspects of project delivery. It is not a direct focus of KDD
Communications	High	It deals with communication in project management. PKM becomes a single point of reference for the entire project knowledge which everyone in the project can access at any point in time. All the efforts are made to keep the knowledge in the model updated in real-time. This helps in planning, execution and communication. Any gap in communication with respect to project knowledge is reduced to minimum. The 20 project artefacts and 15 key performance indicators (KPI) extracted from PKM are the prime reporting mechanism in KDD on project progress.
Risk management	Medium	It deals with project risk management. Risk management can either be a part of the manual review process or it can be a separate building block of PKM as the situation warrants. Currently it is envisaged to be part of review. Key performance indicators and review mechanism also assist in identifying and controlling risks.
Procurement	NA	It deals with purchasing or acquiring products and services for the project team. It is not a direct focus of KDD
Stakeholder management	Medium	It deals with project stakeholder management. KDD is focused on core project delivery and PKM, being the single source of project knowledge, assists in stakeholder management. PKM can extract customised information for most of the project stakeholders.

9.2.2 | PRINCE2

PRINCE2 (an acronym for **PR**ojects **IN** Controlled Environments) is a structured project management method. It emphasises dividing projects into manageable and controllable stages. It is used extensively by the UK Government. It is also used in private sector. PRINCE2 is based on [13] seven principles, seven themes and seven processes, as explained in Table 9.4, along with compliance of KDD with it.

Table 9.4 | KDD compliance with PRINCE2

Category	Item	KDD compliance	Explanation
Principle	Continued business justification	Low	Business Case is not part of KDD although it can provide input to continued business justification of a programme or initiative via the enterprise knowledge it contains. High level estimate can also be assisted by the enterprise knowledge. KDD with its promise to deliver better quality product at less cost, assists in continued business justification.
Principle	Manage by exception	High	Transparency provided by the digitised project knowledge and the quality assurance mechanism around it helps in self empowering different teams of the project. KDD extracts 15 KPIs to indicate the project health based on the information available in EPKM. It gives much needed objectivity in the project status and reduces the burden on the project management helping the theme of managing by exception. The 20 project artefacts also provide much needed transparency in the progress of project delivery.
Principle	Learn from experience	High	Enriching enterprise knowledge and its reuse for project delivery helps in learning from experience of others in the organisation.

Contd.

KDD Compliance with Standards of Project Delivery

Category	Item	KDD compliance	Explanation
Principle	Defined roles and responsibilities	High	The project delivery is implemented by 56 generic activities and each of these steps is assigned one or multiple roles in the project. There are primarily four worker roles (business analyst, business system analyst, system analyst and test analyst) and a management role (project manager) in KDD.
Principle	Manage by stage	High	Quality gates manage stages as explained in chapter 7.
Principle	Focus on products	High	Specification of the software product from business, technical and test perspective helps keep the focus on the product and its quality delivery.
Principle	Tailoring	High	KDD has the concept of selecting project knowledge data points from a superset provided by the Project Knowledge Model. At the later phases of the project, iterations can be done if it suits the project.
Theme	Business Case	NA	Business case is not part of KDD; it starts with the requirement analysis phase.
Theme	Organisation	High	KDD has primarily four workers role and a management role to manage the project as listed earlier in this table. Also, on need basis there may be specialist roles such as performance tester.
Theme	Quality	High	With exhaustive traceability, reuse of enterprise knowledge, negative relationship and manual review, KDD has brought transparency to quality assurance. Digitisation of project knowledge has made the detection of errors simpler.
Theme	Risk	High	Risk can be included either in the manual review or as a separate building block of PKM.

Contd.

Category	Item	KDD compliance	Explanation
Theme	Planning	Medium	Although KDD does not bring any new idea on planning, its cataloguing approach (via inventory and relationship) will certainly help project planning.
Theme	Change	High	Any change, whether originating from the requirement or any other building block, can be accommodated seamlessly by the exhaustive traceability mechanism of KDD representing 171 relationships.
Theme	Progress	High	There are 15 key performance indicators listed in section 5 of chapter 7 and 8 project progress indicators listed in section 4 of chapter 6 which give a good idea on the progress of the project and its quality. They are built into PKM which indicates progress of different phases of the project, both qualitatively and quantitatively.
Processes	Starting a phase	NA	KDD starts at the requirements gathering stage and does not deal with traditional idea generation and feasibility studies.
Processes	Initiating a project	Medium	In KDD, we initiate a project via the three levels of scoping based on the customer supplied requirements. KDD does not deal with areas like resource mobilisation for initiation of a project.
Processes	Directing a project	High	The 15 key performance indicators and 8 project progress indicators of PKM help to direct a project in the right direction. They indicate qualitative and quantitative progress of the project.
Processes	Controlling a stage	High	KDD manages the project via 8 stages and 10 quality gates as described in chapter 7.
Processes	Managing Stage Boundary	High	The 10 quality gates are used to manage the boundaries of 8 stages of KDD. Quality gates have specified entry and exit criteria as detailed in chapter 7.

Contd.

KDD Compliance with Standards of Project Delivery 187

Category	Item	KDD compliance	Explanation
Processes	Managing product delivery	High	KDD brings extreme quantification to the project delivery which makes its management transparent. Project knowledge forms a significant portion of the product delivery, which is fully digitised.
Processes	Closing a project	High	The last stage and the last quality gate drive project closure as described in the chapter 7. It primarily deals with enriching the enterprise knowledge with the project knowledge so that the next project can benefit from the reuse.

9.3 | Service Management Framework

ITIL is the de facto standard in service management. Its main objective is to standardise the service management function and keep it under continuous improvement. It consists of five books [14] and related processes.

The most relevant process where KDD can be of direct assistance is knowledge management process for Service Transition book. KDD, via exhaustive traceability mechanism, provides the digital project knowledge that replaces the tradition documents where the knowledge is currently held. It helps the team in learning the application and doing impact analysis for a new change and keeping the knowledge base updated in real-time with less effort when compared to other methodologies.

9.4 | Enterprise Architecture Framework

Enterprise architecture has 30 years of history. It started with the publication in *IBM Systems Journal* of an article titled 'A framework for Information Systems Architecture', by J. A. Zachman. The enterprise architecture primarily addresses two problems:

- System complexity: Organisations are spending more money building IT systems creating a complex network of ever-growing IT systems.
- Poor business alignment: It is challenging to keep those increasingly complex and expensive IT systems aligned with business needs.

The essential point was that the systems had more cost and less value. These problems have reached to a crisis point now. The cost and complexity

of the IT systems have exponentially increased, while the chances of deriving real value from these systems have decreased. The two most popular enterprise architecture frameworks are:
1. The Open Group Architecture Framework (TOGAF)
2. The Zachman Framework for Enterprise Architectures

KDD primarily focuses on digitised project delivery with reuse from the enterprise knowledge. The enterprise architecture framework and KDD share many areas of concern and in the subsequent sections we have discussed how KDD complies with the thought process of TOGAF and Zachman framework in these areas of concern.

9.4.1 | TOGAF

The Open Group Architecture Framework is best known by its acronym TOGAF, and started in 1995. TOGAF provides an approach for designing, planning, implementing and governing an enterprise information technology architecture. TOGAF is typically modelled at four levels [15]: business, data, application and technology. In Table 9.5, compliance of KDD with these levels is detailed.

Table 9.5 | KDD compliance with TOGAF

Architectures	KDD compliance	Remarks
Business Architecture	Medium	Business architecture defines the business strategy, governance, organisation and key processes of the organisation. KDD has key and detailed processes, both at the project and at the enterprise level, facilitating reusability. The processes and their details are captured and maintained in the process and process step building blocks of PKM and process steps are also connected to inventories of other building blocks such as business rule for completeness. This becomes the core to project and enterprise business architecture.
Data Architecture	Medium	Data architecture describes the structure of an organisation's logical and physical data assets. KDD has logical data (via business data building block) and physical data (via data building block) for a project. Business data and data are also connected to inventories of other building blocks, such as business rule, for completeness. For an enterprise, it has logical data for reuse in a project.

Contd.

KDD Compliance with Standards of Project Delivery

Architectures	KDD compliance	Remarks
Application Architecture	Medium	Application architecture provides a blueprint for the individual systems to be deployed, the interactions between the application systems, and their relationships to the core business processes of the organisation with the frameworks for services to be exposed as business functions for integration. The following building blocks PKM, along-with the intra and inter-relationships of the inventories of the building blocks, completely define the project and enterprise application architecture: • Application • Interface • Process
Technical Architecture	Low	Technical architecture describes the hardware, software and network infrastructure needed to support the deployment of core, mission-critical applications. While KDD recognises the importance of technical architecture, it does not directly deal with it. KDD primarily focuses on linking the technical inventory (data and logic building blocks) of the application with the requirement, solution and test cases so that the coverage can be determined and gaps identified for better quality of project delivery. The detailed technical solution, including hardware, networking and such information are not the focus of KDD.

9.4.2 | Zachman Framework

The main point behind the Zachman Framework is the realisation that the same system or its development can be viewed by different sets of people in different ways, depending on their point of view. This is about the enterprise architecture. The Zachman Framework [16] defines 36 constituents of enterprise architecture. It is in the form of 6 x 6 matrix, where the rows denote how a concept becomes a reality (from Identification to Definition, Representation, Specification, Configuration and Instantiation) and columns denote different interrogations relevant to the evolving enterprise (from What to How, Where, Who, When and Why).

We need to bear in mind that the focus of the Zachman Framework is enterprise architecture, whereas for KDD it is project delivery. There is a strong connection between the two as project delivery forms significant portion of the enterprise activities. KDD, a project delivery methodology, has strong inclination towards delivering projects in a structured manner

and creating and reusing enterprise knowledge which is closely linked to enterprise architecture. Let us understand how KDD complies with the core philosophy of Zachman Framework through different interrogation points (column view).
1. What (Data): Three building blocks of KDD, i.e., scenario, business data and data, and the inter and intra-relationships of their inventories cover the data aspects of the project delivery. Intra business data relationship drives entity relationship model. Physical data drives data entity specifications and provides the data details.
2. How (Function): The process and process step building blocks, along with inter and intra-relationships of their inventories, represent function in the project delivery. Process is hierarchical and has process list at various levels. Inter and intra-relationship of process and process steps inventories represent process diagram, process function specification and process details. Other building blocks of KDD, such as application, business rule, report, communication, screen, message and business scenario complement process and process step.
3. Where (Network): Country, location and channels (indicators of 'where' in Zachman Framework) are attributes of the process building block of KDD.
4. Who (People): The user is an attribute of the process and process step building block of KDD which closely resembles the people aspect.
5. When (Time): Trigger, which is an attribute of process building block, indicates events that are driven by time.
6. Why (Motivation): PKM contains business rules, both at business as well as at technical level. However, the goal list, which helps deriving business rules, is not captured in KDD as it works at more detailed level via business rules.

It is interesting to note that KDD proposes a viewpoint (perspective) approach for the project delivery in a similar way that Zachman Framework proposes a viewpoint approach for the enterprise. As per Zachman Framework [17], there are six perspectives:
1. Executive perspective: It corresponds to an executive summary for a planner who wants an overview of the system.
2. Business management perspective: It represents an architect's drawing which depicts the final building from the perspective of the owner who will have to live in it.
3. Architect perspective: The architect's plans are the translation of the drawing into detailed requirement representation from the designer's perspective.

KDD Compliance with Standards of Project Delivery 191

4. Engineer perspective: It explains how the detailed requirements are expanded into technology details such as physical data model and system design.
5. Technician perspective: This is the programmer's perspective to build the software with the inputs provided.
6. Enterprise perspective: Finally, a system is created and made a part of the organisation.

As we can see, these perspectives cover the relevant stakeholders in an enterprise.

Likewise, KDD caters to the important project delivery roles, as follows:

Business analyst perspective: Where different aspects of the software are understood from the requirement viewpoint.

Business system analyst perspective: Where different aspects of the software are understood from the process viewpoint.

System analyst perspective: Where different aspects of the software are understood from the application viewpoint.

Test analyst perspective: Where different aspects of the software are understood from the test case viewpoint.

Figure 9.2 is a schematic representation of the business analyst's perspective via the requirement viewpoint. Building blocks are shown in their respective phases as explained in chapter 4.

Requirement viewpoint is the journey of requirements across the four knowledge-intensive phases of project delivery by linking them to the inventories of related building blocks. This is how a business analyst will have an overall view of the software from requirement perspective.

In the requirement analysis phase, the remaining four building blocks are traced to requirements, ensuring that the relevant applications, processes, non-functional attributes and products, taken together, can meet all the requirements.

In the solution design phase, all the ten building blocks of this phase, taken together, detail the requirements and, through traceability, ensure complete solutioning.

In the application design phase, technical inventories of the application are traced to requirement, giving the business analyst enough confidence on requirement compliance for the applications being created or updated.

In the test design phase, requirements are traced to test cases to ensure sufficient test coverage. The business analyst would know that even if the development team makes a mistake, it will be detected in the test execution phase.

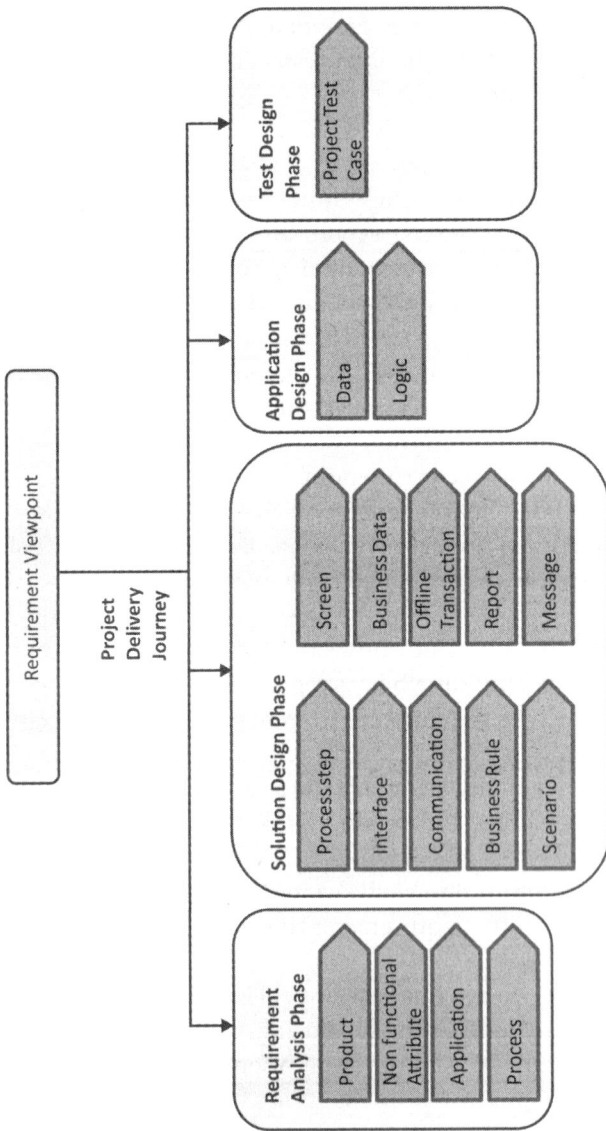

Figure 9.2 | Requirement viewpoint of project delivery

Through this journey, business analysts get a full picture of the software 'in making', across the knowledge-intensive phases from the language of requirement that they understand the most.

Similarly, the project delivery can also be visualised from the perspective of business system analyst, system analyst and test analyst. KDD proposes sixteen constituents of project delivery. It is in the form of 4*4 matrix where rows denote relevant stakeholders of project delivery (from business analyst to business system analyst to system analyst to test analyst) and columns denote different functions of project delivery (from requirement analysis to solution design to application design to test design). This is powered by 189 data points of project knowledge and 327 data points of quality assurance.

9.5 | Business Analysis Framework

IIBA (International Institute of Business Analysis) has come up with BABOK (Business Analysis Body of Knowledge) that is the de facto standard in business analysis. Table 9.6 lists two of six BABOK knowledge areas and its tasks [18] that are core to the project delivery and KDD's compliance with them.

Table 9.6 | KDD compliance with BABOK

Knowledge Area	Task	KDD compliance	Explanation
Requirements Life Cycle Management	Trace Requirements	High	Requirements are linked to 17 other building blocks of project knowledge providing exhaustive traceability.
Requirements Life Cycle Management	Maintain Requirements	High	Version control, requirement review and traceability assist in effective maintenance of the requirements in PKM.
Requirements Life Cycle Management	Prioritise Requirements	High	Digitisation of requirement and other associated inventories assist assigning its priority.
Requirements Life Cycle Management	Assess Requirements Changes	High	Exhaustive traceability helps impact assessment of any requirement change more effectively.
Requirements Life Cycle Management	Approve Requirements	High	Digitisation of requirements increases the efficiency of the approval process, assisted by status of the linked review log.

Contd.

Knowledge Area	Task	KDD compliance	Explanation
Requirements Analysis and Design Definition	Specify and Model Requirements	High	Requirements are specified as user stories (if one chooses) and transformed into solution design inventories.
Requirements Analysis and Design Definition	Verify Requirements	High	Requirements and the resulting solution inventories are quality assured by 327 negative relationships and manual review mechanism. Requirements are also verified while transforming them into solution design inventories.
Requirements Analysis and Design Definition	Validate Requirements	High	Through 17 relationships of traceability of requirements with the solution design, application design and test design inventories, requirements are validated so that they are fit-for-purpose. Test execution is primarily responsible to validate requirements.
Requirements Analysis and Design Definition	Define Requirements Architecture	Low	KDD does not address this directly.
Requirements Analysis and Design Definition	Define Design Options	Low	Design options are not dealt with in KDD. KDD expands on the selected design option. However, design option can be added as a new building block if the project team think it is suitable in the given context
Requirements Analysis and Design Definition	Analyse Potential Value and Recommend Solution	Low	Recommending preferred solution is not in-scope of KDD. KDD expands on the selected solution.

9.6 | Test Management Framework

In the absence of a test body of knowledge, the seven principles of testing, as per ISTQB (International Software Testing Qualification Board) [19], is checked for KDD compliance. Table 9.7 provides the details in this regard.

Table 9.7 | KDD compliance with seven principles of testing

Test Principles	Description	KDD compliance	Explanation
Testing shows presence of defects	Testing can show that defects are present but cannot prove that there are no defects. Testing reduces the probability of undiscovered defects remaining in the software but, even if no defects are found, it is not a proof of correctness.	High	KDD is evolved in compliance with this principle. To reduce the probability of undiscovered defects to a minimum, following steps are taken: 1. Quantitatively prove test coverage not only with the requirements but also with solution design and application design. 2. An exhaustive negative relationship and manual review mechanism improves the chances of getting things right the first time itself. Digitisation of the project knowledge helps in effectively executing these two points.
Exhaustive testing is impossible	Testing everything (all combinations of inputs and pre-conditions) is not feasible except for trivial cases. Instead of exhaustive testing, risk analysis and priorities should be used to focus testing efforts.	High	Test design has a limited effort allocation and creating exhaustive test cases is almost impossible. KDD approaches test case creation in a scientific manner. It reuses inventories of solution design to create test cases. Digitisation of solution design inventory helps in this. Test cases are then traced to requirements and application design inventories for complete coverage. Doing test design digitally helps in risk analysis and prioritising test cases.
Early testing	To find defects early, testing activities should take place as early as possible in the software or system development life cycle, and should focus on the defined objectives.	High	KDD implements three important considerations from the perspective of early testing: 1. Through negative relationship and manual review mechanism, KDD tries its best to arrest any defect introduced in the same phase, as early as possible.

Contd.

Test Principles	Description	KDD compliance	Explanation
			2. Creating test cases via reuse of solution design and then mapping requirements to test cases ensure complete coverage. 3. Test cases are traced against application design inventories ensuring they are statically tested even before a single test case is executed. These actions ensure that the defects are detected and corrected at source and test cases are of optimal quality.
Defect clustering	Testing effort should be focused proportionally on the expected and, later, the observed defect density of modules. A small number of modules usually contain most of the defects discovered during the pre-release testing, or are responsible for most of the operational failures.	High	KDD stores consolidated (from unit test to UAT) test cases for the entire project in one place and in the one format. This helps to identify the complex area where more focus is required. Extreme quantification of the project knowledge also assists in tracing with test cases appropriately. One indicator can be: if a requirement has more review comments, it may need more attention while creating test cases.
Pesticide paradox	If the same tests are repeated over and over again, eventually the same set of test cases will no longer find any new defects. To overcome this 'pesticide paradox', test cases need to be regularly reviewed and revised, and new and different tests need to be written to exercise different parts of the software or system to find, potentially, more defects.	Medium	KDD has an elaborate mechanism to produce test cases where test coverage can be quantitatively arrived at. KDD can be kept dynamically updated with changing requirements and solution via exhaustive traceability mechanism of PKM. KDD can assist in building and maintaining regression test cases to ensure the new or updated features of the software do not impact the existing features.

Contd.

Test Principles	Description	KDD compliance	Explanation
Testing is context dependent	Testing is done differently in different contexts. For example, safety-critical software is tested differently from an ecommerce site.	High	KDD has taken a different approach on this. It has standardised the test case production mechanism, which is exhaustive. It provides for flexibility to prioritise the test cases (reducing the total number), based on preference of quality and budget.
Absence of error fallacy	Finding and fixing defects does not help if the system built is unusable and does not fulfil the users' needs and expectations.	Low	This is related to the area of skill and experience of the project team, not too relevant for a methodology.

CHAPTER 10

Enabling DevOps

DevOps is becoming an increasingly popular concept, trying to optimise the product lifecycle, rather than the product development lifecycle, where the development team and service management team are seamlessly integrated. This chapter tries to understand the details of DevOps, issues in the product lifecycle it is trying to solve and how KDD supports DevOps.

10.1 | What Is DevOps

Before the advent of the personal computers, it was almost the same team that used to develop the software and maintain it, until its decommissioning. The advent of personal computers and other advancements in technology led to the specialisation of skills and the formation of development, quality assurance and service management teams. The IT organisation structure has been based on functional specialisations since then. This structure initiated the development of the popular handover-takeover mechanism to pass information from one team to the other. This mechanism has limited effectiveness, as during handover-takeover, it is practically impossible to pass on all the knowledge that is gathered by one team to the other. Often, the functional splitting of the project acts as a barrier to the work rather than being the enabler of project delivery as widely observed in Waterfall methodology.

   The Agile methodology has brought significant improvement in the way software is developed. For example, Agile forms a joint project development team which is co-located and works together for the success of the project. Formal handover-takeover is no longer needed as the teams are physically or virtually co-located. This has made a working style possible that was difficult to imagine a couple of years ago. For example, testers in a Sprint team do not usually raise a defect. They come to developers, discuss and resolve the issue directly, saving a lot of effort in this way.

However, Agile, like Waterfall, focuses on project delivery. Agile hands over the project knowledge in the form of minimal documents and Waterfall hands over exhaustive documentation that may not be kept updated to service management team. Neither of these two scenarios are ideal from the service management team perspective. There is a need to look into optimising the entire lifecycle of the product and not only product development. In the product lifecycle, the three most important stakeholders are:

- Development team (includes business analysts), which develops the product.
- Quality Assurance team, which ensures the product is as per the specifications of the customer.
- Service management team, which maintains the product until it is decommissioned.

Optimising the delivery and maintenance of the software within and across these teams is the purpose of DevOps. DevOps is a culture like Agile and tries to bring synergy in the delivery and maintenance environment. It is not just about a methodology, tools and techniques, but is a mix of all three. It is not only about integrating delivery and maintenance, but also bringing in agility in every step in these phases.

10.2 | DevOps Focus Area and Assistance by KDD

DevOps is a movement with the ultimate objective of improving the quality of work in the delivery and maintenance environment focusing on a cultural change with a focused approach to automation. Figure 10.1 illustrates how KDD supports the concept of DevOps.

The 189 data points of project knowledge and 327 data points of quality assurance around the project knowledge take centre stage in the KDD and bring together development, quality assurance and service management teams for delivery and maintaining the software. Project knowledge data points are first created by the development team and thereafter the service management team maintains the software. The quality assurance team owns the data points of quality assurance, both in the delivery and maintenance phases of product lifecycle.

DevOps makes an impact on the following four factors relevant to delivery and maintenance. KDD also influences these factors, enabling DevOps.

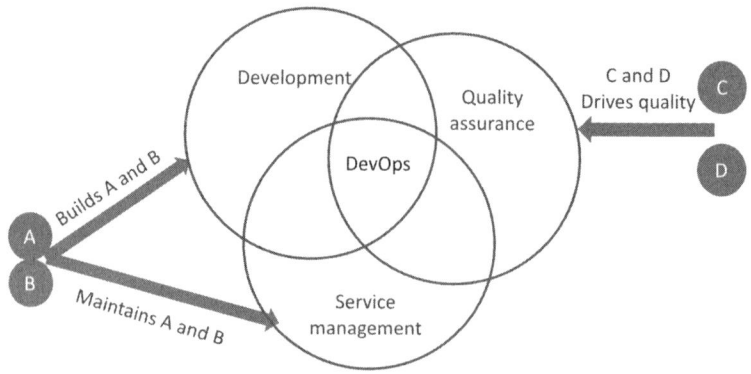

Notation (example):
A – Inventories of 18 building blocks (Requirement-01)
B – 171 relationship types of inventories (Requirement-01 linked to Screen-01)
C – 324 negative relationship potential defect (Test Case-01 not linked to any requirement)
D – 3 manual defect (requirement related defect)

Figure 10.1 | Collaboration between Dev and Ops in KDD

1. Communication: Communication is a significantly impacting factor for a successful project delivery and for product maintenance. Communication, in this sense, is the spreading of correct and updated information throughout the project team in the most effective manner. In Waterfall, the communication is in the form of documents, whereas Agile places greater emphasis on face-to-face communication. With technology advancements, other enablers have emerged, such as easy retrieval of information and collaboration features.

KDD has scoped the entire information relevant to the project delivery. Using PKM, it enables capturing and maintaining that information in a single repository. KDD has made an elaborate provision for quality assurance of that information via static and dynamic quality assurance. Static quality assurance primarily consists of review of information and dynamic quality assurance consists of creating and executing test cases to ensure that the product is as per the specifications before it is deployed.

PKM becomes the single source of information for the project and eases the communication issues in the project. The same information can continue to be used in the product maintenance environment by the service management team.

2. Integration: DevOps integrates all the phases of the project delivery and maintenance in a seamless manner so that the product lifecycle becomes a smooth journey. Integration can be seen at two levels, technical and project knowledge. Technical integration is about integrating the build, test and release to production. Project knowledge integration is about integrating the project knowledge across different phases.

KDD integrates the following four knowledge-intensive phases of the project delivery via PKM:

1. Requirement analysis
2. Solution design
3. Application design
4. Test design

PKM also defines the integration mechanism. They are:

1. Transformation between requirement analysis and solution design
2. Conversion between solution design and application design
3. Reuse between solution design and test design

This integration at project knowledge level helps the technical integration by increasing transparency significantly on how the requirements are translated into code. Traceability of requirements with code is well established by the exhaustive traceability mechanism of PKM. This helps in easier maintenance of the product.

3. Automation: The technical and project knowledge aspects of project delivery and maintenance are predominantly manual, with significant opportunities for automation.

There are tools available that manage the technical aspects. They bring sensible automation in build, test and movement to production, to an extent. Once the development team completes build, the tool automatically compiles it, runs automated test scripts, releases it to production if the test is successful, or else reports the defects to the development team.

The project knowledge evolves over phases and it cannot be automated the way technical aspects can be. PKM, as presented in this book, has the potential to bring order to the current chaos that prevails in the area of the project knowledge. The model digitises the project knowledge in a way that integrates its various aspects, such as requirement, business, application and test knowledge, and the relevant information can be extracted easily. Quality assurance of this project knowledge is also digitised, making the model a reliable single source of project knowledge for the use of the development team and, thereafter, the service management team. The model, when the project is complete, is handed over by the development team to the service management team. Any changes that are required to be made are facilitated by the model due to its exhaustive traceability.

This level of advancement in managing project knowledge is not available in other project delivery methodologies to the best of my knowledge.

4. Measurement: Measurement deals with project estimates and measuring the progress against the estimates.

KDD enables scientific estimates as the in-scope project knowledge inventories can be measured better than the project documents. Even at the start of the project, the enterprise knowledge base provides information for better project estimates. As explained in the case study in chapter 1, based on project overview, in-scope applications, processes and non-functional attributes are selected from the existing enterprise knowledge base (in KDD in the requirement analysis phase).

The entire project knowledge is scoped in 189 data points, its quality assurance is scoped in 327 data points and all these are managed by 24 generic activities. This extreme quantification is missing from the current methodologies. This enables KDD to extract 8 indicators of project completion as detailed in chapter 6 and 15 KPI's as detailed in chapter 7.

CHAPTER 11

Addressing Contemporary Concerns of Project Delivery

As discussed in the earlier chapters, smooth project delivery is still a challenge and the IT industry is continuously working to make the project delivery more effective. This chapter discusses the relevance of KDD to important topics that are of interest for effective project delivery, other than DevOps and automation. The relevance of KDD to DevOps and automation has been discussed in separate chapters.

11.1 | Shift Left

Shift Left refers to a practice in software development where teams focus on quality, work on prevention instead of detection and begin testing earlier than ever before. The goal is to increase quality, shorten long test cycles and reduce the possibility of unpleasant surprises towards the end of the development lifecycle.

Following traditional methodologies results in a substantial testing phase of the project delivery, and significant effort is spent on rework due to oversights made in the pre-testing phases. KDD, via its negative relationships and manual review of the catalogued project knowledge elements (requirement, solution design, application design and test design) that are integrated via exhaustive traceability, creates an effective static testing environment that has been largely absent in the existing methodologies.

The cost of quality in a typical project is close to 50% (in my experience) with the break-up as follows:
1. About 25% effort goes in in test design, execution and management.
2. One-third of the remaining 75% effort typically goes towards review and rework.

Shift left aims to optimise this one third of the remaining effort so that the test execution can be almost defect free. KDD reduces this one third of the review and rework effort through the catalogued knowledge capturing mechanism, the negative relationships review and manual review. Its benefits are:

1. Review and rework is digitised via 516 data points of project knowledge and the related quality assurance. Due to the scientific way of handling review and rework, KDD reduces this effort up to 50% of the existing effort.
2. Test cases are prepared by reusing inventories of solution design. OATS technique is used for optimised coverage. The entire set of test cases (from unit test to UAT) is prepared at one go and in the same format. Considering traditional end-to-end test design by different teams, the KDD approach has the potential to reduce the efforts spent in test design by half.
3. Due to effective reviews, test execution and defect management effort is reduced significantly. Test cases are traced to requirement, solution design and application design digitally and that, again, reduces the test execution and defect management significantly. The reason is that test cases are statically tested (via traceability), thereby reducing the possibility of a defect in execution. As a result, I believe that the test execution and defect management effort is reduced by up to 50%.

All these factors may result in savings of up to 25% of the project delivery effort due to shift left implementation in KDD.

Any defect not detected in the pre-test execution phase multiplies the effort taken to resolve it when detected in the test execution phase. This is because of its impact on all the previous phases and the mechanism of test defect management. KDD aims to detect defects closest to the origin of the defect. Let us understand this by taking requirement review as an example. In KDD, when a requirement is read, it is either fully understood, partially understood or not understood. When it is fully understood, it results in creation of base solution inventory. For partially and not understood requirements, a review log is added, linking the log to this requirement. When the review log is resolved, usually with input from Business, it again results in base solution inventory creation. Through this mechanism, KDD provides enough opportunity to arrest any requirement related defects in the requirement analysis phase itself.

11.2 | Knowledge Management

This book is an attempt to apply the concept of knowledge management to software development.

As mentioned in the first chapter, I have made my own discoveries in knowledge management. I claim that knowledge about anything and everything can be specified in eight building blocks. In chapter 4, I have demonstrated how these eight building blocks expand into 18 building blocks when it comes to software development, giving rise to KDD. In chapter 15, I have expanded on this idea of 8 building blocks, creating a new framework named as Generic Knowledge Management Framework (GKMF) and visualise its usage in other domains.

In this section, let us take a traditional view of knowledge management and understand how KDD tries to improve it.

Let us define knowledge and related terms [20] as follows:
- Data: Data comes in the form of measurement. An example is 5 kg of rice.
- Information: Information is a statement of fact about these measurements. An example is: A new quality management initiative has reduced product defects by 45%.
- Knowledge: Knowledge is the ability to turn information and data into effective action. A majority of knowledge is 'tacit', i.e., it comes with the experience of interpreting data and information.
- Knowledge management: Managing knowledge that is majorly 'tacit'.

Key components of knowledge management are:
- People: Those who produce and those who use knowledge that will be the basis for action.
- Content: The flow of data, information and knowledge, important for the success of the business.
- Technology: The technical infrastructure that enables the capture, storage and delivery of the content to those who need it and when they need it.

Let us understand the current state of knowledge management in the context of IT project delivery. People are the project team, content is the document where the knowledge is kept and technology is the tool that stores the documents. The tool focuses on indexing and cataloguing information so that its retrieval is easier. The tool also concentrates on having an effective folder structure for storing the documents. There are collaboration based tools for real-time audio and video based interactions.

There are wiki pages to store related unstructured information which can be read and kept updated by a group of participants.

Let us now visualise knowledge management from the perspective of KDD. In KDD, via 189 data points, the project knowledge is completely defined and scoped, making it explicit knowledge. KDD is clear that unless you specify what you want, how can you get that in the software that is being built as a part of the project? KDD's viewpoints on the key components of knowledge management are:

- People: Project team as with the traditional methodologies.
- Content: KDD replaces the project documents with PKM, consisting of189 data points of project knowledge.
- Technology: There is no software or tool to assist KDD as it a new methodology which this book is introducing. PKM which is conceptually defined in chapter 4 can evolve into a tool supporting KDD methodology.

There are some key differences KDD has with other methodologies with regard to knowledge management. Other methodologies rely on documents for knowledge management and believe in the 'tacit' nature of knowledge. For example, they may say that testers will have a different point of view of looking at things, based on their experience. Therefore, testers should be able to identify defects without any specific requirement and help the project due to their 'tacit' knowledge. Also, to specify a requirement, the business analyst uses documents that are in the format of free-form texts, which is an attempt to convert their 'tacit' knowledge into explicit knowledge.

KDD provides a mechanism to maintain explicit knowledge of the project. This happens due to the digitisation of the project knowledge via 189 data points of project knowledge. It gives a sense of completeness of the project knowledge and reduces the dependency on SMEs with their supposed 'tacit' knowledge. I believe this is a perfectly valid way of thinking, as codification (making of the software) is 100% explicit knowledge. Tacit knowledge is not necessary for project delivery as the software is based on algorithms which represent explicit knowledge. As said earlier, if we cannot specify something explicitly, how can we expect that in the software?

The key to knowledge management [20] consists of:
- Knowledge storyboard, which shows where the content is used in the business processes.
- Knowledge network, which shows where the content lives in the organisation and who owns it.

These two points drive the considerations of people, content and technology. From KDD perspective, knowledge storyboarding represents process building block and other building blocks associated with it. For knowledge network, in KDD, the content is in PKM and the owners are the four worker-roles of the project (business analyst, business system analyst, system analyst and test analyst) which together own all the 18 building blocks of the project knowledge. KDD does not envisage separate roles to manage knowledge in an enterprise. Instead, in a matured state, it visualises project knowledge to expand or assist enterprise knowledge with ownership assigned to the worker's role such as business architect.

KDD concentrates on knowledge in its fundamental form. The spider-web structure intuitively explains the project knowledge. Most of the fundamental structures in the world follow the spider-web structure. The examples range from atomic structure to planets. A cluster of interconnected webs can fully represent a knowledge base. These are three dimensional structures. The first dimension is the node, the second dimension is the relationship and the third dimension is the time which is spent in either filling them up or transforming one cluster of web to another. Figure 6.2 in chapter 6 shows that PKM of KDD is based on a web structure where the first and second dimensions are inventories and their relationships.

KDD is based on creating or detailing information in the project only when it is not available (neither in the enterprise knowledge, nor in the other portions of the project knowledge). Also, where possible, KDD relates or connects different forms of knowledge in the project rather than treating them separately. This needs to be followed rigorously, but if done properly, it achieves significant results. Following this approach will reduce the volume in the project knowledge at least by half. This would mean reduced duplication of information and, hence, less confusion and less time to maintain the information if it needs updating. Instead of creating a huge amount of information and then trying to think how to correlate it, KDD stresses on creating only fit-for-purpose information.

There are primarily eight activities [21] of knowledge management. KDD represents these activities in the project delivery environment as explained in the following:

1. Represent knowledge: Knowledge is represented in KDD in a typical implementation in 18 building blocks. This is fit-for-purpose for the project delivery.
2. Store knowledge: PKM of KDD stores the project knowledge in 18 building blocks, resulting in 189 data points in a typical

implementation. It is to be noted that PKM is conceptual model, as detailed in this book.
3. Integrate knowledge: Knowledge is integrated in PKM via exhaustive traceability. The information is interconnected and, therefore, its reuse is at its maximum.
4. Deliver knowledge: Knowledge is delivered in KDD via a set of 20 project artefacts extracted from PKM.
5. Facilitate collaboration: PKM, being the single source of truth about the project knowledge, encourages different project teams to look into the model for their project knowledge needs.
6. Manage quality: Quality of knowledge in PKM is assisted by negative relationships and manual review mechanism aided by exhaustive traceability.
7. Measure usage and benefits: Digitisation of project knowledge has assisted in various measurements. The model can quantifiably measure coverage, reuse, rework, effort spent until date and the projected effort to complete the project. There are 15 key performance indicators that measure different aspects of project progress in the project delivery environment.
8. Nurture knowledge management: PKM helps in nurturing project knowledge in the project team. Also, the enterprise knowledge concepts of KDD help nurturing knowledge for the entire organisation.

It is worth noting that at the enterprise level also, KDD has a differentiating proposition. KDD is the only methodology to the best of my understanding, scoping enterprise knowledge (precisely, part of enterprise knowledge relevant to project delivery) as well as project knowledge and linking them together for the benefit of both. Books on knowledge management discuss subjectively about enterprise knowledge as there is no popularly accepted definition of its constituents and varied storage media such as documents, audio, video, images, presentations and sheets. Industry discuss the area of contribution to knowledge base [22] primarily under the topics such as motivation, facilitation and trust. In contrast, as per KDD, contribution can be made to the enterprise knowledge by reviewing the existing digitised enterprise knowledge and adding the further information through structured information addition. Enterprise knowledge is scoped to 22 data points in KDD as discussed in chapter 4. KDD brings more transparency in the area of enterprise and project knowledge.

11.3 | Digitisation

IT helps digitising other industries. Although the meaning of digitisation itself has evolved over the years, let us illustrate it by an example below so that it is clear what I mean by digitisation in the context of this book.

Until 1990s, the banking industry worked with lengthy and bulky books (hard copies) to maintain ledgers. With the help of IT, now all of that is being handled more efficiently by using software. This is an example of digitisation.

The IT project delivery uses a set of lengthy and bulky documents, primarily for project knowledge purposes. KDD tries to replace the set of documents with inventory and relationships of the building blocks as defined in PKM. The model replaces free-form text documents via catalogued project knowledge. I have termed this as bringing digitisation to the project knowledge. KDD, through PKM, is the only methodology (to the best of my understanding) today which addresses digitisation of project knowledge.

11.4 | Collaboration

Technology enables collaboration in today's world. There are numerous audio, video, chat and social media related collaboration tools available. There are also document storage tools working as collaboration tools. KDD enables collaboration by accumulating various forms of project knowledge at one place in a digital format (in PKM) and then encouraging the project team to use and maintain it. It provides a medium of collaboration for different project teams. For example, the list of business rules and scenarios, added by the business system analyst, is used as input to create test cases by the test analyst. PKM does not entertain non-productive collaboration where the effort is spent on personal discussions.

11.5 | Agile Way of Working

KDD complies with the Agile way of working. Let us try to understand this from the statements in the Agile Manifesto:
1. Agile prefers individuals and interactions over processes and tools: KDD provides a broad framework for digital project knowledge management and its quality assurance. It provides a platform for

interaction between individuals in the project for faster project delivery. For example, KDD caters for three layers of project scoping and the project SMEs execute them during project delivery. KDD is lean by nature and has processes directly contributing to effective project delivery. It does not encourage elaborate processes such as formal review and sign-off mechanism for the project documents.
2. Agile prefers working software over comprehensive documentation: The capture and maintenance of project knowledge in a digitised manner is an alternate in KDD to documents. Documents, if required, are extracted from PKM. KDD drives creation of working software scientifically, with the assistance of PKM.
3. Agile prefers customer collaboration over contract negotiation: Not only collaboration with the customer, KDD also caters for effective collaboration within the project team. Making the project knowledge transparent assists collaboration. PKM drives collaboration as it is a single source of truth with respect to the project knowledge and members of the project team collaborate to keep it updated in real-time.
4. Agile prefers responding to change over following a plan: KDD enables impact analysis for responding to change. As the project knowledge is digitised right from requirement to test phases, change management is made simpler due to easier impact analysis, enabled by exhaustive traceability.

11.6 | Systems Thinking

Systems thinking is an integrated approach that focuses on the way that a system's constituents inter-relate and how systems work over time and within the context of larger systems. We can treat the project knowledge as a system that interacts with execution and management activities to produce a working software in the larger context.

The systems thinking concept is implemented in the project knowledge via PKM. PKM divides the project knowledge into four compartments of knowledge (requirement, solution design, application design and test design) that are inter-related via the themes of transformation, conversion and reuse, as discussed in chapter 4. It also has the next layer of components in the form of 18 building blocks that are interlinked by 171 relationships, covering the entire project knowledge.

11.7 | Lean Way of Working

The core idea of lean is to maximise customer value while minimising waste. In simple terms, lean means creating more value for customers with fewer assets.

KDD supports the lean methods. PKM helps visualising project delivery in a manner similar to manufacturing industry. Through catalogued project knowledge, it supports parallel execution of different activities of project delivery effectively. For example, performing test design and test execution in parallel is not a problem as long as there are clearly defined scopes for them. Three levels of scoping assist in performing only necessary activities for project delivery. Information duplication is reduced to a minimum and reuse is encouraged from enterprise knowledge as well as from the other portions of project knowledge. Digitisation of the project knowledge helps reducing waste to a minimum.

As explained in chapter 16, KDD is made further lean by reusing the business rule and scenario for requirements and solution design knowledge for test design knowledge.

11.8 | Software Engineering Modelling

Modelling assists in representing knowledge better than through documents. There are many widely used and known models in project delivery and some examples are:
1. Use Case
2. Business process model
3. Data model
4. Object model
5. Activity diagram
6. Class diagram
7. State transition diagram

If analysed in detail, they consist of information about one or more than one building blocks as defined in PKM. In contrast PKM consists of 18 building blocks, which is more than any of the existing methodologies.

11.9 | Machine Learning and Artificial Intelligence

Artificial Intelligence simulates human intelligence into computer. Machine Learning is a part of Artificial Intelligence that can learn from given data and use it to teach themselves to adapt to new circumstances and perform certain tasks. Natural language and knowledge representation should assist both.

PKM may also be treated as one of the knowledge representation mechanism or close to it and has seeds of intelligence, although not matured enough. Some of the examples indicating that are:

1. Knowledge representation in PKM is structured, representing lowest logical unit of knowledge via attributes, inventories and relationships.
2. Negative relationships extracted by the model has seed of intelligence as in this case the model attempts to bring out all the potential inconsistencies to the notice of an SME to assist in resolving them. PKM can learn from the experience of acceptance and rejection of the potential defects by SME if artificial intelligence is built into the model.
3. Rework and review activities on subject of the previous phase in the current phase (i.e. requirement rework in the solution design phase) is a mechanism allowing PKM to learn from experience to keep updating the estimate during different phases of project delivery.
4. Continuously enhancing the enterprise knowledge of PKM from subsequent projects so that the next project has more knowledge in the enterprise knowledge base for reuse – simulates learning from experience, a feature of Machine Learning.

11.10 | Internet of Things (IOT)

IoT is a system of interrelated computing devices, machines or humans that are provided with unique identifiers and the ability to transfer data over a network without requiring human to human or human to computer interaction. An example could be smart fridge that can tell you if it was out of milk.

Kevin Ashton, cofounder and executive director of the Auto-ID centre at MIT, first mentioned the Internet of Things in a presentation he made to Procter and Gamble in 1999. Here is how Ashton explains the potential of IoT:

[23] The problem is, people have limited time, attention and accuracy – all of which means they are not very good at capturing data about things in the real world. If we had computers that knew everything there was to know about things – using data they gathered without any help from us – we would be able to track and count everything, and greatly reduce waste,

loss and cost. We would know when things needed replacing, repairing or recalling, and whether they were fresh or past their best.

PKM conceptually is closer to the idea above. In using the model, the existence of mandatory and optional attributes of building blocks assist the project team to create structured knowledge that is fit for purpose. Exhaustive traceability ensures that all information is integrated and self-consistent. It is better than leaving them to add information via documents in the free form text.

CHAPTER 12

Helping Existing Methodologies

It is not easy to compare different methodologies as each methodology is evolved by its inventors for specific problems and context in mind, which makes the methodology most relevant in that context. As detailed in the earlier chapters, PKM is based on age old concepts of knowledge management and It is a refreshingly simple and logical approach to a complex problem. The list of most of the well-known methodologies is discussed in chapter 2.

Table 12.1 lists these methodologies again with the context in which they are relevant. The table also explains how the PKM concepts, can be used to assist these methodologies.

Table 12.1 | Existing project delivery methodologies and how PKM assists

Methodology	Usage scenario	Assisted by PKM
Waterfall	It is used in projects where requirements are stable and easily known or derivable.	The biggest issue in Waterfall methodology is difficulty in keeping the documents updated with the changes during project delivery. PKM has resolved the issue as it has digitised the project knowledge, which is now easier to maintain in real-time. Documents, when needed, can be extracted from PKM. The other issue with the Waterfall methodology is that the software is available to test only at the later stages of the project delivery, making defect resolution costly and time consuming. The Extended Project Knowledge Model, with its robust quality assurance and quality control mechanism, helps early detection of errors and defects.

Contd.

Methodology	Usage scenario	Assisted by PKM
		Digitised project knowledge also helps in right sizing a project so that the software can be delivered in time and, if necessary, in increments.
Agile	It is used in projects where requirements are subject to change frequently; small sized projects with stringent deadlines to deliver; and complex projects where the customer has difficulty in defining requirements.	PKM fills a major gap in Agile by providing a robust mechanism to manage project knowledge. The current Agile projects try to manage knowledge via high level documents, face-to-face interaction, wiki style knowledge repository and frequent deliveries. PKM also allows Agile to be used in the DevOps environment more effectively as the model can easily be maintained by the service management team until the product is decommissioned.
Prototyping	Prototype model is used when the desired system needs to have a lot of interaction with the end users. Prototyping is often used to help the business users visualise a solution. This methodology is often used where no existing system or process exists. Prototyping may also be used for proof of cost of production or technical viability.	PKM provides a digitised prototype specification framework that includes solution design building blocks, helping in completeness of the specifications.
Spiral	It is used in research oriented projects where requirements are complex and significant changes are expected. It is suitable for medium to high risk projects where users are not sure about their needs and where cost and risk evaluation is important.	Project knowledge digitisation can replace document production and maintenance, thus providing better maintainability. Requirements are better managed in PKM. Digitisation also helps in risk analysis and remedial actions.

Contd.

Methodology	Usage scenario	Assisted by PKM
Rapid Application Development	RAD should be used when there is a need to create a system that can be modularised in 2–3 months of time. There should be high availability of team with modelling skills.	Digitised project knowledge of PKM can become a single repository of knowledge, driving various teams in RAD, doing various iterations. Digitised project knowledge also assists different modelling used in RAD.
Extreme Programming	It can be used in the environment where requirements change dynamically. Extreme Programming is also used when the project risk is high.	PKM creates an asset that helps the delivery team as well as the service management team in the future. The model assists in project knowledge management, which is a weak point of Extreme Programming. Due to digitisation of project knowledge, tracing it with code becomes easy and helps in quality assurance.
V-Model	It is used for small and medium sized projects where requirements are clearly defined and fixed. High confidence of the customer is required to choose V-model approach. Since no prototypes are produced, there is a risk involved in meeting customer expectations.	PKM takes the test design considerations of V-model to the next level by producing Project Test Cases, together in a single format. Test cases across different test phases can be rationalised following the Project Test Case concept of PKM, resulting in significant savings due to increased quality with reduced effort. Solution design knowledge is core to creating test cases at all the levels (unit test to UAT) as it provides end-to-end knowledge about the project at the lowest level of detail. Traceability ensures coverage of the test cases.
Scrum	Scrum methodology should be used where frequent interaction with the customer is required and the requirements cannot be defined completely at the beginning of the project.	Digitisation of project knowledge complements Scrum with something it is lacking. Currently, in Agile methodologies, there is no real alternative of knowledge other than the source code. This makes life difficult for the service management team and the test team. On capturing knowledge, that the devil is in details, is true. High level documents of Agile will not help in practice if the detailed level knowledge is not captured and maintained. PKM digitises project knowledge, which is the key to delivery as well as service management.

Contd.

Helping Existing Methodologies

Methodology	Usage scenario	Assisted by PKM
Dynamic System Development method	DSDM is suitable for fixed time and fixed budget projects where features can be prioritised.	Four knowledge compartments with elaborate traceability mechanism and selection of the project data points for a particular project, assists in the 80-20 rule, which is also the main philosophy of the DSDM methodology. PKM provides for easy impact analysis for any change that can help DSDM significantly. The elaborate quality assurance framework of PKM should also assist DSDM.
Rational Unified Process	RUP is suitable for large projects where requirements are not clear in the beginning and need to be evolved. A strong discipline is required to follow iterations within phases.	The exhaustive traceability mechanism of PKM which consists of 171 relationships, manages the core proposition (evolution of knowledge) of this methodology better, for example, requirements starting at initiation and getting matured right up to the transition phase. Also, digitisation of the project knowledge enables better management of work products that mainly consist of documents, one of the main features of RUP.
Lean software development	Lean software development methodology is broad in its concept and is suitable for most of the projects, whether large or small.	PKM supports the key principles of Lean software development as follows: 1. Eliminate waste: Via 327 negative relationships and manual review data points, PKM tries to eliminate waste right at the time of its production. 2. Amplify learning: PKM believes in incremental knowledge building and care is taken to reuse information so that redundant information is not added, resulting in reducing the potential of inconsistency hindering effective learning. Also, a single repository of the entire project knowledge in the form of PKM is a big enabler. 3. Decide as late as possible: The evolutionary development of project knowledge reduces this need to some extent. 4. Deliver as fast as possible: Reducing waste via negative relationships review, reusing solution design for creating test cases, reusing enterprise knowledge and a single repository of knowledge base are some of the enablers in PKM to deliver as fast as possible.

Contd.

Methodology	Usage scenario	Assisted by PKM
		5. Empower the team: A single repository of project knowledge in the form of PKM, which is integrated and consistent, is a big enabler for empowering the team, particularly the development team. 6. Build quality in: An elaborate 327 negative relationships and manual review data points, supplemented by test case creation by reusing solution design, brings in quality to the project delivery. Verifying test cases with the build inventory improves the quality of the build. Easy access to the entire project knowledge further adds to its quality. 7. See the whole: A single repository of the project knowledge helps in seeing the whole picture. PKM also provides different viewpoints to see the project knowledge from different perspective.
Test-Driven Development	TDD is suitable for small to medium sized projects. It works well with Java based projects and where continuous integration is required.	PKM provides a robust framework for producing test cases, not only from the developer's point of view but covering the entire scope of the project, including system test, system integration test and UAT. PKM can also predict the coverage of the test cases quantitatively.
Behaviour-Driven Development	BDD fits well where the project complexity is more.	Let us understand how PKM can assist BDD by listing its three core principles: 1. Business and technology should refer to the same system in the same way. The single source of the project knowledge of PKM enables this. 2. Any system should have an identified, verifiable business value. PKM enables this via exhaustive traceability. For example, if none of the requirements is related to a system, the system is not relevant for the project. 3. Upfront analysis, design and planning, all have a diminishing return. This is not so if the planning, execution and knowledge related activities are understood and integrated appropriately. PKM makes this happen.

Contd.

Helping Existing Methodologies

Methodology	Usage scenario	Assisted by PKM
Feature-Driven Development	FDD is intended to be used by large teams working on a project, using object oriented technology. FDD is good for organisations which are transitioning from a phase based approach to an iterative approach, but are not comfortable getting rid of all the tasks and role assignments.	In a typical PKM, 516 (189 + 327) data points of project knowledge and quality assurance ensure the progress is reported much more accurately than in a traditional model. Also, 171 relationships of traceability help in scoping features and their relationships with requirements.
Model-Driven Engineering	MDE is used where there is a need to model a complex system.	Enterprise knowledge of PKM will gradually (with maturity of subsequent projects) emerge as domain models which can drive the next project. PKM, which reuses the enterprise knowledge, drives the project and is compliant with the concepts of Model Driven Engineering. In a way, PKM has gone a bit further than domain models and claims that we have a domain agnostic model which can fit into any domain.
Kanban	Kanban is ideal to be used in support and maintenance environment.	Project Knowledge Model can be used to maintain project knowledge in Kanban.
Joint Application Development (JAD)	JAD is most effective in small and clearly focused projects. JAD works well where the system must be conceived and delivered in its entirety and not in increments.	PKM will help the joint workshops with customers which are the main theme of JAD methodology.
Scaled Agile (SAFe)	Suits large organisation with big projects.	Project Knowledge Model can be used to maintain project knowledge in Scaled Agile.

It is evident that PKM has a universal appeal. PKM may influence a majority of the existing methodologies and try to reduce their difference in approach. It can assist in the rationalisation of the existing methodologies into a smaller number of methodologies bridging the gaps between them.

CHAPTER 13

Technology Enablers: Tools and Automation

Tools can assist to implement a project delivery methodology. PKM provides an opportunity to bring in sensible automation of the project delivery. I believe that a tool can be created to implement PKM, customised to the environment suitable to the organisation needs. The tool may be based on project knowledge and its quality assurance. It may be enhanced by adding other standard features such as collaboration, configuration management and work flow. It may also be expanded to support the execution and management related activities. It may then be used to automate most of the project delivery.

This chapter identifies category of tools existing in the market for project delivery. It visualises how PKM can enhance existing tools. It also visualises PKM as a tool at a conceptual level.

13.1 | Automation Potential in Project Delivery

Let us try to understand the automation potential of project delivery from the perspective of KDD. Project delivery consists of activities related to project knowledge and project execution, as well as management of both.

There are tools around project knowledge that are either requirement driven or test driven, but they are generally weak in solution design and application design. There are tools specialised in certain areas of solution design or application design, such as business process modelling tools.

In project execution, there are packages which have reduced the role of coding and rely more on customising the product. SAP is a representative example. In cases where there are no packages, the latest programming languages have made coding easier assisting the development team.

Automation of build (code generation) from detailed specifications is also possible.

Project management tools are also available in the market. They are used for planning, estimating and monitoring purposes, where the data from the project knowledge and execution phases is fed manually most of the time.

Considering project delivery from the knowledge perspective can bring more maturity to the automation efforts. Let us understand it in details as below.

End-to-end project delivery creates five forms of project knowledge:
a. Requirement and high-level scoping information
b. Solution design
c. Application design
d. Test design
e. Developed Application (Code)

Each of these forms of project knowledge is complete in itself and can be mapped to others at the lowest level. One interesting deviation is requirement. Although it is the complete representation of project knowledge, it is at a higher level than the other forms such as solution design. The unit of information in requirement analysis, therefore, will be significantly less when compared to the other project knowledge forms. The unit of information for the other four forms of project knowledge is almost the same.

The relationship between these five forms of project knowledge is as follows:
a. Requirements are transformed into solution design.
b. Solution design, written in business language, is converted into application design, written in technical language.
c. Solution design is reused in test design.
d. Application design is implemented into the working software via coding.

As per KDD, creating these forms of project knowledge and evolving them consistently using review, reuse and testing, is where project delivery automation has a role to play. Figure 13.1 illustrates how the first four forms of project knowledge collaborate and help to create the fifth form of project knowledge: the software (in the form of code) that the project strives to deliver.

The existing project delivery methodologies lack this maturity. KDD, having digitised the four forms of project knowledge, has provided a credible way of creating and maintaining the project knowledge and hence is probably better placed to bring about end-to-end automation in project delivery. It is interesting to note that under the KDD framework, build and test (execution), that contain execution related activities, relate quite well with the five forms of project knowledge. In fact, KDD is a bridge between the software and the other four forms of project knowledge.

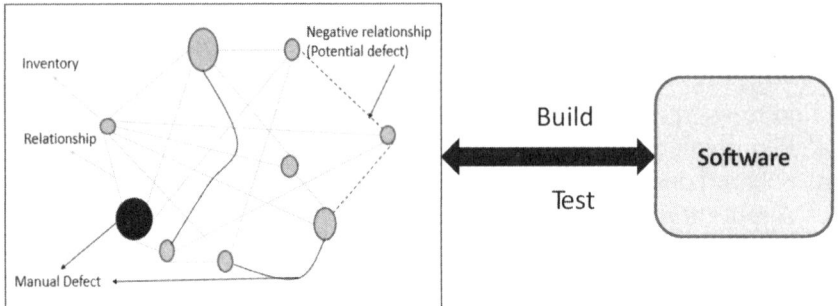

Integrated four forms of project knowledge
Requirements (5 building blocks, 15 linkages)
Solution Design (10 building blocks, 105 linkages)
Application Design (2 building blocks, 35 linkages)
Test Design (1 building blocks, 16 linkages)
Negative relationship (324 potential defect types)
Manual review (3 types of manual review)

Software: the fifth project knowledge form
'Build' implements application design to create the software
'Test' executes test cases and does defect management to ensure the software is created with quality.

Figure 13.1 | Digitised project knowledge for creating the software

Business processes of a domain are inherently stable. KDD has almost standardised the project delivery business processes which, until now, was not understood in the way it should have been understood for effective business process standardisation. In KDD, 56 generic processes manage end-to-end project delivery. Their standardisation in the KDD has paved the way for automating them. Therefore, KDD is now better placed to automate IT industry itself, which until now was outwardly focused in automating the business process of other domains.

One reason the existing project delivery tools are not very effective is that they are mostly led by technologists who lack appropriate domain skills and give more focus to the technology features such as collaboration. This makes the tools less appealing to the users who are members of the project team. KDD has evolved from the domain focus and it is now ready to adopt technology enablement. This is the natural process for a concept to gain maturity.

13.2 | Tools Landscape in Project Delivery Environment and PKM

The project delivery environment is full of tools covering different aspects of delivery. Some of the frequently used category of tools and their relevance to the PKM are discussed in this section.

1. Requirement Management Tool

Project requirements are managed by requirement management tool. The features of requirement management tool include scoping, documenting, analysing, tracing, prioritising and agreeing on project requirements. Requirement management tool may also manage changes in requirements and communicating it to relevant stakeholders. Requirement management is a continuous process which lasts throughout the project.

PKM can implement all the features of a requirement management tool. Additionally, it is closely related to the other areas of project knowledge such as solution design, application design and test design that may not be present in a typical requirement management tool in the way visualised by PKM.

2. Process Modelling Tool

Process modelling tools are diagram oriented software tools which analysts use to create business process diagrams. Simple tools only support diagramming. Professional process modelling tools store each element of the model in a database, allowing for reusability. Many professional tools support simulation or code generation.

Inputs to the process model are primarily contained in the solution design phase of KDD and are stored digitally in PKM. Process step building block of PKM primarily deals with detailed processes contained in a typical process modelling tool.

3. Software Prototyping Tool

Software prototyping is the activity of creating prototypes of the software application, i.e., incomplete versions of the software being developed, primarily via user interfaces.

Inputs to prototyping come from the solution design phase of KDD and are stored digitally in PKM. For example, PKM relates screens to the messages, input data fields, business rules, interfaces, offline transactions, and interfaces. Screen navigation is also covered in PKM as intra-relationship of screen building block.

4. Project Management Tool

The project management tools help plan, organise and manage the project team and track the plan. Depending on the sophistication of the tool, it can manage estimation, planning, scheduling, cost control, budget management, task allocation, collaboration, communication, decision making, risk management, quality management and documentation.

PKM, in its extended form, helps in estimation, quality management, project status tracking and risk management. It will have the ability to extract documents from the available project knowledge. It does not deal with planning, scheduling and resourcing, but provides inputs for all of it, primarily via estimates and the ability to split the project knowledge related work as the project knowledge is digitised.

5. Test Automation Tool

Testing, being a downstream activity in project delivery, has more opportunity for reuse and hence more suited for automation. The various types of testing tools are:
- Test management tool
- Static test tool
- Test specification tool
- Test execution and defect management tool
- Performance and monitoring tool

PKM, in its extended form, contains test specifications, execution and defect logging features and portions of test management capability. It enables test design by reusing inventories of solution design phase building blocks. It makes a provision to create the test cases for the entire project in the same format and execute it when appropriate.

6. Integrated Development Environment Tool

An integrated development environment (IDE) is a software suite that consolidates the basic tools, developers need to write and test software.

Typically, an IDE contains a code editor, a compiler or interpreter and a debugger that the developer accesses through a single graphical user interface.

PKM does not deal with any of the IDE related features as these features relate primarily to the execution related activities. PKM primarily deals with project knowledge related activities.

7. Configuration Management Tool

Configuration management determines the items that make up the software. These include source code and documentation. The configuration management tool manages the configurable items primarily via version control. The tool may have release management, baselining and access control feature.

PKM, in its extended form, can do configuration management of project knowledge, which is traditionally in the form of documents. Digitisation of PKM helps in its effective configuration management. PKM does not deal with code configuration.

8. Enterprise Architecture Tool

An Enterprise Architecture (EA) tool can create models, viewpoints, views and visualisations of the enterprise architecture for different stakeholders of an organisation and generate various reports on it. It mainly consists of three types of applications: the EA Repository application, the EA Modelling application and the EA Reporting application.

KDD is focused on project delivery with elements of enterprise architecture. A total of 22 data points out of the 189 data points of project knowledge have been tagged as enterprise knowledge and are maintained at enterprise level. They are more stable and suitable to be maintained at an enterprise level. The enterprise knowledge is in the same format as the project knowledge and can, therefore, be directly reused by the project. Every project delivery, in turn, enriches the enterprise knowledge and this establishes a close relationship between the project knowledge and the enterprise knowledge.

9. Data Modelling Tool

Data modelling tool helps in documenting a complex software system design as an easily understood diagram, using text and symbols to represent the way data needs to flow. The diagram can be used as a blueprint to construct a new software or for re-engineering a legacy application.

PKM has business data and physical data as its building blocks. Business data and relationships between them can substitute most of what is done in the data modelling tool. PKM links business data to other relevant building blocks such as screens, business rules, processes, communications and so on.

13.3 | PKM: Conceived as ALM Plus Enterprise Knowledge Management

The tools mentioned in the previous section touch upon different areas of project delivery. They may or may not interact with each other, so a manual reconciliation may be needed. This activity becomes further complicated because of the need to produce traditional project documentation where portions of the document will come from the output of different tools, such as portion of FSD comes from the data modelling tool.

We have not discussed so far one of the most popular tools used in project delivery in the previous section because it needs a section by itself. This is the Application Lifecycle Management (ALM) tool. ALM tool provides the widest coverage for project delivery so far and scopes end to end project delivery. PKM, in its extended form, may eventually evolve into a tool that implements KDD. It will go a step further than ALM and can be considered as ALM plus enterprise knowledge management tool.

Table 13.1 lists the typical features of project delivery (generally relevant to an ALM tool) and explains how the Extended Project Knowledge Model (EPKM) may support them.

Table 13.1 | Features of project delivery and the Extended Project Knowledge Model

Project delivery feature	*Assisted by Extended Project Knowledge Model*
Requirement analysis	PKM covers requirement analysis, requirement versioning and its transformation to solution.
Solution design	PKM covers complete solution design via its digitised inventories and relationships of ten building blocks of project knowledge.
Application design	PKM digitises application design and relates it to requirement, solution and test via traceability.
Test design	PKM covers test design completely and for all the stakeholders.

Contd.

Technology Enablers: Tools and Automation

Project delivery feature	Assisted by Extended Project Knowledge Model
Project knowledge reuse	In PKM, via the themes of transformation, conversion and reuse, optimal reuse is facilitated. Reuse is also assisted by digitisation of project knowledge.
Enterprise knowledge reuse	In PKM, direct reusability of the project knowledge is facilitated by 12 building blocks of enterprise knowledge.
Quality management	Negative relationships potential defect and manual review of inventory and linkage is the in-built quality assurance in PKM.
Traceability and impact analysis	In PKM, project knowledge is linked by 171 relations of traceability, enabling impact analysis.
Change management	Change management is assisted by impact analysis capability of PKM.
Risk management	Risk management can either be included in the manual review or be a separate building block of PKM, depending on the situation.
Reporting	A set of 20 project artefacts can be extracted from PKM. Some of them are project documents and some are status reports.
Project scoping	PKM has scoping at three levels: project knowledge, quality assurance and project inventory, as explained earlier.
Test execution and defect management	Not visualised in PKM. The model contains the Project Test Cases. However, test execution and defect managements gels well with the digital approach of PKM and can be easily accommodated under Extended Project Knowledge Model as defined in chapter 7.
Build	PKM has application inventory that drives build. The Extended Project Knowledge Model can track build activities as well.
Task management	Digital project knowledge of PKM assists in task management. There are 56 generic tasks in KDD for end-to-end project delivery.
Workflow	Standard product feature visualised in the Extended Project Knowledge Model.
Integration with other tools	Standard product feature visualised in the Extended Project Knowledge Model.
Support to collaboration	Standard product feature visualised in the Extended Project Knowledge Model.
Support to release management	Standard product feature visualised in the Extended Project Knowledge Model.
Support to multiple projects	Standard product feature visualised in the Extended Project Knowledge Model.
Ease of use	Centralised knowledge repository of PKM helps in ease of use.

After analysing the features in Table 13.1, it becomes clear that critical features not efficiently implemented in a typical ALM tool (such as exhaustive traceability and enterprise knowledge reuse) are visualised in PKM. The Extended Project Knowledge Model can have standard features of project delivery such as workflow management. It may also include execution related activities such as build, test execution and defect management.

The ALM tool can gain from the project knowledge management concepts of PKM. For example, it can expand the coverage to solution and application design as this portion of the knowledge is now digitised in KDD, rather than being available in the document format.

Automation of business processes of the project deliveries is important for practical usage and success of any methodology. The examples are, Microsoft Project Plan (MPP) driving Waterfall methodologies and JIRA driving Agile methodologies. A similar tool that can assist implementing KDD methodology can be developed over time.

13.4 | Benefits of Automation

Automation is driven by data and algorithms. It gains from the repetitive data entry and/or manual execution of the repetitive process. Quality of automation is as good as the quality of the process it is trying to automate. There is a good opportunity for automation in KDD as it has well-defined business processes: in 56 generic activities of KDD, the end-to-end project delivery is covered. In KDD, as the project knowledge is digitised, it can extract the project artefacts out of the digital project knowledge. I believe a saving of 25% of the project delivery effort is possible from the automation visualised in KDD. Figure 13.2 shows indicative benefits per phase.

Indicative shift of effort in different phases are explained as follows:
- Requirement analysis: As more rigour is required in this phase, the effort is slightly more. Initiation activities like project scoping are done in this phase. Base inventory in solution design is also prepared in this phase.
- Solution design: As the base solution inventory comes from the requirement analysis phase, the contents are digitised with 10 building blocks under robust quality assurance. The solution design effort is less in KDD.
- Application design: Due to digitisation of application design via two building blocks, traceability and the robust quality assurance mechanism, the application design effort reduces.

Technology Enablers: Tools and Automation 229

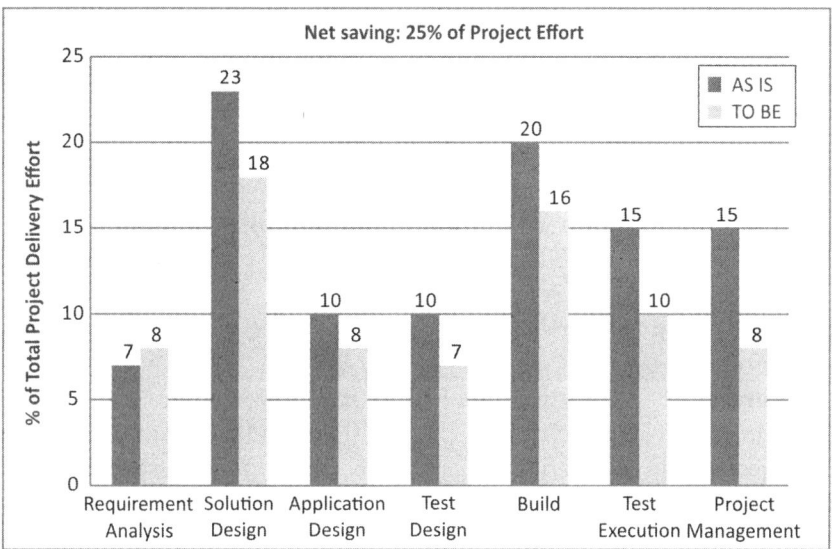

Figure 13.2 | Benefit from KDD automation

- Test design: Primarily due to reuse from solution design, test design effort reduces. KDD also gains from economies of scale as test cases from unit test to UAT are created together in one format. Test coverage with requirement, solution design and test design, or lack of it, can be extracted from PKM.
- Build: Build will take less effort due to better quality of application design, which is digitised and is interlinked with requirement, solution design and test design inventories.
- Test execution: Test execution effort reduces as the defects raised will be less due to better static testing.
- Project management: Project management effort reduces primarily due to digitisation of the project knowledge, enabling generation of key status reports by PKM. In the Extended Project Knowledge Model, even execution related activities are digitised, assisting project management further.

The common factors responsible for 25% decrease in effort are:

- Savings in impact analysis that needs to be done for every change in requirement during the project delivery.
- Savings in review efforts due to negative relationships review extracted from PKM.

- Digitisation of manual review so that review needs to be done only for inventory and relationships of the building blocks. The review log raised can be attached to one or more of inventory or relationship. If members of the project has any difficulty in understanding the inventory or relationship, they should check for an existing review log before raising a new log.
- Due to exhaustive traceability, quality is in-built from the requirement phase itself. This reduces defects in the later phases. This results in savings due to less rework.
- Reuse from enterprise knowledge base also reduces project delivery effort.

Figure 13.3 is a visualisation of PKM. It lists the constituents of PKM in the inner circle (as defined in chapter 4) and in the outer boxes, it lists 20 project artefacts as defined in chapter 6. The 20 project artefacts can be extracted from the knowledge available in the model. The numbers used here are only illustrative.

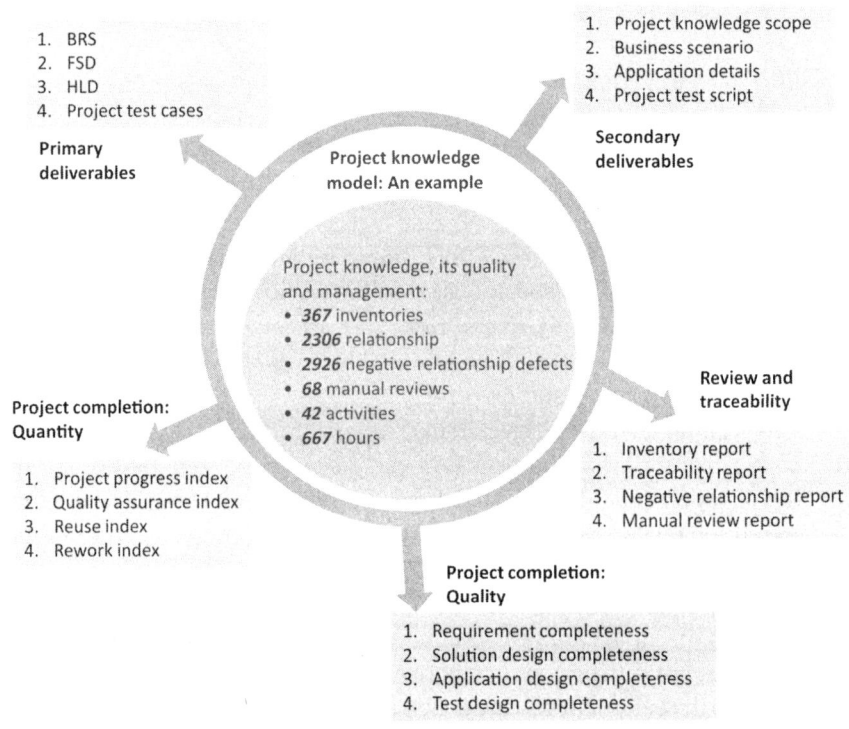

Figure 13.3 | Visualisation of the Project Knowledge Model

The data shown in Figure 13.3 is explained as follows:
- In the middle of the figure we have the number of inventories and their relationships with the selected building blocks, negative relationship and manual reviews of these inventories and relationships. It also has number of activities covering these and the total effort captured to complete these activities. With these six items, the project knowledge is completely digitised via PKM. The entire project team is collectively responsible for maintaining the project knowledge and its quality so that it remains the single version of truth from the start to the end of project delivery. It can then be easily handed over to the service management team to assist in its maintenance.
- The project started with SMEs deciding which of the 189 data points of project knowledge are relevant to the project. A total of 90 data points were chosen to be maintained as a part of this project, keeping in mind the nature of the project and the sanctioned project budget. The given numbers only represent data against 90 data points that are relevant to the project.

The following provides summary of the 20 project artefacts extracted from PKM:
- The complete project knowledge, as represented by the model, consists of 367 inventories and 2,306 relationships between these inventories. These inventories and relationships are quality assured by 2,926 negative relationships potential defects introduced by errors or gaps as shown in the relationships and 68 manual review comments on every aspect of inventory and relationships, as a final check on the quality of project knowledge. This is controlled and managed by 42 project activities in draft, review and rework mode that have taken 667 hours, in total, to complete.
- Out of these inventories and building blocks, eight project documents are extracted from PKM. Relevant documents are extracted at each quality gate, thereby giving it the capability of version control.
- There are four extracts to report on the progress of knowledge related phases which result in:
  - A total of 95% of requirements are linked to other inventories of the remaining four building blocks of the project knowledge in the requirement analysis phase.
  - A total of 63% of requirements are linked to solution design inventories.
  - The entire 100% of the data/logic of application design are linked to one or the other test cases.

- A total of 13% requirements are covered by one or the other test cases.
- There are also four extracts to report on the quality aspects of the project delivery.
  - A total of 667 hours of project effort have been spent and 80% of the project is complete. To complete the project, it needs additional 230 hours.
  - The status of negative relationships and manual reviews are detailed in one of the reports.
  - A total of 5% of the inventories of solution design have been reused from requirement transformation exercise. Just 1% of the inventories of project knowledge are reused from the enterprise knowledge base.
  - A total of 25% of the effort went towards rework.

CHAPTER 14

Suits Factory Model: Needs Cultural Change

KDD can drive the digitisation of project knowledge that may lead to standardising the processes of the project delivery. This may take the IT industry away from being knowledge-based and nearer to being a process-based industry. The factory model is suited to process-based industries and we can now say that KDD may enable IT industry to follow the factory model. However, changing from the current knowledge-based approach to factory approach is not simple. It needs greater appreciation of the digitisation of the project knowledge and a change in mindset to inspire the project team to work in the factory model. This chapter discusses these two topics in detail: enablement of the factory model for IT industry and the cultural change required to make it happen.

14.1 | Bringing IT Project Delivery Closer to Process-Based Industry

Traditional project knowledge is contained in the following set of project documents:
  a. Business Requirement Specification (BRS)
  b. Functional Specification Document (FSD)
  c. High Level Design Document (HLD)
  d. Test Cases

KDD has digitised the project knowledge from these four documents to 189 data points. These data points are integrated with each other and provide a framework to manage the project knowledge via PKM. This will revolutionise the treatment of project knowledge and, in fact, commoditise it. This has brought software development closer to being a process-based industry from being a knowledge-based industry.

Let us understand the document production regime of project knowledge by an example. As a business analyst, I have to produce the BRS document. When I start the day in office, I will have limited idea on how long it will take; I only have an indicative estimate to refer to. With my skills, experience and networking with my colleagues I will try to complete the BRS within the given time. If I am highly skilled and experienced, I can complete the work in half the time allocated and if I am a novice business analyst, it might even take more than twice the effort and the quality of work may not be fit-for-purpose. This is a typical situation while working in a knowledge-based industry.

Let us now understand what typically happens in a factory. At the start of the day, the worker in the factory will get a target of specific output for the day. The worker will have a clear idea of the work involved, which can be quantified. This quantification brings transparency in evaluating the progress of work during the day and its completion at the end of the day. During the day, the worker will or can keep a track of how much work is accomplished and how much is left to be completed. At the end of the day he or she will clearly know whether the tasks assigned are complete or not and probably the reason for not completing the work, if applicable.

KDD tries to simulate the factory model for the knowledge-intensive work in the project delivery. Let us revisit the business analyst work, but this time apply the KDD approach. Instead of producing the BRS document, the business analyst has to populate 20 integrated data points of project knowledge that are relevant in the requirement analysis phase. Breaking the business analyst's work into manageable and measurable smaller chunks will allow for accurate sizing, planning and tracking against the plan. The business analyst's work is now better quantifiable when compared to document production.

This example helps to understand how KDD brings project delivery closer to being a process-based industry. The logical units of work are split into 189 measurable data points, as opposed to the four project documents. The project knowledge capture and maintenance has been standardised to an extent that reduces the dependency on the SME. Mandatory attributes of the building block force the worker to create the project knowledge that is fit-for-purpose. It is easy to miss an important information in the document regime, knowingly or unknowingly. Transparency increases significantly following the KDD approach, helping to bring the IT industry closer to the factory model.

It is important to clarify that splitting 4 documents into 189 data points will simplify things rather than complicate them. The reasons are:
1. The 189 data points are well integrated into PKM of KDD. This helps the project team to find any inconsistency easily (such as a test case not related to any requirement).
2. Data points are the lowest logical unit of the project knowledge that can easily be populated by the project teams. There is a structured format to populate the data points, thus bringing quantification, visibility and transparency of the work to be accomplished.
3. Depending on the nature and budget of the project, the number of data points can be customised. If the project is batch intensive, the number of data points required may be 80, for example. If the project is mission critical and cannot afford any lapse on quality, the same project may need to have 120 data points (for example) of project knowledge. This level of transparency and flexibility is not present in the document production regime.

14.2 | Implementing the Factory Model

Figure 14.1 represents how steel is produced in a factory environment.

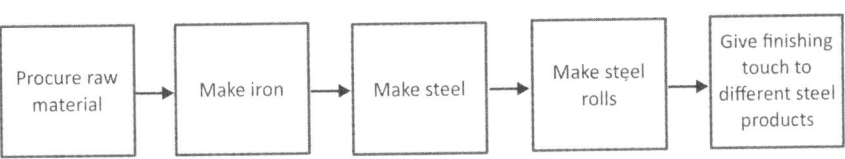

Figure 14.1 | Typical steel manufacturing process

The main characteristics of the factory model are:
1. Suited for mass production.
2. Standard processes; the workers know exactly what is expected of them.
3. Repeatable processes and therefore prone to automation/optimising the efficiency if it is executed manually.
4. Processes can be split to the lowest level, with well-defined logical units of work that can be planned and tracked quantitatively.
5. The effort taken to complete a typical process should not be too long.
6. Executing the processes does not need too much of innovation.
7. The effort taken for executing a process should be almost the same when executed by different workers.

8. Quality of output is ensured via quality assurance and quality control.
9. Process execution results in specific output.

For implementing the factory model in IT project delivery, an important consideration has been the quantification of progress on knowledge related activities. Traditionally, creating project documents are the lowest logical unit of work in project knowledge. Producing a document against a given estimate, without having much variation in quality and maintaining transparency throughout the process of document creation is a challenge. In the factory model progress is transparent.

KDD takes the lowest logical unit of work from documents to data points of project knowledge. Examples of data points are business rules and test cases, whose creation can be much better planned and tracked as compared to documents.

By scoping project knowledge into 189 data points, KDD has split the lowest logical unit of work to such an extent that it is easy to track its progress on a daily basis. This is similar to tracking of project execution activities. This has helped the end-to-end project delivery activities to be of a homogeneous nature and of a similar effort. This enables working in a factory model. It is easy to appreciate that PKM assists in all the nine points stated, about the main characteristics of the factory model.

Figure 14.2 illustrates how KDD visualises the project delivery in the factory model.

Through the following points, we can visualise how the factory model operates for IT project delivery using KDD.

1. Input of the factory is customer supplied requirements, the output is software as per the specified requirements (or amended requirements as the case may be). Four sequential and parallel units drive the core of the project delivery as specified in Figure 14.2 via a total of 189 data points, where information needs to be captured by different roles of the project team at different points of time. Information entry for these data points are quality assured by 327 data points of quality assurance. The 22 data points of the enterprise knowledge assist requirements and solution design. Software creation (Build) is driven by 37 data points of application design that are quality controlled by 17 data points of test design. A total of 56 generic activities drive the end-to-end project delivery. This provides the framework to execute a project in the KDD manner.

2. Knowledge is intangible, implementing this knowledge into the software is tangible. Cataloguing the knowledge, as prescribed by

KDD, assists in this transformation and takes the project delivery closer to the factory model.

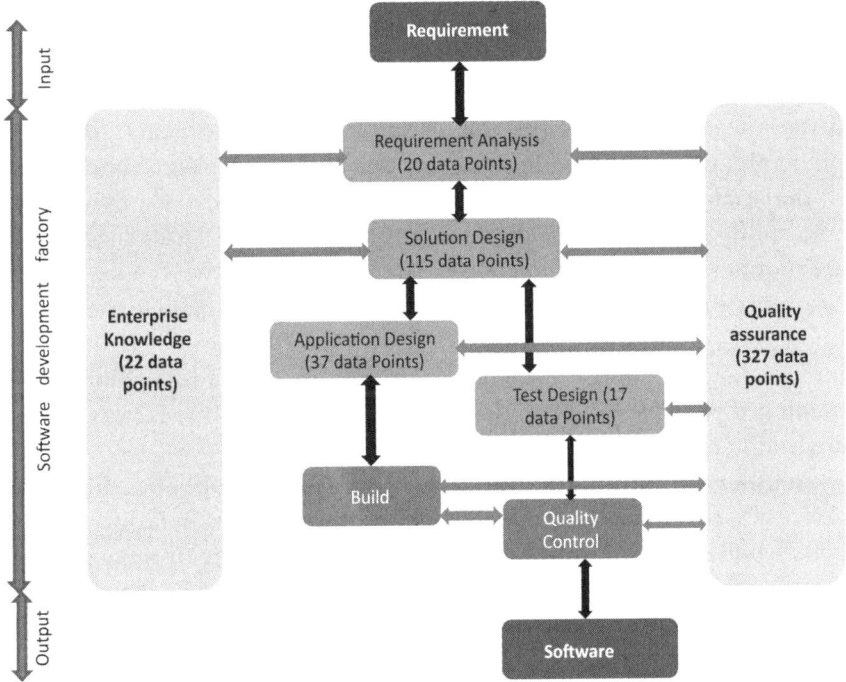

Figure 14.2 | Project delivery factory model

3. Knowledge related processes are contained in four units (requirement analysis, solution design, application design and test design) and each unit has a defined set of activities simulating a factory model.
4. Through 324 data points of negative relationship and 3 data points of manual review, quality of the work in the four units is assured. This simulates quality assurance in the factory model.
5. Traceability provides a transparent framework to maintain the project knowledge in real-time through the 171 relationships.
6. Project knowledge drives execution related activities. Application design drives build to produce draft software. Following successful quality control (test case execution), the software is complete and deemed fit to go into the production system.

A marked difference between a typical factory model and IT project delivery is that in the factory model, the activities are almost sequential, without too much of a feedback loop between different activities. Quality assurance activities (enabling doing things correctly) are mostly built into the execution activities in the factory model. Figure 14.1, representing the steel manufacturing process, illustrates this. Quality is built into the machines performing a majority of the activities.

In the IT project delivery, there is a provision of feedback loop between different activities and the quality assurance (review) activities are predominantly obvious. A requirement defect, for example, can be detected in the application design phase and the feedback loop, via exhaustive traceability, makes sure it is consistently updated. KDD manages these areas quite well by digitising the project knowledge as well as the quality assurance (negative relationships and manual review linked to the project knowledge). The feedback loop between activities and review of the intermediate outputs produced are all transparent and easily manageable, making it possible for IT project delivery to work in the factory model environment.

Another obvious difference between factory model and IT project delivery is two stages in the way factory model operates. In factory model, before mass production starts, it has design phase where the new product is conceived, designed, prototyped and few specimen produced. For IT project delivery, an analogy can be a methodology based on knowledge digitisation is matured (at the design stage) and then used in the project (mass production). This book is the first attempt to mature that methodology which is KDD.

14.3 | The Need for Cultural Change

Existing methodologies do not focus much on project knowledge. IT is considered as a knowledge-based Industry and it is believed that project knowledge is better left with the experience and skillset of the project team. KDD ushers in a new level of maturity by standardising and digitising the project knowledge bringing it closer to a process-based industry. KDD promotes doing the same thing (gaining project knowledge) in a different (digital) way. Well-defined and objective activities with specific outputs are the characteristics of KDD.

Digitised project knowledge via KDD has brought project delivery closer to the factory model. To make it work, it requires cultural changes as described in the following points:

1. Creation, retrieval and management of the project knowledge in KDD is achieved in a digitised way and not via document production and maintenance. Culturally, we are used to creating and managing project knowledge via documents. There is a tendency to feel that the long paragraphs in the documents are really needed and cannot be digitised. This is not true. Appendix E deals with this in detail. KDD has digitised the project knowledge. There is a need for the project team to realise this and train to exploit the benefits of digitisation.
2. Attitude to traceability requires a change. Many project teams create traceability at the end of the project mainly for compliance purposes. Traceability usually links different sections of different documents (e.g., when requirement needs to be linked to solution) accuracy of which are often questionable and subjective. As it is done ex post facto many times, its relevance and importance are also questionable. KDD drives the project right from the beginning through traceability facilitated by PKM. Traditional traceability relationships are not more than ten when compared to 171 in KDD. There is a need to appreciate the usefulness of traceability in the project delivery in driving the project rather than the current approach of proving the coverage of requirements.
3. Knowledge is not a prerogative of a selected few. KDD implements the age old saying that knowledge grows by spreading. Some of the subject matter experts have a fear of losing importance and they are careful about sharing the knowledge they have gained. This is not in the interest of the organisation. The structured information format in KDD ensures that when the information is added, it is added completely and with quality. Making the project knowledge available to all has reduced the dependency on SMEs. As the knowledge is linked within the model, it helps in analysing the impact for any changes in the project.
4. A perspective change in the build team is needed. KDD enables the build team much more than the other methodologies. Currently, inputs to build team are either HLD or FSD, depending on how the team is structured. KDD changes this environment and exposes the entire team (including build) to the project knowledge right from requirements to solution design, application design and test design in a catalogued and inter-connected way. It helps the build team to build the software closer to specifications and they can detect and correct any oversight in the project knowledge as it is digitised. The

build team is the creator of the software and it should be enabled through access to all the information about the software. KDD assists by presenting the entire project knowledge in a single repository. As the requirements, solution and test design are in business language, it should not be difficult for the build team to understand them. The build team needs to support this new way of working so that KDD becomes an enabler for them to enhance their performance.

CHAPTER 15

Global Relevance of KDD: GKMF Assisting Skill Development

KDD, as an IT project delivery methodology, is still in its infancy and this book is the first attempt to bring the concept to the academia and industry. As it relates to knowledge, the concepts of KDD are also relevant to areas other than IT project delivery.

In chapter 1, we have seen how knowledge is split into four levels that can be captured in eight building blocks. In chapter 4, we have seen how these eight building blocks, when customised to IT project delivery, become 18 building blocks. In this chapter we will reverse engineer 18 building blocks and understand how they comply with the Generic Knowledge Management Framework (GKMF) introduced in chapter 1. We will go through examples of KDD in action in areas other than software development.

We will focus on the domain knowledge portion of GKMF. Through examples, we will demonstrate that GKMF has all the capability to grow into a skill development framework.

15.1 | KDD and Generic Knowledge Management Framework

Let's recollect the Generic Knowledge Management Framework that we have introduced in chapter 1. Figure 15.1 is taken from chapter 1.

The four levels of knowledge covering end-to-end knowledge are:
- Abstract knowledge: This is knowledge at the highest level of abstraction. It is manifested in universal truth and statement of fact at the highest level.
- Domain knowledge: It contains knowledge of the domains such as manufacturing, insurance and banking.
- Enterprise knowledge: This is the instantiation of domain knowledge for an organisation such as a banking company.

- Project knowledge: It keeps the enterprise knowledge continuously updated.

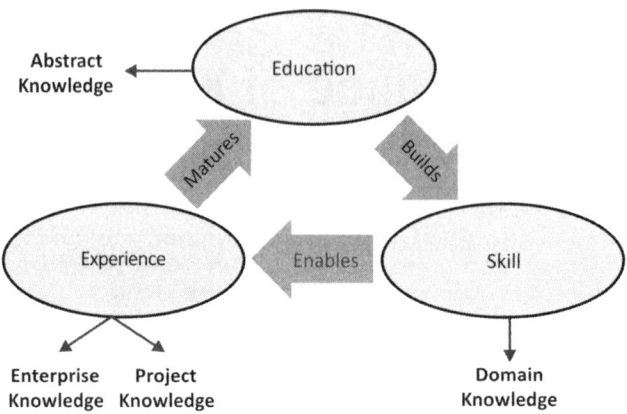

Figure 15.1 | Generic Knowledge Management Framework

The level of knowledge is contextual and something at abstract knowledge level in one context can be at project knowledge level in another context.

The respective stakeholders at these levels of knowledge are:
- Project knowledge: The project team of the organisation
- Enterprise knowledge: The IT and business teams of the organisation
- Domain knowledge: College students, for skill development relevant to an organisation
- Abstract knowledge: Students, for their basic education

The building blocks required to capture knowledge at various levels, as per GKMF are given in Figure 15.2.

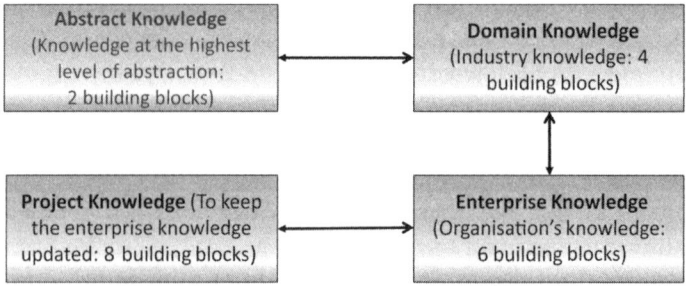

Figure 15.2 | Knowledge maturity: domain agnostic

When we apply this concept to software development, the number of building blocks changes to 18 for project knowledge as shown in Figure 15.3.

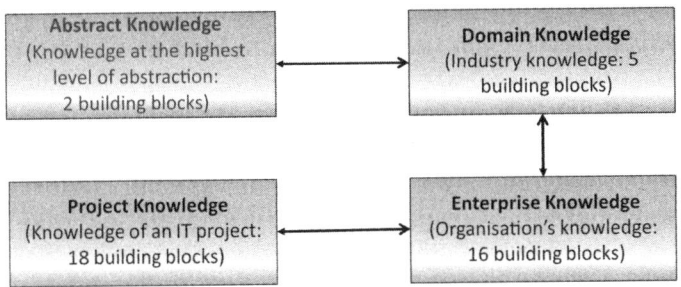

Figure 15.3 | Knowledge maturity in IT industry

Table 15.1 maps the building blocks of GKMF as well as its customisation for software development as per PKM.

Table 15.1 | Building blocks of GKMF and PKM

Levels of knowledge	Building blocks as per Generic Knowledge Management Framework	Building blocks for software development as per PKM
Abstract knowledge	Scenario Business Rule	Scenario Business Rule
Domain knowledge	Product Process	Product Process Process step
Enterprise knowledge	Usage Enabler	Non-functional attributes Business data Communication Report Screen Message Offline transaction Application Interface Data Logic
Project knowledge	Requirement Test	Requirement Project test case

Appendix B describes how the 18 building blocks of project knowledge in software development have evolved from abstract knowledge to project knowledge following GKMF.

Let us understand the four levels of knowledge as per GKMF through two examples, one from IT industry and the other from non-IT industry.

Example 1: Password Management in IT Industry

Abstract Knowledge: The password should be strong enough so that it cannot be easily cracked.

Domain Knowledge: For specialised, high-cost insurance products, a second level password is required.

Enterprise Knowledge: The company has decided that all its passwords must have eight characters consisting of a combination of alphabets, numeric and special characters, and should lock after three unsuccessful attempts.

Project Knowledge: There is a requirement to send an email to the user immediately after he or she changes the password.

Example 2: Managing Customer Details in the Insurance Domain

Abstract Knowledge: Customer details can be of two types, personal details such as the date of birth and contact details such as the mobile number.

Domain Knowledge: For customers of an insurance company, personal habits such as smoking and having hazardous hobbies help in premium calculation.

Enterprise Knowledge: Usage of channels in a specific organisation for change in personal details may be Call centre: 50%, Sending a letter: 25%, Doing it online: 25%.

Project Knowledge: The company may initiate a project tasked with increasing the online channel usage for change in personal details from 25% to at least 75% to reduce expenditure and remain competitive.

15.2 | Examples of Generic Knowledge Management Framework

GKMF, as described in the previous section, has the potential to change the way of storing and reusing knowledge in different domains. The examples in this section try to illustrate this. Generally, one inventory per building block is listed in the examples. Exhaustive treatment of the topic is not given here, but by sprinkling inventories, an attempt is made to give an idea of how the complete work may look like. The examples also show how the information of the same building block evolves gradually when we move from abstract knowledge to project knowledge.

15.2.1 | Password Management in IT Industry

Table 15.2 shows all the four levels of knowledge used in the IT domain for password management.

Table 15.2 | Password management via eight building blocks

Knowledge Level	Building Block	Inventory Id	Inventory description
Abstract: Password management	Rule	Rle_1-01	The password should be strong enough so that it cannot be easily cracked.
	Scenario	Scn_1-01	There are two scenarios for password validation: right password and wrong password.
Domain: Password management in Insurance domain	Rule	Rle_2-01	The strong password should contain a mixture of alphabets, numbers and special characters.
	Scenario	Scn_2-01	Password is created in the following processes: • Registration • Change password • Reset password
	Product	Prd_2-01	For specialised insurance products, a second level password is required.
	Process	Prc_2-01	Password management is used in the 'login' process.

Contd.

Knowledge Level	Building Block	Inventory Id	Inventory description
Enterprise: Password management in an insurance company	Rule	Rle_3-01	It must have 8 characters and should lock after 3 unsuccessful attempts. It must be changed after 6 months.
	Scenario	Scn_3-01	Scenarios for password change: • Successful in first attempt • Successful in 2nd attempt • Successful in 3rd attempt • Locked at 4th attempt
	Product	Prd_3-01	The specialised insurance products requiring second password are: • Aircraft insurance • Marine insurance
	Process	Prc_3-01	During login, password can be retrieved via: • Typing it via the keyboard • Typing it via virtual keyboard available in the portal
	Usage	Usg_3-01	The same password should allow users to access all the relevant applications of the organisation.
	Enabler	Enb_3-01	A single sign on tool helps in accessing all the relevant applications of the enterprise with one password.
Project: A password management enhancement project in an insurance company	Requirement	Req_4-01	There is a requirement to send an email to the user immediately after he/she changed the password.
	Rule	Rle_4-01	If the system does not have a valid email of the user changing the password, it should give a warning message to add email address using the relevant functionality. It should not, however, stop the user from changing the password.
	Scenario	Scn_4-01	The user has or does not have a valid email address in the system.
	Product	Prd_4-01	Aircraft insurance is chosen for this project.
	Process	Prc_4-01	Typing password via keyboard is chosen as the channel for this project.
	Usage	Usg_4-01	There is a need to report the number of users changing their passwords per month.
	Enabler	Enb_4-01	This requirement is for all the five IT systems currently used in the enterprise.
	Test	Tst_4-01	To test that the changed password confirmation message is sent to the email address of the user.

15.2.2 | Plantation: Agriculture

Table 15.3 illustrates how the plantation domain can make use of the four levels of knowledge to structure its knowledge scientifically.

Table 15.3 | Rice seedbed preparation via eight building blocks

Knowledge Level	Building Block	Inventory Id	Inventory description
Abstract: Plantation	Rule	Rle_1-01	Plantation is a means by which plants keep reproducing themselves.
	Scenario	Scn_1-01	There are natural plantations (e.g., forests) and human-made plantations. Human-made plantations can be for gardening, commercial or agricultural purposes.
Domain: Agriculture	Rule	Rle_2-01	Weather plays an important role in the timing of activities in an agricultural plantation.
	Scenario	Scn_2-01	Plantation can be through seeds or a branch of the plant itself.
	Product	Prd_2-01	Plantation is essential for all the agriculture produce such as rice, wheat, pulse and vegetables.
	Process	Prc_2-01	Steps for plantation are: site selection, type of plantation, planting distance, site preparation and planting.
Enterprise: Preparation of rice seedbed for government agriculture department	Rule	Rle_3-01	Seedbed usually takes around 5–10% of the total farming area of the crop.
	Rule	Rle_3-02	Approximately 50 kg of seed is needed per hectare of land.
	Scenario	Scn_3-01	Seedbed types are wet-bed, dry-bed and modified mat nursery.
	Scenario	Scn_3-02	Factors impacting seedbed types are: sunlight, water, labour, land and agricultural implements.
	Product	Prd_3-01	Seedbed is required for all the varieties of rice, e.g., Long grain, Basmati, Jasmine and Japonica.
	Process	Prc_3-01	Examples of the steps to prepare seedbed are: flash irrigate the seedbed area before ploughing, plough the seedbed area and keep it submerged for a week.
	Usage	Usg_3-01	Researching in this area to improve the process of seedbed preparation.
	Enabler	Enb_3-01	Using implements and tools to ease the seedbed preparations.
	Enabler	Enb_3-02	Preparing a portal to help, spread the knowledge of seedbed preparation.

Contd.

Project: Enabling online chat feature for instant query resolution in the portal	Require-ment	Req_4-01	Online chat facility should be provided to both registered and unregistered users visiting the portal.
	Rule	Rle_4-01	Online chat facility should be available from 8.00 am to 11.00 pm and this should be highlighted and displayed on the portal.
	Scenario	Scn_4-01	It should be available to both unregistered user and registered user.
	Product	Prd_4-01	Before someone asks a question, there should be a look-up to select the product (e.g., variety of rice such as Basmati) the question is about.
	Process	Prc_4-01	When the product is known, there should be a look-up for the related process (e.g., plantation, servicing, harvesting) for the selected product.
	Usage	Usg_4-01	A weekly report is needed to report on products and processes of the queries, split by registered and unregistered users.
	Enabler	Enb_4-01	Technology for the chat feature should be the same as that of the portal.
	Test	Tst_4-01	Test via an unregistered and a registered user that the online chat feature works as expected during its available and non-available hours.

It becomes clear from these examples that there may be multiple logical units of the knowledge at lower levels for a single unit of knowledge at higher level, thus providing a mechanism for collecting fit-for-purpose knowledge for an enterprise and its project work. The format used in the examples may be adapted by organisations as a natural way of storing and maintaining knowledge and it is not restricted to the IT industry.

15.3 | Generic Knowledge Management Framework: Used in Skill Development

The examples of GKMF in the previous section deal with all four levels of knowledge. In fact, there can be yet another, wider, application of GKMF in skill development, using the domain knowledge concept of the framework.

Contextualising business rules and scenario with products and processes, which is domain knowledge, provides an excellent mechanism which promises to store the knowledge existing in the text books of related skills. Whereas books will always be useful to explain and expand on the concepts, the fit-for-purpose knowledge (without noise and whistles) can be captured via the domain knowledge format of GKMF. If adopted universally, it can mature scientifically, providing an opportunity to all to gain necessary skills before joining relevant organisations.

Through the examples in this section, selected from diverse areas, an attempt is made to visualise how skill development can be enabled via domain knowledge. Again, the coverage may not be exhaustive, but should be enough to make the reader curious about this proposition.

15.3.1 | Portal Development

Through a typical portal functionality, the power of domain knowledge is demonstrated via the combination of business rule and scenario. The process is 'customer alteration', where the user can update the personal and contact details. This process may be customised to different products of different domains. The current example is related to insurance domain and therefore the related products may be term insurance for example. This was also a part of the case study in chapter 1. Tables 15.4 and 15.5 represent the scenario and business rules for the customer alteration functionality. For the sake of simplicity, the relationships between the two are not listed.

Table 15.4 | Business scenario for 'customer alteration' process

Scenario No.	Scenario Name	Scenario Value
Scn_01	Channel	
		Portal
		Email
		Phone
		Fax
Scn_02	Requester for alteration	
		User
		Authorised representative
Scn_03	Documentary evidence required	
		Yes
		No

Contd.

Scenario No.	Scenario Name	Scenario Value
Scn_04	Customer communication (outbound)	
		Request initiated
		Documentary evidence required
		Request completed
Scn_05	Personal details	
		Name
		Date of Birth
		Marital Status
		Beneficiary
		National ID
		Bank Details
		Gender
Scn_06	Contact details	
		Mobile Number
		Email id
		Address
		Landline
Scn_07	Mode of change	
		Add new details
		Modify existing details
Scn_08	Request actioned by	
		User
		Authorised representative
		Operations (Front End)
		Operations (Back End)
Scn_09	No. of beneficiary	
		One
		More than one
Scn_10	No. of change per request	

Contd.

Scenario No.	Scenario Name	Scenario Value
		One
		More than one
Scn_11	Receipt of documentary evidence	
		Received within 3 weeks
		Received after 3 weeks and within 6 weeks
		Not received within 6 weeks
Scn_12	Type of change request	
		Personal details
		Contact details
Scn_13	Response time in the portal	
		< 2 secs for validation
		< 5 secs for update

Table 15.5 | Business rule for 'customer alteration' process

Rule No.	Rule Name
Rul_01	Customer id and name displayed in the portal should be of the individual who logs in. If an authorised representative logs in, the details shown in the screen header should be theirs and not of the customer who they represent.
Rul_02	Date of birth validations: needs to follow a format.
Rul_03	Date of birth validations: Age must be within a range.
Rul_04	Email check: email should be of a particular format, must have '@' character.
Rul_05	Email check: email must be a valid email.
Rul_06	Names: name must have at least the first name.
Rul_07	Phone number: needs to follow a format.
Rul_08	Mobile number: needs to follow a format.
Rul_09	Customer should be in a status where it is possible to accept the request to change the personal and contact details. For example, the status of customer should not be deceased.
Rul_10	Address: validate details (City/State/Country/Postal Code) where available (e.g., in UK, the postcode validity can be determined by a utility).

Contd.

Rule No.	Rule Name
Rul_11	Address: there must be at least two address lines completed by the user for the address to be accepted.
Rul_12	Following is the relationship between update requested and the document needed: 1. Change in Forename / Surname: Passport 2. Change in Date of Birth: Passport, Birth Certificate 3. Change in Marital Status: Passport, Marriage Certificate 4. Change of Gender: Passport
Rul_13	National ID: needs to follow a format.
Rul_14	There can be only one active authorised representative for one customer at any point in time.
Rul_15	Documents must be received within 3 weeks of raising the alteration request for which the evidence is needed. At this point in time another email should go to the customer requesting to send the document in the next 3 weeks. If the document does not come within 6 weeks, the request is rejected and closed.

After going through Table 15.5, it is not difficult to visualise that the domain knowledge in the table is fit-for-purpose for gaining necessary skills for customer alteration process in insurance domain.

15.3.2 | Insurance Industry

Let us take a specific process related to insurance, 'retirement due to incapacity'. As the name suggests, it is related to pension products.

A policyholder of a pension product can retire at the normal retirement age, which differs in different countries. However, if the person is incapacitated, he or she can take an early retirement. This process of taking early retirement is called 'retirement due to incapacity' from the insurance perspective. This process is detailed in Tables 15.6 and 15.7 via a set of business scenario and rules.

Table 15.6 | Business scenario for 'retirement due to incapacity' process

Scenario No.	Scenario Name	Scenario Value
Scn_01	Channel	
		Online claim form
		IVR
		Unstructured mail

Contd.

Scenario No.	Scenario Name	Scenario Value
Scn_02	Requester	
		Policyholder
		Authorised representative
		Friends and family members
Scn_03	Claim validation	
		Validation of requester
		Validation of medical condition and medical practitioner
		Validation of policy (e.g., status)
Scn_04	Retirement option chosen	
		Open Market Option (OMO)
		Annuity of existing provider
Scn_05	Tax free cash taken	
		Yes: Full
		Yes: partial
		No
Scn_06	Mode of payment	
		Electronic
		Cheque
Scn_07	Payment details available	
		Yes
		No
Scn_08	Payment details received in time	
		Yes
		No
Scn_09	Payment details validated	
		Yes
		No
Scn_10	Inbound communication	
		Notification from Policyholder for incapacity claim
		Filled claim form
		Doctor's certificate
		Notification for OMO

Contd.

Scenario No.	Scenario Name	Scenario Value
Scn_11	Outbound communication	
		Claim form
		Notification of refusal of claim from Company
		Notification of acceptance of claim
		Confirmation of OMO processed
		Confirmation of claim processed (non OMO route)

Note: Open market option (OMO) is an option provided to the pension policyholders to opt for annuity from a provider that may be different to the provider of the pension policy.

Table 15.7 | Business rule for 'retirement due to incapacity' process

Rule No.	Rule Name
Rul_01	Age of the policyholder should not be greater than the retirement age captured for the policy.
Rul_02	Policy fund value should be greater than a defined minimum.
Rul_03	Policy must have been running at least a certain number of years before the claim is made.
Rul_04	Completed claim form must be received by the insurance company within a certain number of days from when the claim notification is first received.
Rul_05	Other requester can be 'friend/family of member whose details are not available with the company', but other requester can only request and not continue in the process, which can only be done by Policyholder/Representative of policyholder.
Rul_06	Bank details consist of bank sort code, account name and account number.

Note: Open market option (OMO) is an option provided to the pension policyholders to opt for annuity from a provider that may be different to the provider of the pension policy.

Again, it is easy to visualise that this domain knowledge builds sufficient skill in 'retirement due to incapacity' process for the pension products in insurance domain.

15.3.3 | Agriculture Industry

Let us see how the set of scenario and business rules helps in capturing necessary skills of a process named 'preparation of seedbed' for the product rice in the agriculture domain.

As we know, the crop of rice is prepared in two stages. First, the seedbed for rice is prepared, which is then transplanted to grow to become a full-grown crop of rice, ready for harvesting. Through Tables 15.8 and 15.9, this process of 'preparation of seedbed' is understood via a set of business rules and scenario.

Table 15.8 | Business scenario for 'preparation of seedbed' for rice

Scenario No.	Scenario Name	Scenario Value	Remarks
Scn_01	Seedbed types		
		Wet-bed	
		Dry-bed	
		Dapog	
		Modified mat nursery	
Scn_02	Factors impacting seedbed types		
		Sunlight	
		Water	
		Labour	
		Land	
		Agricultural implements	
Scn_03	Seedbed preparation method		
		Manual	
		Mechanised	

Table 15.9 | Business rule for 'preparation of seedbed' for rice

Rule No.	Rule Name
Rul_01	Seedbed usually takes around 5–10% of the total farming area of the crop.
Rul_02	Approximately 50 kg of seed is needed per hectare of land.
Rul_03	The soil must be raised by 5–10 cm for the seedbed.
Rul_04	Transplant the seedlings in 15–21 days.
Rul_05	The soil of a seedbed needs to be loose and smoothed, without large lumps.
Rul_06	The soil structure may be improved by the introduction of organic matter, such as compost or peat.
Rul_07	The nitrate and phosphate levels of the soil can be adjusted with fertiliser. If the soil is deficient in any micro nutrients, these too can be added.

Structured repository of domain knowledge in agriculture can thus be created, building necessary related skills. It can supplement the existing literature and provide to-the-point information, when needed. The set of scenario and business rules can be made easier to understand by including the definition of the terms used (such as 'Dapog' in Table 15.8).

Appendix C re-emphasises the relevance of business rules and scenario by proposing a new method to estimate an IT project.

15.4 | Towards Another Ontology Framework

Ontology deals with representing knowledge in different domains. Ontology is a formal naming and definition of class, attributes and relationships of the entities which really exist in a particular domain.

The four levels of knowledge of GKMF have universal applicability. From the examples in the previous sections, it is obvious that GKMF can be easily used to represent knowledge of different domains and, therefore, it is another domain ontology framework. It complies with the definition of ontology with the mapping as follows:
- Class can be mapped to the building blocks
- Attributes of class can be mapped to attributes of the building blocks
- Relationship can be mapped to relationship between two inventories of the building blocks

The evolution of knowledge in the new GKMF from abstract knowledge to project knowledge from two building blocks to eight building blocks have given it both the capabilities, learning and delivering. Whereas the first three levels of knowledge are used for learning purposes, the fourth one, i.e., the project knowledge, is primarily used for delivering purposes. Implementation of GKMF to IT industry via KDD has clearly demonstrated its delivery capability. In comparison, other domain ontology frameworks are more from the perspective of learning. For example, ontology is matured enough in the medical sciences and used extensively in education for learning purposes. Its use for delivery purpose such as building a new medical equipment may not be so obvious.

CHAPTER 16

Lean KDD: Elimination of Requirement and Test Design?

Further analysis of KDD and GKMF leads to two interesting improvements in the KDD. Test design phase of KDD seems redundant. The other compartment of project knowledge, solution design, is in business language and is of similar size to that of test design. Solution design can, therefore, make test design redundant. Chapter 15 has demonstrated the universal appeal of business rules and scenario in knowledge management, which can be used to specify the requirements. This gives rise to Lean KDD, which is KDD where requirement is replaced by combination of business rule and scenario and test design is accommodated in the solution design. This chapter explains Lean KDD.

16.1 | Revisiting KDD: Elimination of Test Design Phase

As stated in the earlier chapters, requirements are transformed into solution design, which is converted into application design and reused in test design.

Let us analyse these four compartments from the perspective of readability and size, keeping in mind that the four compartments are different representations of the same project knowledge. Table 16.1 tries to visualise the language and volume of this knowledge.

Table 16.1 | Project Knowledge compartments

Project Knowledge compartment	Language	Indicative relative size
Requirement analysis	Business language	One
Solution design	Business language	Ten
Application design	Technical language	Ten
Test design	Business language	Ten

Analysis of Table 16.1 clearly shows one fact. In terms of language and size, solution design and test design look similar. They are both written in business language and have approximately the same size. This makes us ask the question that if these two knowledge compartments are similar (rather duplicate as test design is created by reusing the solution design as per KDD), then why cannot the solution design represent test design as well? We have an opportunity to get rid of the test design phase altogether, making use of solution design for this purpose.

Figure 16.1 represents a typical project delivery using KDD by tagging the redundancy of test design.

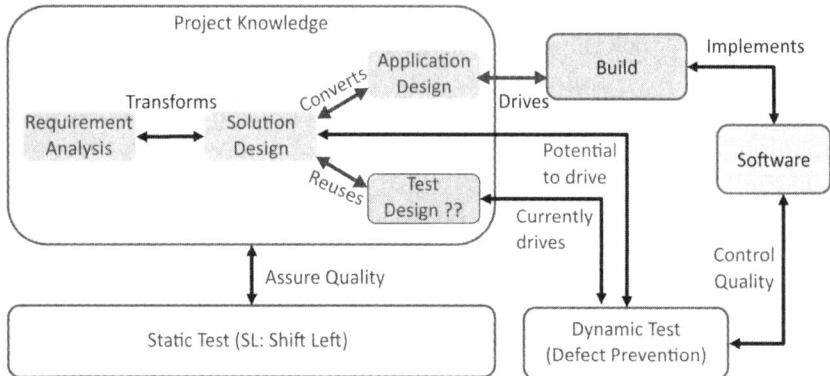

Figure 16.1 | KDD and redundancy of test design

It is interesting to note the different representation of the quality assurance and quality control aspects in KDD. Quality assurance mainly caters to project knowledge via negative relationships review and manual review. They are based on Shift Left concept, which aims to increase the quality of project knowledge on which the software development will be based. Dynamic test represents quality control and its objective is to detect as many defects as possible when the software is ready to test so that, when implemented, the software will run smoothly.

16.2 | Influence of Business Rule and Scenario on Project Delivery

The importance of business rules and scenario is demonstrated in chapter 15. It represents the domain knowledge (when contextualised with processes and products) as per GKMF and has the potential to drive the project delivery. Figure 16.2 illustrates this.

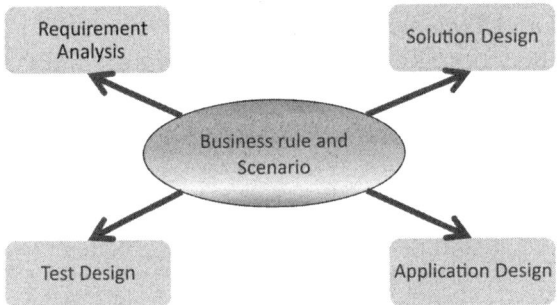

Figure 16.2 | Relevance of business rule and scenario in IT project delivery

The central oval in the figure represents available in-scope domain knowledge as part of enterprise knowledge for the project in the form of business rule and scenario (contextualised by product and process). It can help:
- Requirement analysis phase, by specifying requirements in the form of business rules and scenario.
- Solution design phase, based on expansion of the business rules and scenario.
- Application design phase, by ensuring that the detailed business rules and scenario are considered while designing for build.
- Test design phase is, anyway, driven by business scenario and rules, which become the basis for creating test cases using enabler techniques such as OATS.

16.3 | Lean KDD: without Requirement and Test Design

The previous two sections detailed that the test design can be made redundant by the solution design knowledge compartment, and business rules and scenario may be used to specify requirements. I visualise a situation when the business analyst sits with the customer and specifies requirements in the format of business rules and scenario which get further expanded into solution design and traced in application design. In fact even better, based on the understanding of the project, the business analyst collects the relevant business rules and scenario available in the enterprise knowledge base and matures it further (i.e. by adding new business rules and scenario) to capture requirements for this project. Examples in section 3 of chapter 15 are representative enterprise knowledge in this regard.

Figure 16.3 helps visualising how the end-to-end project delivery can be accomplished under this changed environment. This new way of delivering a project is called 'Lean KDD' as it eliminates the redundant activities.

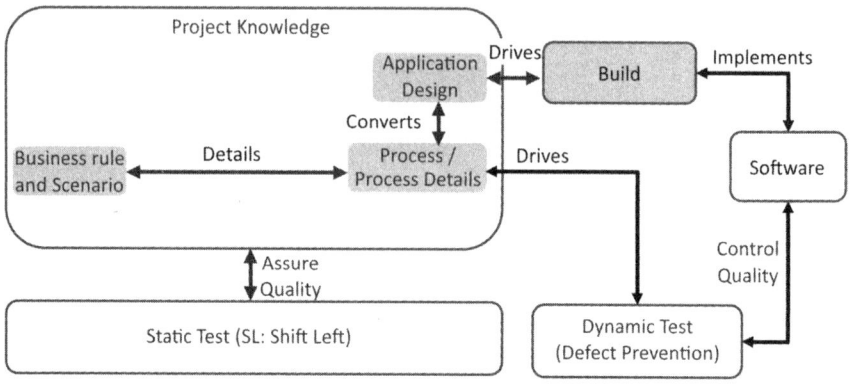

Figure 16.3 | Lean KDD

As represented in Figure 16.3, the project starts with capturing business rules and scenario. It is then expanded into process details, which represents solution design. Process details are directly tested, eliminating the test design phase. The rest of the phases are typical of KDD. Lean KDD is an interesting topic and needs more research to make it practical to use.

CHAPTER 17

Conclusion

Mind, which is the warehouse of knowledge, is ever elusive. On one hand, it is so powerful that, according to Indian spiritual belief, it can visualise objects thousands of miles away in no time, and on the other hand, it is so weak that it may not even recollect what was said a minute earlier. This can be the situation of the same mind at different times. Variation in the way the mind works is dependent on the person's nature and upbringing. When many people (minds) get together to work in an IT project which is knowledge intensive, chaos is expected, by default. Even if a small portion of these minds can be synchronised to work together, project delivery can be significantly improved. KDD is an attempt to assist in synchronisation of the minds by giving a tangible structure to the intangible knowledge. It encourages people (minds) to work together on knowledge intensive areas. Through this book, an attempt is made to provide a mechanism to structure knowledge, both in IT industry (via PKM) and in general (via GKMF).

PKM

PKM, with its 18 building blocks, helps digitising project knowledge. This leads to the evolution of KDD methodology to manage end-to-end project delivery. KDD emphasises on enterprise knowledge reuse as much as possible, which differentiates it from other methodologies. The initial phases in KDD are more like Waterfall, where a certainty of requirement and solution is required. The later phases in KDD are more like Agile, where the bulk of the work is accomplished in a parallel and iterative manner, splitting the work into logical units.

Let us look at the knowledge gap in different methodologies. Figure 17.1 indicates the knowledge gap in the lifecycle of the product, from software development to its decommissioning. In Waterfall, the knowledge gap is widened, particularly at the point of handover and takeover between different teams since the mechanism for recording and storing knowledge is documents, which are costly to be reviewed and difficult to be kept updated. In Agile, the knowledge gap is relatively smaller in the software development phase, remains the same in the business area and increases in the service delivery area as there is a lack of reliable and exhaustive project knowledge to be handed over. In KDD, the knowledge gap is much less and the handover-takeover is smooth across the product lifecycle and not just in the software development phase. This is possible due to PKM used in KDD.

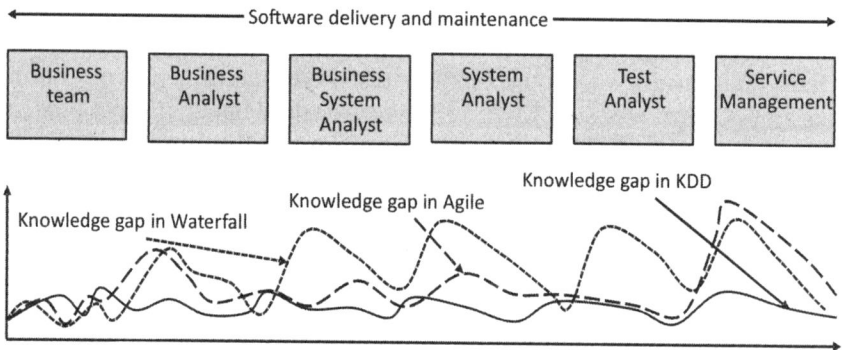

Figure 17.1 | Knowledge gap in Waterfall, Agile and KDD

It is interesting to note that there is no reason why knowledge gap cannot be reduced in Waterfall and Agile if they adopt PKM, just like KDD. This leads us to believe that PKM reduces the difference between different methodologies of project delivery and paves the way of their rationalisation and consolidation. PKM, through its digitisation of project knowledge, has seeds to move the IT industry from a knowledge based industry to a process based industry.

PKM assists in making the project teams self managing reducing the overhead on project management. Project knowledge is one of the most crucial and complex area of project delivery and PKM by digitising project knowledge and extracting various artefacts out of it has made different project teams self sufficient in many aspects. One such example can be, the project manager may get all the updates of the other teams based on how much units of project knowledge they have added in the model.

GKMF

GKMF is a new Generic Knowledge Management Framework, which captures fit-for-purpose knowledge of any domain with four levels of

Conclusion

knowledge and eight building blocks. It also represents the knowledge cycle of humankind, which starts with gaining education. It then learns skills for livelihood and gains experience of those skills that may ultimately enhance the related education. This is how the knowledge cycle works and is depicted in Figure 17.2.

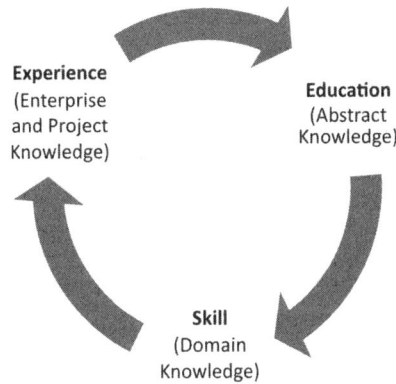

Figure 17.2 | Knowledge life cycle

The four levels of knowledge, based on GKMF, have done something interesting. They have bridged the gap between learning and execution. The first three levels (abstract, domain and enterprise) of knowledge are primarily aimed at learning and the last level (project knowledge) is aimed at executing projects. All the four knowledge levels are seamlessly connected to one another, providing an environment to learn and execute projects at the same time. This is a unique proposition, with a great potential to solve real-life problems in the IT and other industries.

The second layer of knowledge, that is, domain knowledge, has the capability to develop skills required for a person to be productive in the competitive industrial environment of today. It is accomplished by the set of business rules and scenario contextualised by processes and products. This is explained via examples in chapter 15.

The journey from PKM to GKMF is depicted in Figure 17.3.

Sufficient details about PKM, KDD and GKMF, are provided in this book. However, as these are new concepts, one limitation is that not enough real case studies are available to be added as examples.

I hope that the academia and the industry consider these concepts, test them, adopt them and get benefitted from project delivery at low cost and better quality.

There is also a great opportunity to progress these concepts further, for example, in elimination of test design and requirements phases from the project delivery (Lean KDD) as detailed in chapter 16.

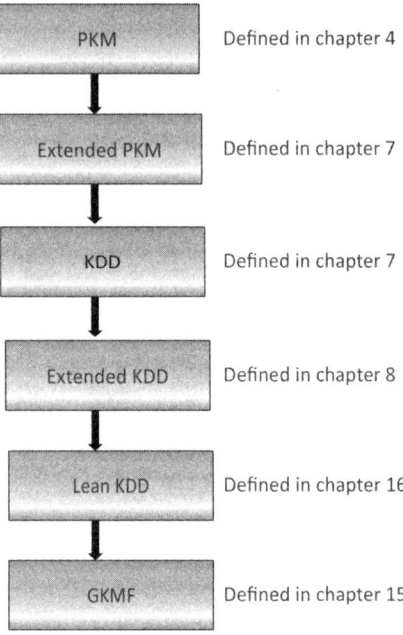

Figure 17.3 | From Project Knowledge Model to Generic Knowledge Management Framework

APPENDIX A
Illustrative Non-Functional Attributes

Non-functional attributes (NFAs) are one of the building blocks of PKM and they are domain agnostic. NFAs specify criteria that can be used to judge the operation of a system, rather than specific behaviour. They are relevant across the system for all the functionality unless specified otherwise. An illustrative list of non-functional attributes is provided in Table A.1 which can be customised as per the discretion of the SME.

Table A.1 | List of non-functional attributes

Parent non-functional attribute	Child non-functional attribute
Maintainability	Modifiability
Maintainability	Co-existence
Maintainability	Analysability
Maintainability	Reusability
Maintainability	Testability
Maintainability	Modularity
Maintainability	Archive
Maintainability	Interoperability
Overarching Functional Attribute	Report
Overarching Functional Attribute	BPM
Overarching Functional Attribute	IT
Overarching Functional Attribute	CRM
Overarching Functional Attribute	Portal

Contd.

Parent non-functional attribute	Child non-functional attribute
Overarching Functional Attribute	Regulatory
Performance Efficiency	Capacity Planning
Performance Efficiency	Service Level Agreement
Performance Efficiency	Response Time Behaviour
Performance Efficiency	Batch
Portability	Installability
Portability	Replaceability
Portability	Adaptability
Reliability	Fault Tolerance
Reliability	Recoverability
Reliability	Availability
Security	Authenticity
Security	Accountability
Security	Confidentiality
Security	Integrity
Security	Authorisation
Security	Non-Repudiation
Usability	Screen Aesthetics
Usability	Learnability
Usability	Accessibility
Usability	User Error Protection

APPENDIX B
Compliance of PKM with GKMF

18 building blocks of PKM can be classified into 4 levels of knowledge as defined by GKMF proving its relevance in IT. Through Table B.1 and subsequent explanations, 18 building blocks of PKM are classified into abstract knowledge, domain Knowledge, enterprise knowledge and project knowledge.

Table B.1 Project Knowledge analysis for finding knowledge at the highest level of abstraction

Project Knowledge building block	Knowledge characteristics	Highest level of abstraction?
Requirement	Requirements are detailed and project specific. Requirements specify the project knowledge of other building blocks such as business rule and therefore cannot be considered as knowledge at the highest level of abstraction.	No
Process	At the level of identifying a list of processes, they represent a good mechanism to contain the detailed project knowledge and create a framework to contain knowledge at the highest level of abstraction.	No, but can be used for filtering purposes
Product	At the level of identifying a list of products, they represent a good mechanism to contain the detailed project knowledge and create a framework to contain knowledge at the highest level of abstraction.	No, but can be used for filtering purposes
Application	Applications implement the detailed project knowledge for the project scope and cannot be knowledge at the highest level of abstraction.	No
Scenario	Generic knowledge can be easily accommodated via a set of scenarios and business rules.	Yes

Contd.

Project Knowledge building block	Knowledge characteristics	Highest level of abstraction?
Business rules	Generic knowledge can be easily accommodated via a set of scenarios and business rules.	Yes
Non-functional attribute (NFA)	NFAs are relevant primarily to IT project delivery. Moreover, they can be accommodated in the set of business rule and scenario that are identified as knowledge at the highest level of abstraction.	No
Interface	They will be varying for different organisations as they are related to applications and may change, based on subsequent projects. Not suitable when looking for knowledge at the highest level of abstraction.	No
Communication	Communications are specific to organisation and requirements. When generic, they can be accommodated in the set of business rule and scenario.	No
Screen	Screens are application specific and hence not stable enough to qualify for knowledge at the highest level of abstraction.	No
Report	Reports are closely linked to requirements and are organisation specific. Generic reports can be covered in the set of business rule and scenarios.	No
Business data	Business data is company specific and changes with every project. Generic business data can be covered in the set of business rule and scenario.	No
Offline transaction	Offline transactions (batch processing) are circumstantial and depend on the enterprise architecture of the organisation. Some organisations prefer most of the transactions occurring in real-time and for others they perform a hybrid of transactions both online and batch. Offline transactions are, therefore, not a suitable candidate for the knowledge at the highest level of abstraction.	No
Process step	Process steps deal with detailed implementation of the business processes of an organisation. They will be customised to an organisation and not suitable to be counted as knowledge at the highest level of abstraction.	No
Message	Messages are primarily a communication mechanism when using application or portal-user interfaces. They are not suitable to be knowledge at the highest level of abstraction.	No

Contd.

Compliance of PKM with GKMF

Project Knowledge building block	Knowledge characteristics	Highest level of abstraction?
Data	They are details of application specific data and are not suitable to be knowledge at the highest level of abstraction.	No
Logic	These are detailed logic of application in a technical language and are derived from the previous knowledge such as requirements and solutioning. They cannot be treated as knowledge at the highest level of abstraction.	No
Test case	Test cases are derived knowledge from the solution design knowledge and do not qualify to be knowledge at the highest level of abstraction.	No

Table B.1 brings out an interesting fact that, until now, has almost been hidden amid various forms of the project knowledge.

Knowledge at the highest level of abstraction is a combination of:

1. Scenarios
2. Business rules

This combination is called 'abstract knowledge'. It is the same for IT industry as well as for any other domain.

The next detailed level of knowledge is the domain knowledge. Domain knowledge pierces business rules and scenarios with products and processes for domain contextualisation. Products and processes are distinctly domain specific and help capturing and reusing the domain knowledge. Policy issue and claim are examples of processes and term insurance and endowment products are examples of product in the insurance domain.

Domain knowledge, therefore, maps to these three building blocks of PKM.

3. Product
4. Process
5. Process step

These five building blocks are sufficient to capture domain knowledge in IT industry. To make it generic domain knowledge for all the domains, it makes sense to combine the process and process steps. Therefore, we can say that four building blocks cover the domain knowledge for all the domains.

Let us now try to understand enterprise knowledge. Enterprise knowledge is the next level of knowledge that evolves from the domain knowledge. The enterprise knowledge is knowledge of an organisation, related to a domain. The organisation may operate in multiple domains, but for simplicity let us assume that the organisation operates in a single domain. Enterprise knowledge customises the domain knowledge to suit the needs of the organisation. The enterprise knowledge building blocks for IT project delivery, are as follows:

6. Non-functional attribute
7. Business data
8. Communication
9. Report
10. Screen
11. Message
12. Offline transaction
13. Application
14. Interface
15. Data
16. Logic

On careful examination of these building blocks, it is clear that they represent the details of the organisation, indicating how it operates. It is interesting to note that from reusability perspective we have excluded four building blocks namely Data, Logic, Screen and Offline Transaction while defining enterprise knowledge for PKM in Chapter 4 that consists of the remaining 12 building blocks of the 16 building blocks listed above.

There are two clear themes that come out from these 11 building blocks of enterprise knowledge. The first seven building blocks represent various usage perspectives of the organisation detailing on how they behave. For example, communication details specific letters issued to the customer during implementation of the business processes of the organisation. The number of communication and the exact wording may be different in different organisations. This is what makes an organisation distinct from another organisation. The last four building blocks essentially enable these usages via IT applications. At the generic level, I have identified two building blocks, 'usage' and 'enabler' that should cover the enterprise knowledge. Usage is the details in which the organisation conducts itself and enabler is how the users of the organisation implement the detailed business processes of the organisation. Therefore, at a generic level, enterprise knowledge consists of 6 building blocks, with four from the abstract and domain knowledge.

Let us now try to understand project knowledge. This is the most detailed knowledge and is required to execute projects in an organisation to keep its enterprise knowledge updated to remain competitive. Every project will have requirements and a mechanism to ensure that the requirements have been added to the enterprise knowledge. The mechanism is via test cases. So, the two building blocks constituting the project knowledge for the IT industry from the list of 18 building blocks are:

17. Requirement
18. Project test case

APPENDIX C

Project Estimate and Business Rule/Scenario Framework

One of the biggest issues that the IT industry is facing today is the lack of an effective mechanism for sizing a project. There are many techniques existing to size projects which are sometimes dependent on the technology used for the software and sometimes not. The main project sizing mechanisms are:
- Function Point estimate: The function point is a unit of measurement to express the amount of business functionality an information system (as a product) provides to a user. Function points are used to compute a functional size measurement of software. The sizing is independent of technology.
- Feature Point estimate: It is a modified function point to improve applicability to systems with significant internal processing (e.g., operating systems, communication systems). This allows accounting for functions not readily perceivable by the user, but essential for proper operations. The sizing is independent of the technology.
- Use Case based estimate: Use case represents the functional aspect of the project. The use cases and their complexity add up to scope the project and determine the size of the project. The sizing is independent of the technology.
- Component based estimate: The software is broken into multiple, manageable IT components and an estimate is done for each of the IT components. The technology influences the sizing.
- Line of Code: Line of code is another mechanism that determines the size of the software. The technology influences the sizing.

In practice, these methods are not very popular with the project teams. Estimates are still the prerogative of the SMEs, who often get them wrong. Techniques like Work Breakdown Structure (WBS) that calculate effort and not the software size are still widely used to estimate a project.

Project Estimate and Business Rule/Scenario Framework 273

If we look at the three technology independent software sizing techniques (function point, feature point and use case), it becomes clear that they are primarily trying to count the functionality of the software. They represent the unit of project knowledge for sizing the software. As explained in chapter 15, a combination of business rule and scenario can be used to represent project knowledge. Combination of business rule and scenario is more suitable to become the basis of sizing a project – a well researched discovery made in the book as explained via GKMF and Lean KDD. As it is digitised in PKM, it becomes even better to quantify the project size. This may become one of the techniques to size the software if proper attention is given to this concept. This technique may be more granular when compared with the existing techniques, such as use case based technique, and can be widely used across different types of project and domain. If an organisation adopts KDD approach, the estimation is enabled even better as business rule and scenario are anyway captured as enterprise knowledge.

Agile methodology goes for practical approach on estimation via simple techniques like Planning Poker and worries more on accommodating the work via capacity of the team rather than spending too much time on trying to come up with an accurate estimate.

I think the new way of estimation suggested here may be a useful approach for both Waterfall and Agile methodologies.

APPENDIX D

Inventory Relationship for Setting up of Security Questions – as per Example in Chapter 6

Solution Design Building Block Inventory Relationships

Intra-relationship of the Process Step Building Block

Table D.1 | Intra-relationship of process step

Process step–1	Process step–2	Remarks
Process_Step_01	Process_Step_02	
Process_Step_02	Process_Step_03	When system validation fails
Process_Step_02	Process_Step_04	When system validation passes
Process_Step_03	Process_Step_01	Prompts user to edit the input

Inter-relationship of the Process Step building block:

Table D.2 | Inter-relationship of process step

Process step inventory	Other inventory
Process_Step_01	Business_Data_01
Process_Step_01	Business_Data_02
Process_Step_01	Business_Data_03
Process_Step_01	Business_Data_04
Process_Step_01	Business_Data_05
Process_Step_01	Business_Data_06
Process_Step_01	Business_Data_07

Contd.

Inventory Relationship for Setting up of Security Questions

Process step inventory	Other inventory
Process_Step_01	Business_Data_08
Process_Step_01	Business_Data_09
Process_Step_02	Business_Data_01
Process_Step_02	Business_Data_02
Process_Step_02	Business_Data_03
Process_Step_02	Business_Data_04
Process_Step_02	Business_Data_05
Process_Step_02	Business_Data_06
Process_Step_03	Business_Data_01
Process_Step_03	Business_Data_02
Process_Step_03	Business_Data_03
Process_Step_03	Business_Data_04
Process_Step_03	Business_Data_05
Process_Step_03	Business_Data_06
Process_Step_04	Business_Data_01
Process_Step_04	Business_Data_02
Process_Step_04	Business_Data_03
Process_Step_04	Business_Data_04
Process_Step_04	Business_Data_05
Process_Step_04	Business_Data_06
Process_Step_04	Business_Data_07
Process_Step_04	Business_Data_08
Process_Step_04	Business_Data_09
Process_Step_04	Business_Rule_01
Process_Step_04	Business_Rule_02
Process_Step_02	Business_Rule_03
Process_Step_04	Business_Rule_04
Process_Step_01	Business_Rule_05
Process_Step_01	Scenario_01
Process_Step_01	Scenario_02
Process_Step_01	Scenario_03
Process_Step_04	Scenario_03

Contd.

Process step inventory	Other inventory
Process_Step_03	Message_01
Process_Step_03	Message_02
Process_Step_04	Message_03
Process_Step_03	Message_04
Process_Step_01	Screen_01
Process_Step_02	Screen_01
Process_Step_03	Screen_01
Process_Step_04	Screen_01

Intra-relationship of the Business Data Building Block:

Table D.3 | Intra-relationship of business data

Business data–1	Business data–2
Business_Data_01	Business_Data_04
Business_Data_01	Business_Data_07
Business_Data_02	Business_Data_05
Business_Data_02	Business_Data_08
Business_Data_03	Business_Data_06
Business_Data_03	Business_Data_09

Inter-relationship of the Business Data Building Block:

Table D.4 | Inter-relationship of business data

Business data inventory	Other inventory
Business_Data_01	Business_Rule_01
Business_Data_02	Business_Rule_01
Business_Data_03	Business_Rule_01
Business_Data_04	Business_Rule_01
Business_Data_05	Business_Rule_01
Business_Data_06	Business_Rule_01
Business_Data_07	Business_Rule_01

Contd.

Inventory Relationship for Setting up of Security Questions 277

Business data inventory	Other inventory
Business_Data_08	Business_Rule_01
Business_Data_09	Business_Rule_01
Business_Data_07	Business_Rule_02
Business_Data_08	Business_Rule_02
Business_Data_09	Business_Rule_02
Business_Data_01	Business_Rule_03
Business_Data_02	Business_Rule_03
Business_Data_03	Business_Rule_03
Business_Data_04	Business_Rule_04
Business_Data_05	Business_Rule_04
Business_Data_06	Business_Rule_04
Business_Data_01	Business_Rule_05
Business_Data_02	Business_Rule_05
Business_Data_03	Business_Rule_05
Business_Data_04	Business_Rule_05
Business_Data_05	Business_Rule_05
Business_Data_06	Business_Rule_05
Business_Data_01	Scenario_01
Business_Data_02	Scenario_01
Business_Data_03	Scenario_01
Business_Data_07	Scenario_02
Business_Data_08	Scenario_02
Business_Data_09	Scenario_02
Business_Data_01	Scenario_03
Business_Data_02	Scenario_03
Business_Data_03	Scenario_03
Business_Data_07	Scenario_03
Business_Data_08	Scenario_03
Business_Data_09	Scenario_03
Business_Data_02	Message_01
Business_Data_03	Message_01

Contd.

Business data inventory	Other inventory
Business_Data_01	Message_02
Business_Data_02	Message_02
Business_Data_03	Message_02
Business_Data_04	Message_03
Business_Data_05	Message_03
Business_Data_06	Message_03
Business_Data_01	Message_04
Business_Data_02	Message_04
Business_Data_03	Message_04
Business_Data_07	Message_04
Business_Data_08	Message_04
Business_Data_09	Message_04
Business_Data_01	Screen_01
Business_Data_02	Screen_01
Business_Data_03	Screen_01
Business_Data_04	Screen_01
Business_Data_05	Screen_01
Business_Data_06	Screen_01
Business_Data_07	Screen_01
Business_Data_08	Screen_01
Business_Data_09	Screen_01

Intra-relationship of the Business Rule Building Block:
None.

Inter-relationship of the Business Rule Building Block:

Table D.5 | Inter-relationship of business rule

Business rule inventory	Other inventory
Business_Rule_03	Scenario_01
Business_Rule_02	Scenario_02
Business_Rule_03	Scenario_02

Contd.

Inventory Relationship for Setting up of Security Questions

Business rule inventory	Other inventory
Business_Rule_02	Scenario_03
Business_Rule_03	Message_01
Business_Rule_05	Message_03
Business_Rule_03	Message_04
Business_Rule_01	Screen_01
Business_Rule_02	Screen_01
Business_Rule_03	Screen_01
Business_Rule_04	Screen_01
Business_Rule_05	Screen_01

Intra-relationship of the scenario building block:

Table D.6 | Intra-relationship of scenario

Scenario–1	Scenario–2
Scenario_02	Scenario_03

Inter-relationship of the Scenario Building Block:

Table D.7 | Inter-relationship of scenario

Scenario inventory	Other inventory
Scenario_02	Message_02
Scenario_03	Message_02
Scenario_01	Message_04
Scenario_02	Message_04
Scenario_01	Screen_01
Scenario_02	Screen_01
Scenario_03	Screen_01

Intra-relationship of the Message Building Block:
None.

Inter-relationship of the Message Building Block:

Table D.8 | Inter-relationship of message

Message inventory	Other inventory
Message_01	Screen_01
Message_02	Screen_01
Message_03	Screen_01
Message_04	Screen_01

Intra-relationship of the Screen Building Block:
Not applicable as there is only one screen.

Inter-relationship of the Screen Building Block:
None, as the relationship is covered in the above building blocks.

APPENDIX E
KDD: Response to Criticism

Although KDD is not in the open forum for discussion about its merits and demerits (this book is the first attempt to take it to the industry and academia), while evolving this methodology and writing the book, it was exposed to many academicians and practitioners of software engineering. A list of concerns expressed by the experts and my responses to these concerns are given here.

Criticism 1

Computers cannot generate a fully readable document set representing complete project knowledge. Knowledge can never be fully defined (and will always be subjective) in a way that can be automated by a computer.

Response

Documents referred are related to project knowledge such as BRS, FSD, HLD and Test Cases. People who are sufficiently skilled in producing these documents have enough knowledge about them. But everyone has an individual style, whether it is writing, presenting or explaining. The personal experience of the author influences the document produced. Different people can present the same information differently. Some would write crisp and clear descriptions and some would write details covering detailed background information as well.

This suggests that, because computers cannot think, they cannot produce a project document as the project documents need creative thinking. Computers can only process information based on algorithms and it is assumed that it is difficult to write an algorithm to capture knowledge.

However, KDD has done something noteworthy. It has created a framework which defines and scopes the entire project knowledge. It expects the project team to capture the project knowledge using the same framework. It minimises the variations that are caused in a typical documentation regime. PKM provides a mechanism to capture the project knowledge in such a format which allows a computer to extract it in a document format.

Let us appreciate the robustness of PKM. Any information related to the project can be captured completely via the combination of inventory and relationship. There are only two activities involved here. The first one is defining the inventory of a building block via a set of mandatory and optional attributes. The second one is linking all the inventories together. When all the inventories are traced, it clearly brings out their many-to-many relationships, completing the nested knowledge. This brings the rigour and maturity to the model which makes it easier for a computer to extract a document based on an algorithm.

The project documents contain inventory and relationship with some additional background information. Every line in the document is either trying to indicate an inventory or a relationship or some background information. Documents, as they contain free-form text, do not encourage a writer to follow the inventory and relationship concept rigorously.

It should now be clear that when the information is captured by the project team in accordance with PKM, the document extracted by the computer may be more readable and consistent than the document produced in free-form text format. It may not have a lot of background information, but the information will be fit-for-purpose. As KDD is a new concept, it will take more time for people to realise that a computer can extract a sensible document out of the project knowledge in the model.

A part of the reason for this criticism is due to the fact that there are many outputs generated by a computer that need significant effort before they can be used. For example, many tools claim to generate test cases automatically, but computer generated test cases often require significant effort to make them usable. These instances have created a belief that computers cannot generate a ready to use document. But the issue is the maturity of the input information and the algorithm rather than in the extraction of the document.

Criticism 2

Too much of information needs to be added in KDD to create and manage the project knowledge. It will take more effort when compared to project delivery with the document regime.

Response

Project documents are the de facto mechanism for project knowledge management. KDD manages project knowledge via PKM. We first need to understand that in the KDD project delivery environment, there is no need to produce documents for managing the project knowledge as PKM can extract the documents when needed. PKM replaces project documents in entirety.

Now let us compare the project documents and PKM. Project documents, if produced with quality, take significant effort, from draft to sign-off. Also, it is significantly effort intensive to keep the document set updated. It is difficult to keep the documents updated in real-time as they need to undergo version control with a sign-off process for the new version. Often, documents may lag the latest project knowledge to get the approval for publishing the next version. It also takes significant effort to make all the documents consistent with one another when one of the documents changes. As the documents are written by different members of the team at different intervals, the information contained in them might be duplicate, making them redundant and difficult to keep consistent.

In KDD, PKM makes project knowledge more manageable via the elaborate inventory and relationship framework where it scopes the project knowledge via 189 data points. Adding project knowledge is a matter of adding information to these data points. Adding, updating and assuring the quality of the information becomes easy as the knowledge is digitised now via 189 data points. Digitisation may also assist in versioning the project knowledge.

Let us now address the main point that information addition is too much in KDD. One point is clear that if we want to maintain project knowledge with quality, it will take effort. What I want to convey here is that managing project knowledge in KDD will take less effort than trying to manage it via documents of the same quality. The best part of PKM is the flexibility that it provides to decide how much information is enough for a project. At the beginning of the project, the project SME will decide how many of the 189 data points are needed for the project. For example, if it is a portal related project, it may not include offline transaction. The nature of the project and project budget also influence this scoping. For a project where precision is crucial (e.g., a software to be used for aircraft navigation), more data points will be selected to make sure all means are used to detect the defects. Project budget is important to decide how many data points to select. As the data points have a clear indication about their priority, the project SME can keep the most relevant data points and remove the data points that are meant to give additional quality assurance. For example, under a budget constraint, the data points linking test cases with inventories of application design may be dropped, if the data points linking test cases with requirements and solution design are kept in scope.

Prioritisation of project knowledge in KDD brings out an interesting differentiator when compared to a similar prioritisation in the document production regime. It is difficult to instruct the author to complete a document using less effort if the budget is lower. Prioritisation in the document regime may lead to scrapping of one or more documents due to project budget and timelines. This leads to truncation of project knowledge captured in the project documents. In contrast, prioritisation of the project knowledge in KDD provides a scientific way of letting go the information that is less relevant. KDD attempts to take the most relevant information in scope, based on budget and scoping by the SME, leaving the less relevant out of scope. The truncation of project knowledge prevalent in the documentation regime is effectively replaced by removing less relevant project knowledge in KDD.

KDD has structured information addition. In the document system, the document has free-form text, which may have more background information than necessary and/or less structurally complete information (e.g., inventory without necessary linkage) than the information in KDD. It is now easy to visualise that for information of same quality, KDD will take less effort. Additionally, digitisation of quality assurance in PKM assists in correcting any oversight faster than the document regime.

From volume perspective also, the PKM will have less units of information than the document system equivalent, as in the document there may be many redundant and repeated information.

Criticism 3

Document production that KDD tries to replace is anyway not an important consideration in project delivery in the Agile method, reducing the relevance of KDD in project delivery.

Response

Having an alternate source of project knowledge, other than in the code of the software, is always a good idea. Understanding knowledge via the code is always difficult and costly. Waterfall methodology, which is the oldest method of project delivery, has rightly identified the need for keeping the project knowledge in an alternate format, which are documents. In the initial phases of the Waterfall method, documents are the only output. This results in maturing the project knowledge to an extent that the code written subsequently may be more stable. Jumping directly to the code might mean a lot of iteration in the code. The limitation of the Waterfall method is not in the concept but the way it is implemented. It relies on project documents which are not easy to maintain in real-time.

Agile has made many positive impacts on project delivery but, fundamentally, it does not provide an alternative to the project knowledge management mechanism of the Waterfall methodology. Documentation is minimal in Agile and cannot be used for understanding detailed project knowledge. This creates a problem in the service management area and inhibits the DevOps environment due to lack of an effective and alternate project knowledge. For knowledge management, Agile also uses wiki based tools but in my view they are inherently unstructured and has not yet provided a reliable alternate to the document production regime.

KDD resolves this issue. It adopts Agile practices and, at the same time, provides an alternative to the document production regime which is more scientific and effective. As a result, it enables the DevOps environment and reduces people dependency, which is a major concern in Agile.

In summary, KDD is a futuristic methodology. It is not trying to bring Waterfall method back. In fact, it brings the concepts of Waterfall and Agile together and enables the DevOps project delivery environment.

Glossary

Term	Description
Agile methodology	Agile methodology for project delivery insists on parallel activities and does not wait for a phase to be signed-off for starting the next phase, unlike Waterfall.
ALM	Application Lifecycle Management; ALM tool assists project delivery covering all the phases of its development lifecycle.
Bespoke	Bespoke is when a product is developed from scratch instead of buying a readymade product.
BRS	Business Requirement Specification; this is a document that details requirements from customer's point of view.
Building block	As per Oxford Dictionary, building block is a basic unit from which something is built up. In our context building blocks constitute project knowledge.
Chunk	Chunk is a logical split of the entire project scope primarily based on in scope business processes.
Class diagram	A class diagram represents the static structure of an application. It defines classes having attributes and operations and depicts relationships with other classes.
CRM	Customer relationship management framework and tool that aims to optimise the interaction between customer and the company (generally via its call centre).
DevOps	DevOps (development and operations) is an enterprise software development phrase used to mean a type of Agile relationship between development and service management business units. The goal of DevOps is to change and improve the relationship between these two business units.
Digital	Digital is the name given to the initiative to enable access of information to stakeholders via latest channels such as browsers and smartphones.

Contd.

Glossary

Term	Description
Domain	Domains are different industries such as manufacturing, retail, insurance, banking.
EKDD	Extended Knowledge Driven Development; It starts with business case and continues in service management primarily driven by the Project Knowledge Model.
EPKM	Extended Project Knowledge Model; The Project Knowledge Model is expanded into Extended Project Knowledge Model to include majority of execution and management related activities to bring sensible automation to the end to end project delivery.
GKMF	Generic Knowledge Management Framework; This new knowledge management framework claims that all knowledge can be contained in eight constituents (building blocks) spread across four levels of hierarchy.
HLD	High Level Design; this is an application design document converting business knowledge into technical knowledge.
ISTQB	The International Software Testing Qualifications Board is a software testing qualification certification organisation that operates internationally.
IT	Information Technology.
IVR	Interactive voice response.
KDD	Knowledge Driven Development; is a project delivery methodology based on digitisation of the project knowledge and blends the structure of Waterfall and dynamism of Agile.
KPI	Key performance indicator.
LKDD	Lean Knowledge Driven Development; KDD where requirements are replaced by a combination of business rules and scenario and test design is accomplished by solution design.
MoSCoW	Requirements are generally prioritised using MoSCoW. The classifications are: Must have, Should have, Could have and Won't have.
NFA	Non-functional attribute; these are non-functional behaviours of a software product, such as security features.
OATS	Orthogonal Array Test Strategy is a test optimisation technique that is systematic, statistical way of testing pair-wise interactions and provides uniformly distributed coverage of all pair combinations.
Off-the-shelf	These are software products that can be bought and used with minimum customisation.

Contd.

Term	Description
Phases of SDLC	Project is delivered in the following generic phases of Software Development Life Cycle: 1. Requirement analysis 2. Solution design 3. Application design 4. Test design 5. Build 6. Test execution 7. Implementation
Physical data model	A physical data model is the design of a database showing all the table structures, including column name, column data type, column constraints, primary key, foreign key and relationships between tables.
PKM	Project Knowledge Model; It is a project knowledge repository, an output of the knowledge intensive phases (requirement analysis, solution design, application design and test design) of the project delivery lifecycle. The project knowledge in the model is digitised in the form of 189 data points. It has 327 data points of quality assurance of the project knowledge. All of them are accomplished via 24 activities.
Regression Testing	Regression Testing is defined as a type of software testing to confirm that a recent program or code change has not adversely affected existing features.
SDLC	Software Development Life Cycle; this is a mechanism to deliver software projects in multiple phases.
Sequence diagram	The main purpose of a sequence diagram is to define event sequences that result in some desired outcome.
Shift Left	It is a concept in project assurance that focuses on detecting the defects early.
SME	Subject Matter Expert; someone who is an expert in the area specified.
State transition diagram	It is a diagram describing the individual states and outputs throughout a process.
System use case	System use case is a way in which a user of a computer system can make use of the system to get the result they want.
TBOK	Test body of knowledge – being prepared by ISTQB; it may contain glossary and exhaustive information about the testing best practices and guidelines.
Time-Box	A time-box is a previously agreed period of time during which a person or a team works steadily towards completion of some goal.

Contd.

Glossary

Term	Description
Transaction	Transaction in software development is a consistent retrieval and/or update of the database of the IT application, usually to accomplish a business process.
UAT	User acceptance test; this is the final test by the users or representatives of the users before the product is put into production.
UT	Unit Test Cases.
Waterfall methodology	Waterfall is a project delivery methodology which implements SDLC phases in sequence.
WBS	Work Breakdown Structure; is deliverable oriented hierarchical decomposition of the work to be executed by the project team.
Wiki	A wiki is a Web site that allows users to add and update content on the site using their own browser.

References

1. Despa, Mihai Liviu. 2014. 'Comparative study on software development Methodologies.' *Database Systems Journal* 5 (3): 51–54. Accessed 1 January 2018. Available at http://dbjournal.ro/archive/17/17_4.pdf.
2. The Standish Group. 'Books by Jim Johnson'. Accessed 3 February 2018. Available at https://www.standishgroup.com/
3. Campion-Awwad, Oliver, Alexander Hayton, Leila Smith and Mark Vuaran. 2014. 'The National Programme for IT in the NHS: A Case History.' MPhil Public Policy dissertation, University of Cambridge. Accessed 1 January 2018. Available at https://www.cl.cam.ac.uk/~rja14/Papers/npfit-mpp-2014-case-history.pdf.
4. Clark, Lindsay. 2004. 'Sainsbury's Writes Off £260m as Supply Chain IT Trouble hits Profit.' *ComputerWeekly.com*. Accessed 1 January, 2018. Available at http://www.computerweekly.com/news/2240058411/Sainsburys-writes-off-260m-as-supply-chain-IT-trouble-hits-profit.
5. Kozak-Holland, Mark. 2007. 'Titanic lessons for IT projects.' Paper presented at PMI Global Congress 2007, North America, Atlanta, GA. Newtown Square, PA: Project Management Institute. Accessed 1 January 2018. Available at https://www.pmi.org/learning/library/improve-performance-it-project-teams-7244.
6. Subramanian, Samanth. 2013. 'India's low-cost tablet scheme doesn't compute.' *The National*. Accessed 1 January 2018. Available at https://www.thenational.ae/world/asia/india-s-low-cost-tablet-scheme-doesn-t-compute-1.292569.
7. Ballard, Mark. 2013. 'Why Agile development failed for Universal Credit.' *ComputerWeekly.com*. Accessed 1 January 2018. Available at http://www.computerweekly.com/news/2240187478/Why-agile-development-failed-for-Universal-Credit.
8. Signatories of the Agile manifesto. 2001. 'Manifesto for Agile Software Development.' Accessed 1 January, 2018. Available at http://agilemanifesto.org.
9. Brooks Jr., Frederick P. 1995. *The Mythical Man-Month*. Boston, Massachusetts: Addison-Wesley Professional.
10. NPTEL / Indian Institute of Technology, Delhi. 2009. 'Themes of six sigma.' Accessed 1 January, 2018. Available at http://nptel.ac.in/courses/116102019/32.
11. 'The CMMi easy button.' Accessed 3 February2018. Available at http://www.software-quality-assurance.org.

References

12. Project Management Institute. 'What is Project Management?' Accessed 1 January, 2018. Available at https://www.pmi.org/about/learn-about-pmi/what-is-project-management.
13. AXELOS Limited. 'What is PRINCE2?' Accessed 23 February 2018. Available at https://www.axelos.com/best-practice-solutions/prince2/what-is-prince2.
14. AXELOS Limited. 'ITIL® - IT Service Management' Accessed 23 February 2018. Available at https://www.axelos.com/best-practice-solutions/itil.
15. Josey, Andrew. 2011. 'TOGAF® Version 9.1 Enterprise Edition – An introduction.' The Open Group. Accessed 3 February 2018. Available at https://publications.opengroup.org/w118.
16. Zachman, John. *The Zachman Framework*. Accessed February 3 2018. Available at http://www.zachman.com.
17. Wikipedia. 'Zachman Framework.' Last updated 19 September 2017. Accessed 3 February 2018. Available at https://en.wikipedia.org/wiki/Zachman_Framework.
18. International Institute of Business Analysis. 'IIBA Global Business Analysis Core Standard'. Accessed on 3 February, 2018. Available at http://www.iiba.org/babok-guide/core-standard.aspx.
19. International Software Testing Qualifications Board, ISTQB. Accessed 3 February 2018. Available at https://www.istqb.org/downloads/send/2-foundation-level-documents/3-foundation-level-syllabus-2011.html.
20. Applehans, Wayne, Alden Globe and Greg Laugero. 1999. *Managing Knowledge: A Practical Web-Based Approach*. Addison-Wesley Information Technology Series.
21. Suresh, J. K. and Kavi Mahesh. 2006. *Ten Steps to Maturity in Knowledge Management: Lessons in Economy*. Oxford: Chandos Publishing.
22. Bokowitz, Wendi R. and Ruth L. Williams. 1999. *The Knowledge Management Fieldbook*. Upper Saddle River, New Jersey: F. T. Press.
23. Ashton, Kevin. 2009. 'That 'Internet of Things' Thing In the real world, things matter more than ideas.' RFID Journal. Accessed 1 January, 2018. Available at http://www.rfidjournal.com/articles/view?4986.

Index

Abstract knowledge, 3, 70, 85, 242-245
Agile, 4-29, 61-62, 209-210
ALM, 226-228
Artificial Intelligence, 211-212
Audit, 127, 146, 147
Automation, 201, 220-229

BABOK, 44, 193
Behaviour Driven Development (BDD), 42, 218
Building Block, 2-7, 56, 68-76
Business Analysis, 35, 193
Business Analyst, 35, 37, 119
Business Case, 169, 185
Business Requirement Specification (BRS), 54, 138
Business Rule, 134, 268-269

Change management, 29, 131, 227
Chunk, 27, 152
CMMI, 44, 175-176
Collaboration, 28, 209
Collaboration Driven, 61
Communication, 99, 200
Comparison between Waterfall and Agile, 17
Comparison of project delivery attributes, 28
Comparison of Waterfall, Agile and KDD, 23, 206
Configuration Management, 66, 146, 177, 225
Consolidated test design, 118

Continuous Improvement, 84-85, 92-93, 109-111
Cost of quality, 165, 203
Cultural Change, 233-240

Data, Information and Knowledge, 205
Defect Clustering, 196
Defect density, 165
Defect management, 22, 227
DevOps, 198
Digitisation, 97, 209
Digitised project knowledge, 23, 87, 119, 222
Document Driven, 60
Domain Agnostic, 57, 68, 111, 242
Domain knowledge, 68, 241-244

Enterprise Architecture Framework, 187
Enterprise Knowledge, 69, 243-244
Enterprise Knowledge Management, 226
Enterprise Knowledge Reuse, 25, 92, 227
Error Fallacy, 197
Exhaustive documentation, 5, 17, 28, 61
Exhaustive traceability, 24, 48, 97
Extended KDD, 171
Extended PKM, 146, 147
Extreme Programming, 41, 216
Extreme Quantification, 105

Factory Model, 233-240
Fault tolerant, 153
Feature Driven Development (FDD), 43
Functional Specification Document (FSD), 11, 54, 60, 233

High Level Design (HLD), 54, 138, 238

Impact Analysis, 28, 51, 114, 227
Information Technology, 30-33, 48
Internet of Things (IoT), 212
Inventory, 79-82, 133-138, 143
ITIL, 44, 87

KDD - Focus Area, 141
Key Performance Indicators (KPI), 164
Knowledge Based Industry, 32, 238
Knowledge Building Blocks, 70-76
Knowledge equilibrium, 114
Knowledge Evolution, 68
Knowledge Intensive Phase, 201
Knowledge Management, 8, 59, 205, 236, 241-256
Knowledge maturity, 108, 242-243

Lean KDD, 257-260
Lean Software Development, 42, 217
Lean Way of Working, 211

Machine Learning, 211
Maker and Checker, 116
Manual review, 8, 21, 51, 102, 230
MoSCoW, 41, 287

Negative Relationship, 8, 21-22, 86, 139, 212
Non-Functional Attributes, 73, 74, 265
Non-Functional Test, 12

OATS, 22, 113, 204, 287
Offline Transaction, 73, 75, 268
Ontology Framework, 256

Pesticide Paradox, 196
PMBOK, 180
PMP, 44, 180

PRINCE2, 44, 180, 184
Process Based Industry, 30, 233
Project documents, 17, 50, 121-139, 282
Project estimate, 182, 202, 272
Project Execution, 65, 220
Project Knowledge, 52
Project Knowledge Tree, 81
Project Management, 35, 105, 177, 180, 224
Project Scope, 156
Project Test Case, 138, 145, 227
Prototyping, 40, 215, 223

Quality assurance, 28, 35, 84-86, 139, 172
Quality Assurance Framework, 172
Quality Control, 237
Quality gate, 153-163
Quality Management, 65, 146, 227
Quantitative techniques, 112

Rapid Application Development (RAD), 40, 216
Release Management, 147, 225, 227
Requirement Analysis, 10, 19, 37, 64, 117
Requirement Compliance, 78
Requirement Management, 24, 117, 176, 223
Reuse, 109
Reuse Index, 139
Review, 100
Review effectiveness, 165
Rework, 28, 129, 166
Rework Index, 139
Risk Management, 65, 146, 178, 183, 227
Root Cause of Project Delivery Pain Areas, 52

Scenario, 2, 70, 134, 245, 272
Scrum, 14, 41, 216
Separation of concern, 115-116
Service Management, 36, 48, 170

Index 295

Service Management Framework, 187
Shift Left, 203-204
Six Sigma, 173-174
Skill Development, 241-256
SME, 8, 29, 52, 113, 286
Software Engineering, 211
Sprint, 14, 105
Static Test, 100
Suits Factory Model, 233-240
System Integration Test, 22, 71, 166
System Test, 71, 166
Systems Thinking, 210

Task Management, 66, 146, 227
TBOK, 44
Test Analyst, 12, 37
Test Coverage, 165

Test Design, 22, 37, 145, 151, 257
Test Driven Development (TDD), 39, 42, 218
Test Management, 194
TOGAF, 44, 188
Traceability, 28, 82, 87, 97, 114, 142

UAT, 35
Unit Test, 12, 71, 118

Validation, 178
Verification, 179
Viewpoint, 190-191
V-Model, 41, 118, 216

Waterfall, 4, 39, 214
Wiki, 61, 206

Zachman Framework, 189-190